TRACING
YOUR
ANCESTORS

SIR ROB.T TROUTBECK
of Newton who died in 1637
MARY WILKINSON

William	George	Christoph.r	Lancelot	Iohn	a Daughter	a Daughter
who lived at Blencow	Rector of Bownas he died in 1691	who lived neigh Wigton	who died young	lived at Ravenhead		

William	a Daughter	a Daughter	a Daughter		a Son	a Son
who succeeded his Father					who went abroad but where it is uncertain	who went abroad but where it is uncertain

a Daughter	a Daughter
married to Hodgson of Easton	married to Lawson of Bownas

George	Iohn	William	Ralph	Robert
who also lived at Blencow	of Willenbro in Northamptonshire	who lived at Grays Inn Lane Lond		of Corbridge in Northumberland he died unmarr.d

William	George	Iohn	Iames	Edward	Thomas	William	Samuel	Benjam.n
who died unmarr.d at the Age of 21	who succeeded his Father at Blencow	a Clergyman had a living in Bedford shire	who lived at Blencow	a Surgeon at St Albos and Died without Issue	Rector of Haughton in Bedfordshire still Living	who also live in Grays Inn Lane London	who went to Madras and is still living there	who Died without Issue

William	Iohn	Martin	Iohn	George	William	Charles	Iames
still living and Settled at Blencow	a Surgeon in the East India Company's Service	who Died Young	a Clergyman still Living & holds a Living under L.d God.n of John in one of the Scilly Islands	who Died young	still Living	still Living	still Living

Sarah	Hannah	Iohn
still living	still living	still living

TRACING YOUR ANCESTORS

An Illustrated Guide to Compiling Your Family Tree

Christine M. Morris

5126: Tracing Your Ancestors

Produced by Stonecastle Graphics Limited
for Quadrillion Publishing Limited,
Godalming Business Centre,
Woolsack Way,
Godalming, GU7 1XW, UK

This edition published in 1999 by CLB,
an imprint of Quadrillion Publishing Limited

Distributed in the USA by Quadrillion Publishing Inc.,
230 Fifth Avenue, New York, NY 10001

Credits
Designed and packaged by: Sue Pressley and Paul Turner,
Stonecastle Graphics Limited
Editor: Christopher Westhorp
Picture research: Dan Brooks and Carlotta Cooper,
Brooks Krikler Research
Production: Neil Randles, Karen Staff, Sandra Dixon
Color reproduction: Emirates Printing Press, Dubai

Printed and bound in the United Arab Emirates
by Emirates Printing Press, Dubai

ISBN 1-84100-140-6

CONTENTS

INTRODUCTION

FAMILY HISTORY and genealogy is one of the fastest growing and most rewarding hobbies in the world today. The dictionary definition for genealogy is, "the history of the relationship and descent of families or the pedigree of a person or family." The family tree is a genealogical tree, working back from one generation to another, step by step, and creating one will take you on a fascinating journey back in time. You will learn about your family, their social life and history. It seems a daunting task, but with the investigative mind of a detective you will find it relatively simple to trace your family back to the mid-nineteenth century.

With so many people migrating to other parts of the world during the eighteenth and nineteenth centuries, people often feel the need to find their roots; to find out why their ancestors emigrated, where they came from in the beginning, and who was their family. Is there someone famous in the family? Are you descended from English royalty? What did your ancestors look like? What was their occupation? What genes have you inherited? Do twins run in your family?

WHY START?

Why are you starting to trace your family tree? Is it to find out why great uncle John Logan Turnbull was the black sheep of the family? What did he do that was so bad no one would talk about it?

Do you have a general interest in history, or specifically local and social history? What are the cultural differences between your ancestors' life then and your life now? Perhaps it is the need to prove your identity, find those family traditions or occupations, or even just to reclaim the family grave.

Could it be the need for something to leave to your grandchildren and great-grandchildren? Whatever the reason for your search you will soon find yourself hooked on this fascinating activity and craving for more and more knowledge. Family vacations take on a new meaning. When you go to investigate the places where your ancestors lived and worked your holiday snaps will be of houses, churches, and tombstones.

WHERE DO YOU START?

Has it been done before? Always check this out; it would be a shame to waste time when an uncle, a cousin or someone in the family has already made a start. Are they still working on it? Offer to help. Have they given up? Offer to take it over, but always let them know how you are progressing. Has a distant relation, someone you never knew existed, worked on your family tree? This could have been registered with a family history society, a lineage society, the Society of Genealogists in London, or Ancestral File which is maintained by the Church of Jesus Christ of Latter-day Saints (the Mormons). Do not forget to check the websites, where there are more and more genealogical sites listing names

Opposite left: Many Irish families emigrated to North America in the 1800s both to escape starvation during the potato famine and in search of a better life.

Below: Old photographs of your family are a useful source of research, and may help you to trace your ancestors back several generations.

and researchers; individuals have their own websites for one-name studies. If you have a common name, it is always a good idea to start by checking the website of the Guild of One-Name Studies (GOONS).

Whom do you start to look for first, the maternal or paternal line? There are no hard and fast rules, the choice is purely up to you. Why not do both?

Are you descended from Native American Indians? If so, what tribe? Were your ancestors convicts? If so, were they sent to North America or Australia on the convict ships? Were your forebears from Ireland, perhaps fleeing from the potato famine and hoping for a better life on the other side of the ocean? Whatever the reason, the records are there, waiting for you to use them.

PITFALLS AND PLEASURES

Whatever your ethnic and/or nationality group, everyone must follow the same basic steps in genealogy. Always be aware of the spelling of your surname, and remember that most surnames will have variants. Keep an open mind on spelling, not only with people's names but with place names too. Try to be aware of the

customs and history of the country; know about the country's archives, their maps, libraries and, of course, their genealogical sources. Read books, join the societies and go on courses—but most of all enjoy it.

Anyone can trace their family. Just by starting with yourself and going back five generations—about 120 years—will give you sixteen great-great-grandparents. Go back one more generation and you will have thirty-two great-great-great-grandparents, not forgetting their brothers and sisters and their children. Just from one person, your family has increased to quite a size. In the case of most people this will have led back to the late 1700s or early 1800s and you will start to lose the odd generation, either because there are no records, they have moved or through marriage (remember that cousins and second cousins often married in centuries gone by).

Above: Nineteenth-century graves at Sonora Pioneer Cemetery, California. Headstones can reveal many useful details about your family.

Above: Are you descended from royalty? This picture shows the British monarch King Edward VII and Queen Alexandra.

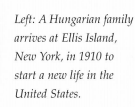

Left: A Hungarian family arrives at Ellis Island, New York, in 1910 to start a new life in the United States.

Your Heritage, Your Family

Royal Families of Europe on CD-ROM contains a great deal of information for Royal Watchers and includes the genealogy of all European royal families.

• Available from TWR Computing:

http://www.dungeon.com/~clapstile

COMPUTERS

One of the more modern tools of genealogy today is the computer; it is becoming more and more important to family historians. Computers can give assistance to the researcher working with notes, not to mention the contact with others through the Internet and the growing number of indexes and information now becoming available through the computer network. A computer will not solve your family history problems, but it will make it easier for you to solve them by having the information there at the touch of a button or two. Some researchers put all their notes onto the computer, others have a printed copy (or hard copy) as well. But, most importantly, do make a back-up disk of your data and never throw away your original notes, however messy they look. Store them in the basement if need be, because there will always be an occasion when you need to check back on them.

Computers will not do your work or research for you but, by inputting the information found, they will provide a more convenient way of storing and retrieving data. Having decided to computerize your notes and research, what software package do you buy? Never rush out and buy the first one you see. Analyse your needs and expectations: what do you want from a program? Talk to fellow researchers; what do they use? Also talk to the experts—you will find many of them advertising their specialized software in family history magazines.

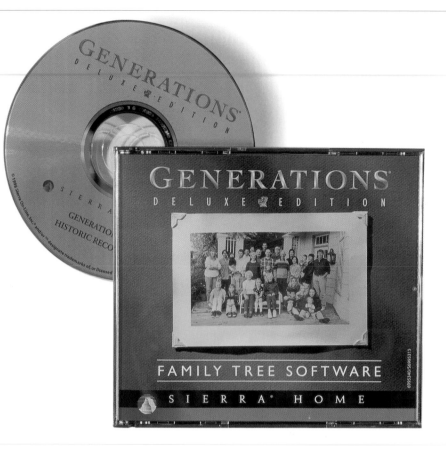

SOFTWARE

There are three categories under which you can store your research. Either a word processing program, a database program or a genealogy program. With word processing, you can put notes and research in the format that you want, and it is easy to retrieve and print. Databases are designed to store data, and to offer easy retrieval, and these programs are often used by researchers doing a one-name study. The last program, the genealogical package, is designed to keep track of specific data of interest. They can deal with pedigree links, they can make various indexes and some are able to produce reports. Others enable the user to have photographs scanned into the program, which gives a nice effect when a family tree is printed off, showing not only the information about a person but a picture as well.

One other way to decide on a genealogical program is to try out several shareware packages. Many of the suppliers of software programs do sell shareware disks for a much lower cost, even putting several on one CD-ROM. This gives you a better chance to try them all out and decide which is the best for your needs. Once your chosen program is loaded you can input the information you have collected. You can soon start printing off family trees, individual reports and family reports. You can

Above: Genealogical software packages are designed to help you keep track of your family history data and prepare your family tree in a professional manner. There are a number of good programs that you can buy, and most can be ordered from specialist Internet websites.

Left: Computers have become increasingly important tools in undertaking genealogical research. They ease the process of entering and retrieving research notes and allow you to access a wealth of information from CD-ROMs and Internet websites.

Right: Genealogy Online: a useful Internet website for family historians can be accessed at: http://genealogy.org

see at a glance what research you still have to do on a person or family group.

If you compare a computer with the use of a card index, one great advantage of the computer is that the information can be sorted and arranged in many different ways; for example, by surname, first name, year and/or date, or a selection of records by county and century. Another advantage is that records are easy to print off so you have the information ready to take to the archive offices or library without having to take your original work.

THE FUTURE

Family historians accumulate vast quantities of paper as a result of their research—what do you do with it? Computers are certainly the way forward, and with modern technology we must continue to look ahead, because eventually more and more records will become available on the Internet. Where a few years ago researchers turned up at national archive offices and local repositories with their note pads and pencils, they can now be seen arriving with their laptop computers—this is the changing face of family history and genealogy.

Whatever the reason for you tracing your ancestors, now is the time to start. Ask those questions, find those records and leave your own little bit of history to future generations.

Above: Many of the suppliers of genealogical software programs also sell shareware CDs at much lower cost. You will be able to find programs that will help you to prepare family trees and create family reports.

Below left and below: If you have a scanner attached to your computer you will be able to scan photographs and add them to your reports and family trees.

CD-ROM RESEARCH

FOR SOME years archive material, typed transcripts, and indexes have been copied onto microfilm and microfiche; but with the modern-day explosion in the use and ownership of computers, with all the benefits of their advanced technology, things are improving and should continue to do so for years to come. The CD-ROM is the latest technological revolution to come to the aid of the family historian. Whether it is just an index or something more substantial, the CD-ROM offers a means of doing more and more research from your own computer chair. The items discussed here are just a small sample of the type of CD-ROMs on the market today.

Australian Vital Records

Contains four CDs, indexes to births, christenings, marriages, and deaths from New South Wales (1788–1888), Tasmania (1803–1899), Victoria (1837–1888), and Western Australia (1841–1905).

• Available from S & N Genealogy Supplies: http://www.genealogy.demon.co.uk

PEOPLE INDEXES

From both sides of the Atlantic, more and more companies are introducing information in the CD format. The US company Broderbund, which created the *Family Tree Maker* computer program, produces a vast number of CD-ROMs ranging from CDs with thousands of family trees, including a database of over 1,300,000 names, to the Social Security Death Benefit Records CDs which contain more than 50 million US names. Broderbund's *FamilyFinder Index* lists the names of more than 130 million people who appear in the US state and federal records. When you find the data you want you can simply import it from the disk directly into your own family lines and link it together.

GENEALOGICAL DIRECTORIES

The *Genealogical Research Directory* (*GRD*) for the years from 1990 to 1996 is also available on CD-ROM. This is certainly a quicker way to find those other researchers who are tracing your family name, rather then having to wade through seven years' worth of books—and it is cheaper as well. The *GRD* is produced in Australia but it covers the world.

The *South and West Wales Genealogical Index*, a reference CD-ROM, contains six indexes assembled and privately published by Richard James in Wales. The researcher will find it a good starting point for additional research; it covers marriage indexes, marriage bonds and a wills index for the southern parts of Wales. Remember when purchasing any CD-ROM to check the information it holds and the period covered by the indexes, also check whether there will be any updates.

A periodical called *The Genealogical Helper* is published in the United States which contains pages of advertisements for genealogical services. There are lists of CD-ROMs for sale covering American birth, marriage, and death records, collections of genealogical records, tax records, and the Social Security Death Benefit Records from 1937 to 1993 (a must for those missing family members who emigrated to the United States at the turn of the century). Automated Archives have published a large number of CD-ROMs and to get you interested they will sell you their *Master Name Index*, which consolidates many of the millions of names featured on their other disks.

Below: Broderbund's Family Tree Maker *is an excellent genealogy program and is available in basic, standard, and deluxe editions.*

Above: Taking the census in London in 1861. Many census records are available on CD.

Above: US software producer Broderbund's Family Tree Maker *CDs are available to provide access to a huge range of indexes, records and family trees.*

TELEPHONE DIRECTORIES

The US telephone directories can also be purchased easily on a CD-ROM; it contains more than 80 million names. A CD-ROM for the British telephone directories is also available, as is one of the commercial and domestic Australian telephone directories.

STATE REGISTRARS

In Australia the Royal Melbourne Institute of Technology, in association with state registrars of births, marriages, and deaths, produced a series of indexes to vital records which will leave all researchers in other countries green with envy. Others have also been produced: *New South Wales, Pioneers Series 1788–1888; Federation Series 1889–1918; Victoria, Pioneers Series 1837–1888; Western Australia, Pioneers 1841–1905;* and *Tasmania, Pioneers 1803–1889.*

UK CENSUS

The *1851 UK Census Extract* contains 500,000 names from the 1851 UK census, as prepared by the Economic & Social Science Research

British Vital Records

Six CDs contain 4.5 million births, christenings, and marriages from the British Isles 1538–1888—produced by the Church of Jesus Christ of Latter-day Saints.
• Available from S & N Genealogy Supplies:
http://www.genealogy.demon.co.uk

The Royal Melbourne Institute of Technology

The Royal Melbourne Institute of Technology, in association with state registrars of births, deaths, and marriages, has produced a series of CD-ROM indexes to vital records. Details as follows:

New South Wales: Pioneers Series 1788–1888;
Federation Series 1889–1918; Between the Wars (death and marriage) 1919–1945.
Victoria: Pioneers Series 1837–1888.
Western Australia: Pioneers 1841–1905.
Tasmania: Pioneers 1803–1889.
• All available from INFORMIT, RMIT Libraries, PO Box 12477, A'Beckett Street, Melbourne, Victoria 8006, Australia

Council, and it also contains a number of additional data files from nineteenth-century censuses from other contributors. The data tables contain the full set of information recorded in the census: Forenames, Surname, Relationship to Head of Household, Marital Status, Age, Occupation, and Place of Birth. It must be remembered that this is not a full coverage of the 1851 census, it covers just 2 per cent of all individuals from the census, but it is still reasonably priced and a good search aid.

To find further CDs read the family history and genealogical journals; more and more societies, groups and companies are producing these search aids, and genealogical researchers should write to them to make their needs known.

Abelmann—(German) meaning "dweller near the poplars."
Abbot(t)—from the Middle Eastern word of *Abba*, meaning "father." A name given to a servant rather than to an offspring.
Ackroyd—Old English for "oak clearing" or local to a place in West Yorkshire. Possibly from the Yorkshire surname of Royds which meant "roads" or "clearings."
Adam, Adames, Adams Adamson—baptismal name from the son of Adam; meaning of "red" in Hebrew. A prime favorite as a font-name in the thirteenth century. Adams is well represented in the United States, a glance in the index to *Hotten's List of Emigrants* shows that many Adams, Addams and Adamsons were among the early settlers.
Adlard—baptismal name, the son of Adelard or Athelard; also meaning "noble" or "hard."
Albery, Albury—the son of Albray or Aubery, a local name from the parish of Aldbury in Hertfordshire.

SOFTWARE PACKAGES

WHAT IS software? The term means programs which can run on a computer for any reason, these could be programs written by the user or pre-written programs which are available from various computer manufacturers or other people who specialize in the writing of software. The computer world falls, essentially, into two main operating system camps, with IBM-compatibles (running mostly Microsoft Windows) and Apple Macintoshes. The software available is designed to run on one or the other; CD-ROMS can often be read by both. Because fewer people use Apple Macintoshes, there is a more limited range of packages available, and the content on familiar ones may differ too (some better, some worse). Systems apart, in the UK most people seem to be using database software packages for their family history needs, whereas in the United States more genealogy software packages are sold.

Family Tree Maker 11 CDs version 5

Contains vols 1 to 5 of the *World Family Tree* CDs, the *European* CD containing trees from the UK and the rest of Europe, and includes a new 170 million name index and US Social Security Death Benefit Records. The program now has Hourglass trees displaying ancestors and descendants on the same tree.

Also available: Family Tree Maker Basic

• Available from S & N Genealogy Supplies: http://www.genealogy.demon.co.uk

WORD PROCESSING

Straightforward typing can be done using a word processing program. They also provide a good way of producing family trees. With a word processor transcripts of wills, indentures, deeds, and any other historical miscellaneous items can be stored and retrieved easily; the disadvantage is that records cannot be sorted automatically.

DATABASES

Database packages are an excellent way of storing events and indexes of names. A database is really an electronic form of putting the information onto card indexes, but with the advantage that it is far easier to sort in different and quicker ways. In addition, if the wrong information has been entered, it is just as easily changed. It is possible to sort people by name, birthdate, birthplace, marriage, census place, or by any "field" (or category) which you have entered. It is possible to link people together, either by marriage or parent, and cross-reference them to bring the family group together. As a newcomer to databases, you would be advised to experiment with various ways and fields.

GENEALOGY PROGRAMS

More and more complex commercial genealogy programs are now available on the market. They maintain pedigrees, family groups and individual records. Such a program will store most information from the records which are

Below: There are many genealogy programs available to the family historian, most of which offer a wide range of useful functions.

available today, but care must be taken with the inputting of details. There are more than fifty packages on sale in the United States (a list of them is published in *Genealogical Computing*, a popular journal). Packages vary a great deal; some are very basic, only allowing for direct ancestors to be entered, and others take a vast amount of unrelated family information.

There are different ways of printing information from your program: a family group sheet, an individual sheet, a birth brief, a

Opposite: It is useful to use a straightforward word processing program to transcribe details of family documents, such as this apprenticeship indenture, dated 1850.

descendants' chart or an indented family tree, as well as sorted lists. Some of the most popular packages in the United States are *Family Roots*, *Roots 2*, *Family Tree Maker* and *Personal Ancestral File* (*PAF*), the last one is produced by the Church of Jesus Christ of Latter-day Saints. All these programs accept data in the standard GEDCOM format. (GEDCOM—GEnealogical Data COMmunications—is the means to transfer data from one software package to another. You could not take file data from *PAF* and read it directly in *Family Roots* format; the data has to be transferred from *PAF* into GEDCOM, then transferred into *Family Roots*.)

ENDLESS SOFTWARE

Before buying your software package talk to other users, see what packages they use and whether they have any problems. Write or telephone the genealogy suppliers who will be only too happy to discuss their products with you. Ask if they have a shareware of the program you are interested in, buy this at a greatly reduced rate, try it out and if you like it, pay the extra for the full version. Sometimes free trial versions can be had with limited functions or life; they will help you to decide.

The ranges of software packages are large on both sides of the Atlantic: *Family Tree Maker* comes in a basic, a standard, and a deluxe version; *Brother's Keeper* for Windows, has photo charts; *Kith & Kin* has family trees and reports;

USEFUL WEBSITES:

http://www.familytreemaker.com
http://www.whollygenes.com
http://www.dungeon.com

GenServ is a database of GEDCOM files (one free search):

http://soback.kornet.nm.kr/~cmanis

I FoundIt! (a link to 2,600 websites):

http://www.gensource.com

Treedraw creates drag-and-drop charts. Most of the genealogy computer magazines and journals review programs and these give a fuller picture of what the program will do. (Most software is American-produced; one of the few UK-written programs is *Genealogy for Windows*. Version 4 runs under Microsoft Windows version 3.1, 3.11 or Windows 95.)

One other software to mention is *GENMAP UK*, a Windows program that displays genealogical or historical data as maps. This is an ideal program for plotting the distribution of surnames or tracking the movement of families over a period of time. It will allow you to read the data in several different ways.

Whatever the program you choose, the results of your research will be well displayed, but one important detail: never forget to back-up your work and place a copy of your computer files at a different address for safekeeping.

Allard—(Huguenot) "the son of Alard," shortened name of Adelard, Adlard.

Allgood, Elgood, Elegood—a baptismal name meaning "son of Algod," a forgotten personal name.

Allpress—a nickname "the holy priest;" earliest entry found a Thomas Alprest in Cambridgeshire in 1273.

Anderson—meaning "son of Andrew," ninth commonest surname in Scotland in 1958 and eighth in the USA in 1939.

Arbuckle, Arbuckel—a corruption of the local place of Harbottle. This surname has crossed the Atlantic and is spreading in the USA.

Armstrong—meaning "strong in the arm," found in Northumberland, Cumberland, and Durham, in England, and south Scotland; a tough Border surname.

Arnold, Arnoll, Arnott, Arnold—(Huguenot) "the son of Arnold." French for Arnoud. The United States has the continental spelling of Arnhold and Arnholt.

THE INTERNET AND WEBSITES

THROUGH THE Internet and websites you have a facility which allows you to contact and exchange information with millions of computers and computer users throughout the world. You can use the Internet to assist you with research for your family tree because so many genealogists are now established users of the Internet. The Internet changes rapidly and it is useful to keep abreast of these developments by reading the specialized magazines which are on the market today.

New Legacy

This UK release provides a comprehensive genealogy program suitable for both research and family history.
• Available from S & N Genealogy Supplies:
http://www.genealogy.demon.co.uk

To get on the Internet you need a computer, a modem (either internal or external), a telephone line and a subscription to an Internet Service Provider (ISP). The ISP is an organization with its own computer system, and it will provide you with the access software. It is the software which will give you the user screen in which to type, send and receive messages. The software will also provide the means to look at websites, which are pages of information which have been stored by different organizations and individuals. You can even produce your own webpage, and it could be as simple as just a single screen showing the family names you are interested in.

Many ISPs have their own on-line service, information services, shopping and discussion groups. Some have very good genealogical forums and also support for genealogy packages. One of the most useful aspects is the ability to send and receive e-mail: just type in

the person's e-mail address, then type the message onto the computer, tell your computer to connect to the telephone network and send the message. This is stored in a central computer and then transferred to your correspondent's computer the next time they connect it to the Internet. They can then display, print and store your message. E-mail is fast, simple and very effective, a lot easier than sending things by mail to friends, colleagues and family. Replies come back rapidly from any part of the world.

A lot of family history societies and genealogical groups now have mailing lists and discussion groups. By joining a group, you can register your family names, the area they were in and the timescale. Any queries you have can just be typed in and sent to the group, your message will then be displayed to everyone within that group. If someone out there knows the answer they will either send it back via the discussion group or direct it to your own e-mail

Left: To get on the Internet you will need a computer, a modem, a telephone line and a subscription to an Internet Service Provider (ISP). Many ISPs supply free CDs containing all of the software that you will need to get started, and some offer a free trial period before you start your subscription.

address. By sending it back via the discussion group, you let everyone know the answer and it means you don't receive lots of e-mails with the same answer. There are many questions that you can ask: Where are certain records kept? Is a particular church still standing or was it pulled down? When? Does anyone know if there are still family members living in that area? The list is endless. You will make so many new friends this way—you may never meet, but that doesn't matter.

The greatest use of the World Wide Web (hence the "www" in addresses) is in giving you access to pages and pages of information from other computers. Some websites have words which are underlined, and these are links to other pages and can be from anywhere in the world. Each webpage has an address, a Uniform Resource Locator or URL, and a title page. You find websites either by typing in the URL or by searching for a topic using a search engine; once located and in, you can move about the site just by clicking the mouse. Webpages will display text and graphics (but you can disable the graphics via your web browser); clicking on a link can take you to other pages, a video recording, or can run another program. You can print pages or copy a file to your computer.

There are collections of surnames and pedigrees on the Internet, which are available for you to search. It is always well worth submitting your own surnames to these lists, because you could get in touch with someone searching for your names and discover distant cousins through the Internet. Roots Surname

Above and right: The Internet provides a wealth of information for any genealogist who wishes to surf the World Wide Web.

List (RSL) contains more than 65,000 surnames, each line of a submission to this list is a surname, the first and last date to which the researcher has any information and places to which the family has moved. To find the name, e-mail and mailing address of the person researching the name just click on the code. Then contact the person and see if you have any common ancestors.

There are always articles and news on how to use the Internet for genealogy, see some of the following magazines: *Computers in Genealogy* (quarterly from the Society of Genealogists in the UK), *Family Tree Magazine* (monthly), *Genealogical Computing* (quarterly from Ancestry Publishing) and *NGS/CIG Digest* (bimonthly to members of the National Genealogical Society).

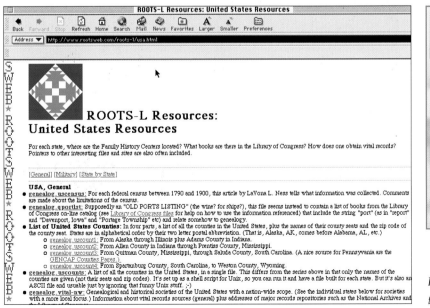

Left: A page from the Roots Surname List Internet site that can be found at: http://www.rootsweb.com

WHERE AND HOW TO START

ALWAYS START with yourself. Write down all the facts as you know them: date of birth, baptism, marriage, where these events happened, the houses you have lived in, the schools you have attended. A good exercise is to write your own autobiography and include brothers, sisters, cousins, aunts, and uncles. This makes you remember people who have moved away over the years and with whom you have lost touch; include dates and school friends. This is all in the process of remembering.

To form your first family tree, start by writing your full name, your mother and father's full name. What was your mother's maiden name? Your four grandparents' full names? Form these names into a family tree (right).

You can add your great-grandparents to this tree, even if you only know their names, this is a start. Now start to add the dates to these people: when they were born, when they got married, and when they died. Two further dates can be added: baptism and burial. Also, give the place of the event. This is the beginning of your ancestral tree, starting with you at the trunk and each family line becoming a new branch to your tree. You must be methodical, working back one generation at a time, whether you keep with just the paternal line to start with, or work on all lines at the same time.

Those missing gaps could well be filled later, when you start to question your relations. Each step back is a step to reconstructing the lifestyle of your ancestors. It is an exciting and rewarding task, which will keep you occupied for years to come. It is a hobby in which you can put in as many or as few hours as you want, and also govern how much or how little it will cost. It is a hobby which can be put to one side and just as easily restarted again. Although once you have dealt with the initial stage you will not want to stop.

One other good point is to read as many books as you can on the subject. As you go

Grandfather	Grandmother		Grandfather	Grandmother
	Father			Mother
		You		

further back into your family history there are many specialized books on a variety of subjects. When you start to record more and more information, record the date and source at the top of the page because this saves time later and will stop you duplicating work. Now you are ready to start the serious work.

Below: Collect as many old family photographs as you can and look in old family Bibles for names and dates that help to fill the gaps in your search.

20

FTM: World Family Tree—Volumes 1–26

Pre-1600 to present. Each CD-ROM contains thousands of actual family trees contributed by *Family Tree Maker* customers and family history enthusiasts. Millions of individuals are named, complete with event dates and family links where known. Produced by Broderbund Software.

• Available from Appleton's Online: http://www.appletons.com/genealogy/genebbcd.html

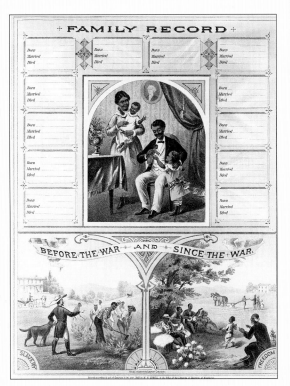

Above left: A family tree depicting the contrast of life before and after the American Civil War.

Above right: An illustrated family tree showing the descendants of Queen Victoria.

Left: Look for clues in old photographs; the style of clothes and details of the photographer may help to place a relative on your family tree.

PERSONAL AND FAMILY MEMORABILIA

START YOUR search for memorabilia by sorting out those boxes, letters and photographs that you have saved and hidden in the basement following the clearing out of the house of a relative. What do you do with all that paperwork of your own which you said you would sort out? Look around your home; what is there? Have you any family birth, marriage or death certificates? These all help to save money, as ordering duplicates can be costly. Look for marriage contracts and licences. Have you a family Bible? Even a small one given to a grandparent at school or Sunday school for good conduct and attendance—note the names, the school, and the date.

Look for autograph books, giving details of your parents' or grandparents' friends, brothers and sisters—even a future spouse. There might be diaries, journals, letters, birth announcements, and wedding invitations, or even funeral memorial cards, which were given to family and friends on the death of someone close, a very common practice in the nineteenth and early twentieth century. Look for those early photographs; are the name and date on them? If not, leave them to one side ready to show to an elderly relative. Are your photographs named and dated for your descendants?

Even look at the glassware which you inherited. It could be engraved with the date of a twenty-first birthday, or a ruby wedding. Look at the inscriptions on watches; to whom was it presented and why? Have you checked that old clock in the attic? It may not have worked for years, but there could be a small inscription inside somewhere. Do you have your father's or grandfather's war medals? Maybe even medals for an unmarried uncle or great uncle; if they died in action with no immediate family they could have been given to their parents.

Other clues could be found in samplers and other family pieces of needlework that have been passed on. Have you a friendship quilt? Quilting is a very old craft (like so many customs and crafts it crossed the Atlantic with the pilgrim families who emigrated from Europe to the USA), and in addition to recording family history, quilts became an important part of social life with friends and family coming together to help to make a marriage or friendship quilt. Samplers were made by young girls at school during the eighteenth and nineteenth centuries to show their ability at basic skills, sewing alphabets and numerals on marked linen, which they would finish off with their name, age, date and possibly their address.

Gather as much personal and family memorabilia as you can. Old autograph books, Bibles, letters, certificates, and postcards may uncover a wealth of important details that will assist you further with your research.

Look for legal papers, attorney's letters, real estate deeds or household records, diplomas, insurance records, passports, business records from an old family business, citizenship papers, house or land purchases and sales, scrapbooks, and old postcards. The list is endless. Add to that your wills, probate documents, yearbooks from schools and churches, degrees and graduation certificates, and there is a considerable volume of material.

The practice of entering family details in a Holy Bible is extremely old. A newly married couple would be given a Bible as a gift, with their marriage details already entered. The couple would then continue entering into the Bible the birth details of their children: a name, a date, the time but very rarely the place. They were popular in the eighteenth and nineteenth centuries, when large pictorial books were published, often containing a page for family records. If you are borrowing a Bible from some other member of the family, try to have it photocopied rather than write it out by hand. Mistakes can be made in the transcribing.

SOURCES OF FAMILY HISTORY

Address books might not contain just names and addresses of friends and relations; there could possibly be lists for parties—Christmas, weddings and even reunion details.

Birthday books could contain any sort of date possible. For example, from the record of a relative's eightieth birthday celebration you will have the day and the month of their birth, and you just need to work back to calculate the year they were born.

Scrapbooks can contain newspaper cuttings, birthday cards, postcards, letters, and odd little snippets of information. These will bring back memories to your older relations when you start

to interview them. Having a baby book is a fairly modern idea, but they not only contain a lot of information about the child's first five years, but names of godparents, details of what they received for their first Christmas or birthday and, most important, who from.

Certificates might include not only those for birth, marriage or death, but baptism or burial too. This would indicate the person's religion and help when it comes to tracking down those inscriptions on gravestones. Certificates can also help with place of residence. Others give details of schools, education, and prizes.

There could also be a certificate of membership of various societies: Freemasons, Lodges, and other similar fraternities. These can add to the family history of a particular person, but not to the pedigree details.

Aschendorf—(German) meaning "ash tree village." Asch(e) meaning Ash.

Ashwood—a local name for ash-tree wood, a place name in Staffordshire.

Attwood, Atwood—a local name meaning "at the wood." Every English county has a representative of the surname. The earliest name found was a Geoffrey Ate Wode in Huntingdonshire in 1273.

Baker—an occupational name "the baker;" the earliest name found was a Walter le Baker in 1273 in Devon. The bakehouse or village oven was owned by the lord of the manor, the villagers would pay the baker for his services. This is a common name found in the UK and USA.

Bailey—an occupational name, a bailiff or crown official, the king's officer or agent, a man of great importance. A Scots alderman is still called a bailie. It is also an English surname of Huguenot derivation.

Baldrey, Baldry—meaning "the bold one," brave in combat; also son of Baldric or Balderic. The name is found in the Domesday Book of a Hugo fil Baldrici.

Left: If your relatives had connections with the Freemasons or other societies, you may be able to find certificates of membership which add to their history.

WHAT CAN YOUR RELATIVES REMEMBER?

SOME OF your relatives may live some distance away, perhaps even on another continent. For these you can prepare a detailed questionnaire, remembering to list all the details which you are hoping to find out. Try to pre-warn these relatives with a phone call; let them know about your interest in the family, say you are sending a letter and questionnaire requesting family history details. Some relatives could object quite strongly to the questions. Others enjoy talking about their family and will remember and reminisce with you quite happily. Never be pushy, if they don't want to talk and fill in your questions, leave it for another time.

> **The Compendium of American Genealogy**
>
> *The Genealogical Encyclopedia of the First Families of America.* This *Family Archive* CD contains images from Virkus' *Compendium of American Genealogy*—perhaps the most famous work in all of American genealogy. It contains the lineage records of the first families of America.
> • Available from the Genealogical Publishing Company: http://www.genealogical.com/cdrom.htm

Using a computer to prepare the questionnaire would certainly help. The form can easily be changed to suit whichever relative you are sending it to. The preparation of your questionnaire is most important. You do need to think of all the details you would like to ask questions about. The following list will give you a guide as to some of the queries you will want answered or need checking.

- What is your full name? Have you any nicknames? If you are married, what was your maiden name?
- Your date of birth, place of birth, when and where you were baptized?
- The date and place of your marriage?
- Whom did you have as witnesses?

- Husband/wife's full name; nicknames?
- Dates and places of birth?
- What brothers and sisters do you have? Their names, dates of birth, places? When and to whom did they marry?
- What were the full names (including maiden) of your parents? Do you know when and where they were born?
- Can you remember your aunts and uncles? Which side of the family did they belong to?
- Where and when did your parents marry? Did either of them marry twice (have a little tact here)?
- When did they die? Were they buried or cremated? Where did this happen?
- What was your father's job? Was he employed or did he have his own business? Did he fight in the war?
- Do you have any certificates (birth, marriage, death) or a copy of a will?

With the assistance of a photograph album filled with old pictures, many relatives will be able to remember people and events that help to fill the gaps in your family tree.

inhibit some people. Take those photographs you have found to see if people can be identified; also take some of your more modern photographs: an elderly relative would like to see your growing family. Make the person feel at ease, explain exactly why you are doing this; show them some of your work and point out the gaps in your information which they might be able help you with.

FAMILY HEIRLOOMS

If they have any family heirlooms, take photographs of them. If your relative has any photographs which are not in your collection, ask if you can borrow them to have copies made. Assure them that you will return them within a couple of weeks. A quick way of copying is to get a laser copy; they could also be scanned into your computer (when you start to prepare your family tree on the computer, these pictures can then be scaled down to be placed next to the name on your tree; many of the commercial family tree programs have a section for you to place your pictures).

Family legends are fun to listen to and perhaps you could try, at some point, to prove them, but always remember some are just tales passed down and changed until the real tale is lost. Do not waste time in trying to prove a story that is not based on any factual evidence.

Another important point to remember: if the relative is interested in your work make sure that a copy of the family tree is sent to them.

- Do you have any photographs of the family?
- What other family members might be able to help with details of family history?

Start with the older generations. Go on your visit prepared and take just enough information to jog the person's memory; if possible take a tape recorder, although the presence of this can

Beard—a nickname meaning "the bearded one." This was an early name in England, about the time of the Norman Conquest and therefore possibly of French origin, also know as a Huguenot derivation.

Beaumont—of Norman extraction meaning a "lovely hill."

Bellingham, Billingham —a local name; parishes can be found in England in Northumberland and Durham, also possibly in Norfolk. A family of Bellinghams who came from a manor near Hastings were mentioned in the Domesday Book.

Bennet, Bennett—the son of Bennet or Benedict. Bennet was the usual English form. While Furness Abbey was administrated under the Benedictine Order, Bennet was one of the most common names in the area.

Bergmann, Bergman— (German) a miner or mountain man.

Billard—this is an occupational name from Bellhird. A popular name from Sheffield in the UK and also in New York and Philadelphia.

Birch—from living near a birch tree.

Left: If you can borrow any family documents or letters which are not in your collection, get laser copies made of them or scan them into your computer so that you have a permanent record for future use.

CHECKING FAMILY RECORDS

HAVING NOW collected information, certificates, copies of wills, and any other documents from your relations, the time comes when you must assess and begin to record your research. Certificates, or any other official documents, we know will give confirmed and correct dates, names and places. Details taken from birthday books, Bibles, and even any oral history must be confirmed by further research. Family historians like confirmed facts; we need accurate details of names, places, and dates, and of relationships too.

Now is the time to divide the resource material into two piles, the maternal line and the paternal line. It will help and save a lot of confusion later if you stay with this division. When checking the birth certificates, look for the name or names of the child, the date of birth, place of birth, and the parents. When transcribing any documents, certificates or letters, always write what is there; if a name does not look correct, don't change it to the modern-day spelling. As you go further back in time, different spellings will occur more and more. In a parish register in Essex, England, during the mid-1800s a family of ten children were baptized over a twelve-year period, and their surname of Filby was spelled five different ways. This could be due to any number of reasons, perhaps dialects and accents: a priest would write the name down as he heard it, the parents may have been unable to read or write and so the spellings were never checked and changed.

Looking at all the different things you have collected will present you with a selection of varying types of information:

• A memorial card was very popular in the mid-Victorian period onward. They were edged with black and would contain precise information: the name of the deceased, their home address, the date of death, where they died and the place and date of interment.
• Family group photographs were taken on special occasions; find out what this one was, the date and the names of the members of the family. So many photographs were left unlabelled and unless you can find an elderly relation to identify them, the names will be lost for ever. Make a resolution to label and date all your own photographs.

• Photographs of gravestones give us more details. A grave can contain several members of one family and the stone will give names, date(s) of death, and age(s).
• Autograph books may contain signatures of family and friends, even future husbands or wives. List these names, with their dates, and keep it as a working document. (You do not want to keep flicking through your book because it will soon disintegrate.)

Try to preserve as much of your original documentation as possible, work with your notes and photocopies. Birthday books can contain dates, not only of birthdays but also anniversaries. These dates and names must also be recorded for they will go a long way toward providing a full family picture.

Every piece of family archive material will have a story to tell; this is the point where you must record them, something missed or incorrectly written at this time could cause problems later on. Once you have recorded all the information from your family memorabilia, either return the things you have borrowed, or put the things you have been given in a safe, dry place.

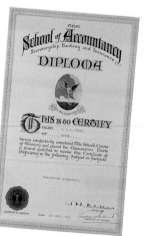

Once you have collected as many family pictures, certificates and documents as you can, start to divide them into two piles: your maternal and paternal lines. Carefully preserve the original material and work with photocopies to record names and dates.

Headstones, Graveyards and Memorials

One of the most peaceful places to wander around is your local churchyard, somewhere quiet to take that break from a busy life. With the effects of weather and the passage of time monumental inscriptions are being lost to us daily, and this should be one of the first ports of call for family historians. Inscriptions can give more information than can be found in the parish registers or the census—and they can also provide that missing link to your family tree.

Early graves were marked with wooden boards or posts, which today have long since rotted away. The use of wood was followed by that of small stones set at the head and foot of the grave. As fashion changed the stones became bigger with more and more inscriptions engraved on them. The Victorians went in for very big and ornate stones, as well as the large tomb-shaped grave or mausoleum in which whole families were buried. Many stones weathered, split or became covered in lichen. Slate, which is often used in Wales, is an ideal medium as it will last for centuries.

Memorials were also placed within the church itself, either as a carved stone on the walls, a brass plaque or as a window. This does not necessarily mean that the person was buried in the church, they could still have a grave in the churchyard.

All Saints Church in Hertford shows two up-ended mill stones, the last resting place of the millwright Robert Fincher and his wife Elizabeth. At Henbury, near Bristol, is the resting place of the Earl of Suffolk's black servant, Scipio Africanus, who died in 1720, aged just eighteen; his stone has African faces painted on it. The following is on a headstone in St Chad's in Rochdale:

Here lieth the body of Samuel Kinshaw
of Church Stile, a Blacksmith
who departed this life October 8th 1810
in the 78th year of his age.
My anvil and my hammer lie declined
My bellows, too, have lost their wind
My fire's extinct, and forge decayed
And in the dust my vice is laid
My coal is spent, my iron gone
My last nail driven, my work done.

Many local family history societies have recorded the churchyards and cemeteries in their area and it is worth contacting them to check what has been transcribed.

Every village, town and city has its own war memorials, and in the UK many of these have been recorded. For further information about UK memorials contact: National Inventory of War Memorials, Imperial War Museum, Lambeth Road, London SE1 6HZ.

Left and below left: Graves of early settlers in the United States at the Sonora Pioneer Cemetery in California. Below: An English graveyard provides a wealth of family history for the genealogist.

Bissett, Bessett, Bissatt, Biset—"the son of Biset." It is said that the name of Bissett is a diminutive of the German name of Bis. It is also said to be of Huguenot derivation.

Black, Blake—a nickname from a dark complexion or hair. Earliest name found is Hamo le Blake in Buckinghamshire in 1273. Mainly found in London and Philadelphia.

Blackadar, Blackadder—a local name "of Blackadder," not far from the English border in Scotland. A river of that name runs there.

Blair—a name of Irish descent, meaning "from the plain."

Bondman, Bonman—an occupational name meaning "the bondman." Bonman is a modified form of the name.

Bonner, Bonnor, Boner—a nickname from "the debonair" meaning civil, gentle or courteous. Earliest name is found in England about 1273,

BASIC FAMILY TREES

RELATIONSHIPS ARE very complex; quite obviously, as we go back further into our family tree, the number of grandparents doubles. By going back ten generations to our eight-times great-grandparents, we will find that we are descended from 1,024 people. This figure would be reduced if cousins or second cousins had married each other. If you now assume that each of your ancestors had brothers and sisters, people descended from them would be your eighth cousins; you could be living in the same town and not know each other. In fact, few of us would even know or recognize our third cousins, yet we share a common set of two-times great-grandparents. We therefore have many more living relations around us than we could possibly know, but finding them is more difficult then finding our ancestors.

It is a very popular task for those living overseas to find living descendants of people who emigrated years ago. In the nineteenth century and early twentieth century, European emigration to the United States, Canada, Australia, New Zealand, and South Africa was very popular. During this period, millions of Irish people, for example, emigrated there and to mainland Britain, also a steady stream of people from Scotland, Wales, and England left to find their fortune overseas and many millions from mainland Europe (Germany, Italy, Spain, Scandinavia, and Central Europe) went to the Americas, both North and South.

To determine relationships, the chart (Chart A) shows that people with a common great-grandparent are second cousins and with a common great-great grandparent are third cousins and so on.

A similar problem can arise from an ancestor marrying more than once (Chart B):

A & B are half-brothers or -sisters to C & D
E & F are also half-brothers or -sisters to C & D
A & B are stepbrothers or sisters to E & F

Understanding these layouts will help when drawing up your own family chart and trees. The most common tree layout is the drop-line—in this you can insert as much or as little information as possible. To cope with the large amounts of offspring it is possible to draw a tree on the blank side of a roll of wallpaper. Drawing up sets of lines to keep the right

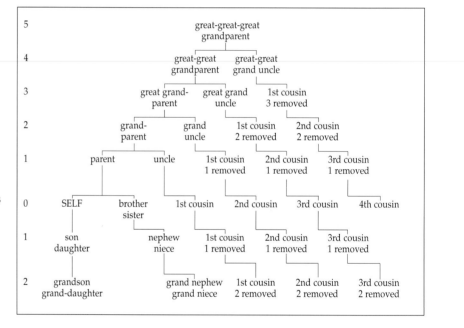

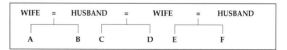

Above: Chart A.

Left: Chart B.

generation on the same line will be a difficult task; as you find more and more ancestors, you will need to erase and insert those extra relations. Our Victorian ancestors had very big families and they, in turn, would have had a large family.

Nowadays we can type all our information into a computer and the machine will lay it out for you, the usual way being the common "drop tree." Tree 1 shown here has been produced using a word processing program. Tree 2 was produced from a genealogical program, but it is

Top: Greek immigrants arriving in Germany in the 1950s. You may need to carry out a great deal of detective work to trace your ancestors if they emigrated to another country in the past.

still a type of "drop-line" tree. The problem here is that as the information increases so does the tree and many programs will only print onto A4 size paper (this will therefore mean having to stick trees together with sellotape). It is possible to show only one "drop-line" of parents and children and then use a reference number to link them to earlier or later generations.

Other types of trees are the circular and the semi-circular; the person on whom the chart is based is placed in the center of the circle and the direct ancestors only are displayed working outward. Two more are the "descent format" (Tree 3) and an "ancestors birth brief" (Tree 4).

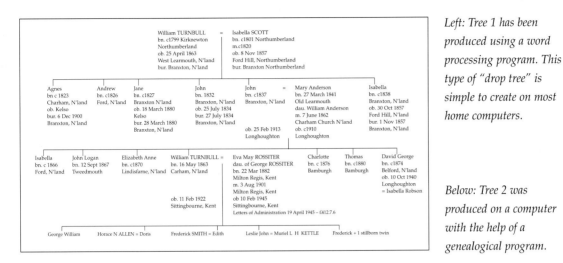

Left: Tree 1 has been produced using a word processing program. This type of "drop tree" is simple to create on most home computers.

Below: Tree 2 was produced on a computer with the help of a genealogical program.

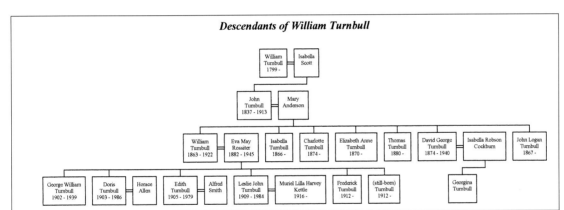

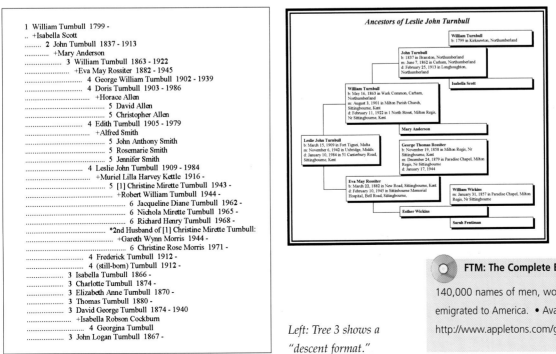

1 William Turnbull 1799 -
.. +Isabella Scott
.... 2 John Turnbull 1837 - 1913
.... +Mary Anderson
.... 3 William Turnbull 1863 - 1922
.... +Eva May Rossiter 1882 - 1945
.... 4 George William Turnbull 1902 - 1939
.... 4 Doris Turnbull 1903 - 1986
.... +Horace Allen
.... 5 David Allen
.... 5 Christopher Allen
.... 4 Edith Turnbull 1905 - 1979
.... +Alfred Smith
.... 5 John Anthony Smith
.... 5 Rosemarie Smith
.... 5 Jennifer Smith
.... 4 Leslie John Turnbull 1909 - 1984
.... +Muriel Lilla Harvey Kettle 1916 -
.... 5 [1] Christine Mirette Turnbull 1943 -
.... +Robert William Turnbull 1944 -
.... 6 Jacqueline Diane Turnbull 1962 -
.... 6 Nichola Mirette Turnbull 1965 -
.... 6 Richard Henry Turnbull 1968 -
.... *2nd Husband of [1] Christine Mirette Turnbull:
.... +Gareth Wynn Morris 1944 -
.... 6 Christine Rose Morris 1971 -
.... 4 Frederick Turnbull 1912 -
.... 4 (still-born) Turnbull 1912 -
.... 3 Isabella Turnbull 1866 -
.... 3 Charlotte Turnbull 1874 -
.... 3 Elizabeth Anne Turnbull 1870 -
.... 3 Thomas Turnbull 1880 -
.... 3 David George Turnbull 1874 - 1940
.... +Isabella Robson Cockburn
.... 4 Georgina Turnbull
.... 3 John Logan Turnbull 1867 -

Left: Tree 3 shows a "descent format."

Breviter, Brevitor, Bretter, Brevetor— official name "the brevetour," a private clerk, a writer of brevets for his lord; from brevet, a diminutive of brief, meaning letter; one whose duty was to write household expenses; a clerk to the steward.

Brown, Browne— meaning the "son of Brun," also Brownson. Also referred to brown hair or skin. In the Domesday Book Brun appears as a personal name; also the German Bruno. It is a popular name on both sides of the Atlantic.

Bruger—also meaning brown, variation of Bruno; also a spear.

Bulmer—a local of Bulmer in Essex, recorded in the Domesday Book as Bulenemera. Also from Old English "bulena" (of Bulls) and "mere" (lakes).

Burnett—son of Bernard or Barnard, a seller of fine woollen cloth originally dyed brown. Also a place cleared by burning.

Burward—an occupational name of a fortress guard.

Left: Tree 4 is an "ancestors birth brief."

SURNAMES

HAVE YOU ever wondered how your surname originated and where? In England, it was the Norman Conquest that introduced hereditary surnames, but then it was only for the landowning families and a limited number of others. Over several centuries the fashion to have a surname spread, until most of the country was included. There are many books on the subject, but the best known must be the *Dictionary of British Surnames* and *The Origins of English Surnames* by P. H. Reaney. *A Dictionary of English and Welsh Surnames* by Charles Wareing Bardsley, MA, includes surnames with special American instances.

Surnames have five main origins: place names, location of abode, occupations, nicknames, and lastly patronymics.

PLACE NAMES

Place-name surnames come from the names of villages, towns and manors. In early English documentation the name would be prefaced by "de", of Norman origin, meaning "from" or "of." In Huntingdonshire in 1273 there is an Alan de Chartres, which could mean he was from Chatteris, a place in Cambridgeshire, or Chartres, a place name still in modern-day France. By looking through Bardsley's book many examples of this name can be found. The name Kenworthy might be from the manor of

Kenworthy in eastern Cheshire. Over time the first few letters could have changed, making the surname Langworthy.

LOCAL NAMES

Local names, or location of abode, can be derived from living at or near the well, giving the name of Atwell or Attwell, or perhaps Attwood from "living at the wood." There are many examples of this kind of surname: Firtree, a local of/at the fir tree; or Crabtree, Plumtree, and even Rowntree, which might be from "rowan" tree or have become Roundtree, as in living around a group of trees or a small wood. Underhill would have resulted from living under or at the bottom of a hill. Hazell, Hazle or Hazel, from a local living at the hazel or hazeltree—note how the variations come about. In German the word for Ash is Asch, therefore the name of Aschendorf comes from the "ash tree village." The list is endless.

OCCUPATIONAL NAMES

Occupational names are self-explanatory, as they came from the occupation or status of a person (see page 109). Falder or Faulder means the falder of a herd, one who tended cattle. The name Hobman, from the servant of Hob (or the hobman), is from the hobbyman, or one who looked after or rode a hobby, meaning a small horse. The occupational name for the smith is common is most countries: Smith, Smyth, and Smythe, not forgetting that this is translated into most languages (Schmitt, in German) but still means "the smith." In Britain this practice was repeated in Welsh, for smith is *gov*, which could have contributed to the surname Gough. In

Above: Occupational names are very common and are usually self-explanatory. In rural communities names such as "thatcher" and "shepherd" were often used to describe particular individuals or families.

Above: The occupational name "smith," and its foreign language translation is common in most countries.

Left: Family surnames have five main origins: place names, location of abode, occupations, nicknames, and patronymics.

Cornish the surname Angove means "the smith." Notice the middle syllable in Angove, is the same as the Welsh, *gov.* Carpenter, Wright, Wainwright, and Cartwright are also examples of occupational names.

NICKNAMES

Surnames derived from nicknames are a varied batch. They can be a description of the ancestor's face, build, temper, tastes and much more. Examples are: Smart, Chick, Daff, Fairweather (the latter having the meaning of a happy sunshine man), Herdson (from the son of the herd or herdman), Thrush (could be a person in good voice rather than the bird). From the appearance we have Long, Short, Ballard, and Pollard—the last two being English names for bald men. The color of one's hair or face, leaves us with Black, Gray/Grey, Reed, Reid, Faire, Fairfax.

PATRONYMICS

Patronymics are names which are derived from the personal name or occupation of the person's father—or even mother, but this is rarer. The first Richards may have been Richard's man or Richard's son; similarly, Robert, Roberts, Robson, and Robertson. If you see the additional letter of "s" or the word "son," this indicates that this person was "the son of"—the same as the Irish "O" and Scottish and Irish "Mac" prefixes. These types of names could be what Charles Wareing Bardsley calls baptismal names, still meaning "the son of."

One thing to remember is that just because several people have the same surname, they are not necessarily descended from the same common ancestor. One should never draw a quick conclusion about the origin of a surname from its modern-day spelling. Over the centuries, pronunciation of sound and spelling can corrupt the name severely: for example, the

Above: Carter, a common name in England, is an occupational name for the maker or driver of carts.

English surname of Kettle proves this with its wide variants of Cetal, Cettel, Kettell, Kettlee, Ketal plus many, many more. We must keep an open mind as we delve further back into our ancestral line; just because the spelling has changed, you cannot say with certainty that this is not the correct line.

One thing to look at is the first name. During the 1800s it was fairly common in both the United States and Britain to give the child a second name, usually the mother's maiden name. This was given to boys and girls alike and sometimes followed down several generations. It is a great help when the surname is a common name.

Another particularly American trend was to name children after famous people and celebrities and in the twentieth century children have been given the first names of sports, film, radio, and television stars.

Cambray—local name "of Cambray" a city in the Netherlands. It is often the name of an early immigrant.

Camero—a "dweller in" or a "worker at" the hall.

Cameron—a Scots Gaelic name for "crooked" or "hook nose." Also a local name with places found in Fife, Scotland.

Capper—occupation "the capper," a maker or dealer in caps. Thomas Pendilton, a capper, 1562, found in the Preston Guild Rolls. The capper made caps in a woollen material, then later in felt.

Carey—a local "of Carey" a great West Country surname. Also a known Jewish name.

Carter—the maker of carts or driver of carts; car is a diminutive of cart. Found in London and Philadelphia.

Below: Cornish Roots is a useful local area CD-ROM.

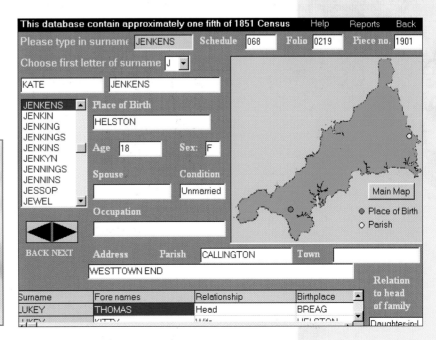

ORGANIZING YOUR SEARCH

*A*S FAMILY historians we like nothing better than to collect masses upon masses of paper. What do we do with it all? Notes and documents should be arranged in a clear and logical way. Further research can be hindered by a lack of organization—so start as you mean to go on.

Keep your notes legible. If you rewrite anything when you get home, check it to make sure no error has occur in the transcribing—get someone else to read it through. Always write the source of the information and the reference number of the documents, microfilm or microfiche, as well as where the source was located. For example, if you have been checking a census return for England in 1871, the reference of the film would be "RG 10 Reel ?," then mark "Census 1871."

RESEARCH PROGRESS RECORD

Prepare a Research Progress Record, for each of your ancestors. Put their full name at the top of the page, leaving a gap to allow you to write in dates and places of birth, marriage and death, and wife or husband's names, as you find them. Divide the remainder of the sheet into three columns, heading them Source, Year(s) Searched, and Findings/Conclusions. So, if you were to check the baptismal registers for John Doe, first write his name at the top of the page, then write the name of the parish, the type of register and the repository (work out a list of abbreviations for the repositories you use), any reference number, in the next column put the year searched or years—1850–1876 or 1843—and in the last column put your findings or any remarks: "Nothing found," "The film was unreadable," or "Have found his baptism."

In recording information from documents and monumental inscriptions, there may be parts which you cannot read, or can only read a little; in which case, place square brackets and a question mark around them, eg. John [red?] Doe. Some researchers type forenames and surnames in capital letters, e.g. JOHN ALFRED DOE. Any information you find should be recorded in exactly the same way as the archive document. One important thing to remember is that you need to distinguish between facts and your analysis of the information. If you have a fairly unusual surname, collect as many certificates as possible, for they can help expand your family search. When checking a surname index, the golden rule is always to check back to the original name.

When you first start with your family tree and haven't much paperwork, use a concertina file, with one for the maternal line and another for the paternal line. Name each pocket with a surname, and as you find further names, add these as well. As you accumulate a little information, write up a small family tree and keep it in the front pocket. If you start off with a neat, simple system it will become easier to expand the filing system later, as more and more information is found.

Below: If you are using a computer to compile your family search, you will find a wide choice of genealogy software programs available to make the process of organizing your material as easy as possible.

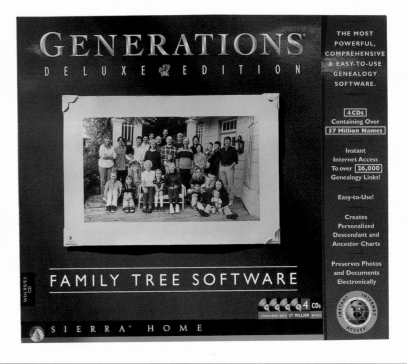

USING YOUR COMPUTER

If you do have a computer and a family history software package, start using it now. Open a directory, one for each of the maternal and paternal lines, and if you have an unusual name, open a database. If the data is entered from the start and added to as you acquire further information you will never let it get on top of you. For the family historians who have been researching their family history for twenty years or more, their work began before personal computers were available. As they started to become computerized the graft really started, for it can take months, or even longer, to input all those years of research. Then just as it seems that you have finished entering it all, a new and far better software program comes on to the market. But if you have software packages with GEDCOM files, transferring from one program to another is an easy matter. Many researchers will stay with just one program, while others will have several programs, perhaps because they like the way one package prints out the family tree, and another stores information in a better way.

Whatever system you start with, try to keep your filing and your notes up to date. It is an easy matter to say, "I'll do that tomorrow," but tomorrow never comes.

Above: Use a Research Progress Record to note all of the documents you can find, such as this birth certificate, for each family member.

Above and left: Home computers and the wide availability of genealogy software have helped to revolutionize family searches. Some researchers work with one program only, while others prefer to use several types of software for specific areas of research.

FILING SYSTEMS AND CARD INDEXES

ONCE YOU find you have two bulging concertina files it is time to move on. However, even with my family history entered into a computer, I still like to have family files available containing hard copies of everything.

To expand on the concertina file, it now makes sense to have a separate ring binder for each name which you are researching. In the front, place your Research Progress Records. If your first file is for your grandmother, write her maiden name on the binder's spine and file all of your paperwork inside. Try to have some sort of order: all certificates together (copies only, the original should be safely filed away), all census copies, wills, newspaper cuttings; or section it with the names of the person—your grandmother's mother's information together, her father's, his father, and so on. As you are the person working with the files, you should decide which method to use, and then stick to it.

As you start to correspond with people who are perhaps researching the same names, keep a separate ring binder. Use dividers to give each surname its own section. On the opening page write the names and addresses of the correspondents, the date received and the date answered. Answer your post within a couple of days, don't say "I'll do it at the end of the week"—which week? Remember, just as you are waiting for a reply to your letters, then so are they waiting for your reply.

CARD INDEX SYSTEM

Another way to keep information to hand is a card index, these cards can be retrieved easily and are portable enough to take with you when you are researching a certain person. The best size is 8 in x 5 in, although there are smaller sizes. I prefer the larger size as this allows room for the information I want to keep on them, but this is up to the individual. The following is an example of my grandmother's card index.

FRONT SIDE:

Name: Lilla Edith Harvey daughter of George Harvey & Elizabeth Filby

Born: January 27, 1890, at Van Diemans Lane, Chelmsford, Essex

Bapt: February 25, 1890, at St John's Church Moulsham, Chelmsford

Marr: June 5, 1915, at Minster Abbey Church, Minster, Isle of Sheppey, Kent, to Henry George Kettle

Died: July 15, 1969, at 59 Rock Road, Sittingbourne, Kent

Cremated: July 22, 1969, at Charing, Kent

1890— in Chelmsford, father agricultural labourer. source: birth cert.

1891— in Chelmsford, father market gardener. source: 1891 census

1896— in Chelmsford. source: brother's birth

1898— in Minster, Isle of Sheppey, Kent. source: Bible from school

1915— living at Little Woottons Farm, Minster. source: marriage cert.

1921— living at Kenilworth, Minster. source: deeds of house

1923— qualified as midwife. source: PRO nurses list

1938— moved to Park Road, Sittingbourne. source: info from her daughter.

Above: Make copies of all of your original documents, such as this birth certificate registered in Malta, to keep in order within your filing system.

1939—moved to Rock Road, Sittingbourne. source: solicitor's bill

1969—in Rock Road, Sittingbourne. source: death cert.

Notes: Served on the Isle of Sheppey as a midwife until 1938. Then transferred to Sittingbourne; trained pupil midwives until her retirement in 1950.

Children: Muriel Lilla Harvey Kettle and Gregory George Kettle

REVERSE SIDE:

Details from birth cert:
Father: George Harvey, agricultural labourer, Mother: Elizabeth Harvey, formerly Bannister, registered by mother February 13, 1890

Details from parish register:
St John's Church Moulsham, baptized February 25, 1890, father ag. lab., resident at Van Diemans Lane, Chelmsford

Details from marriage cert:
Age 25 years, Spinster, resident at Little Woottons Farm, Minster. Father, George Harvey, a farmer. Witnesses George Harvey and Edith Rosalind Chesters (father and step-sister)

Details from death cert:
Cause of death: Chronic bronchitis, asthma and heart failure. Death registered by Muriel Lilla Harvey Turnbull—daughter

Details from will:
Ref: 1969, Page 323, died July 15, 1969. Rock Road, Sittingbourne. Probate Brighton, 14 October 1969, £12,639.00

Right: Old wills are a useful source of family history.

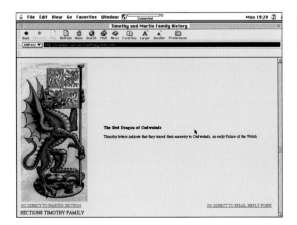

GO DIRECT TO MARTIN SECTION   GO DIRECT TO EMAIL REPLY FORM
SECTIONS TIMOTHY FAMILY

New Computer Aided Genealogy Book

Comes with free Top Ten CDs of genealogy demos and shareware. Contains *Generation/Reunion*, *Family Tree Maker*, *Family Origins* 6, *Genealogy for Windows*, *Winfamily*, *TMG*, *Brother's Keeper* 5.2F, *Cumberland Tree* Win/Win 95, *A-Tools*, *GED Commander* and the *TMG* 3 to 3.5 upgrade.

• Available from S & N Genealogy Supplies: http://www.genealogy.demon.co.uk

From this sort of information, so much has been learned about one person, and parts of her family. This card is then a very handy thing to take with you when looking for further records for her. It will also mean you will not duplicate your research and therefore waste precious time. Keep a note pad handy and use it for a "to do" list. The life of a happy researcher is a good filing and record-keeping system.

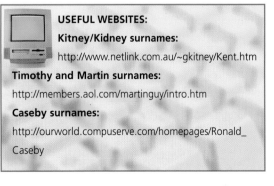

USEFUL WEBSITES:

Kitney/Kidney surnames:
http://www.netlink.com.au/~gkitney/Kent.htm

Timothy and Martin surnames:
http://members.aol.com/martinguy/intro.htm

Caseby surnames:
http://ourworld.compuserve.com/homepages/Ronald_Caseby

Left: The Timothy and Martin Family History website.

Castellan—an official, "the castellan" or the constable of the castle. It could be that Castleman is a corrupted form of Castellan.

Castillo, Castro—a dweller living near a castle or a castle servant.

Chapman—occupation "the chapman." Probably the early chapman was stationary; the traveling chapman was of a lower grade. An Act during Edward VI's reign speaks of "person or persons commonly called Pedler, Tynker or Pety Chapman."

Churchill—local parishes of Churchill are found in Bath and Wells, Bristol, Oxford and Worcester. The earliest person found was a Richard de Churchulle in Somerset in 1273.

Winston Churchill.

Clark, Clarke, Clerk—official name "the clerk," the clergyman, a clerk in holy orders. A scholar who could read and write. Taking Clark and Clarke as one name they are the ninth commonest name in England. Also found in Boston.

Clay—name for someone who lived in an area of clay soil, or an occupation for a person who worked with clay; possibly a brickmaker.

COMPUTER PROGRAMS

T HERE CAN be little doubt that there has never been a better time to get a computer: they are faster, more powerful and easier to use than ever before. Computers are also cheaper than they have ever been and the range of software packages and additional useful pieces of equipment continues to grow while prices come down. Always check to ensure a package is appropriate for your computer system and that your equipment is powerful enough to run it. Finally, try to get opinions from friends who already use packages regarding the sort of features to look out for.

Generations

Generations is the latest version of *Reunion*, the only program to feature both drag and drop customization of charts and the customisation of reports automatically on your word processor. It comes with *Netting Your Ancestors* by Cindy Howell, plus lots of extra CDs.
• Available from S & N Genealogy Supplies:
http://www.genealogy.demon.co.uk

FAMILY TREE MAKER

This excellent program by Broderbund Software Ltd is available in three editions: basic, standard and deluxe. The basic is powerful and designed for people who are starting out on genealogical research; the standard includes the *FamilyFinder Index* and the Internet connections; the deluxe contains all the items mentioned plus six world *Family Tree* CDs and two Social Security Death Benefit Records CDs. The *Family Tree Maker* program has the ability to handle unconventional relationships, such as foster, step-, half- relationships and multiple marriages; it has a sources database to track research; it is compatible with GEDCOM and PAF formats; and you can insert Kodak Photo CD, TIFF and other common image file formats to help you to make colorful albums, scrapbooks and professional family books. Sound and video clips can also be stored on the program.

(See http://www.broderbund.com)

FAMILY HERITAGE DELUXE

This started out as Corel *Family Tree Suite*, which was acquired by IMSI and has now been taken over by The Learning Company (Mindscape). The package includes the *US Social Security* CDs and *Corel Photo House* plus a manual. Data can be entered in two ways, either into a data window or tree window. It has the usual printouts of ancestors, descendants and family

groups, but each tree can have customized backgrounds, border lines and much more, to enable you to create a series of beautiful, timeless family trees.

(See http://www.mindscape.com)

ULTIMATE FAMILY TREE

This is available from Palladium Interactive. As with many software packages, this one also includes an Internet system with which you can create and publish a website. It has an impressive charting facility, and a range of fan charts can be produced in quarter circles, semi-circles and full circles with excellent results. It can also store a large range of details on each person, and it has a rapid GEDCOM import.

(See http://www.palladium.net/)

ANCESTRAL QUEST

Supplied by Incline Software in Salt Lake City, this is claimed to offer the complete family history solution, combining a powerful genealogy program with advanced multimedia scrapbook features. It is ideal for storing your family history information, while making it educational and fun. Data entry is easy through either of the two main data entry screens:

Family Origins version 7

Contains new multiple parents list, sortable marriage list, indented descendant book chart and photo editing tools.
• Available from S & N Genealogy Supplies:
http://www.genealogy.demon.co.uk

USEFUL WEBSITES:
David Hawgood (writes the computer section in *Family Tree Magazine*)
http://ourworld.compuserve.com/homepages/David_ Hawgood/

Pandect Services, supplier of general genealogy programs:
http://ourworld.compuserve.com/homepages/pandect

Above: Family Origins is a firm favorite with genealogists due to its ease of use and modest price. There are genealogy programs to suit all tastes and pockets, so ask other family historians to recommend their favorite software before you buy.

Pedigree View and Family View. It includes guides to Genealogy Resources and a Beginner's Guide to Genealogy.

FAMILY ORIGINS

This can be purchased on-line by credit card from Parsons Technology and is a long-time favourite with genealogists due to its modest price and ease of use. It is possible to edit all facts associated with the individual from one screen, and the number and type of facts entered is unlimited. A new feature it has added is the To Do List, a very handy reminder. It is a good all-round software package for both the beginner and more experienced genealogist. (See http://www.parsonstech.com)

REUNION 5

This Macintosh program is classed as one of the best packages, and it will run on almost any Mac, PowerMac or Mac clone running system 7.0 or later. Included in *Reunion 5* is a Speed Names feature, which will guess place names or surnames as you type them, but does not work on first names. Its Superchart is one of the few charts you can edit, once created.

(See http://www.leister.com)

US President Clinton

Clinton—local name "of Glinton" a parish in Northampton, three miles from Market Deeping. The change from the initial G to C was quite common.

Coles—from "the son of Nicholas," from the nickname of Cole, a diminutive of Colin. It is also said to be a Jewish surname.

Cook, Cooke, Cookson —"the cook," one who bakes pies, etc. for sale. Son of Cook.

Cooper—an occupational name, a maker or repairer of wooden tubs, caskets or buckets. Comes from German and Low Latin. Common everywhere except in the north of England; twenty-eighth commonest name in England and Wales.

Cozens, Cousen, Cousine, Cussen— meaning "the cousin," a kinsman or near relation. Also thought to be of Huguenot descent.

Cronberger, Cronberg *see also Kronberg*— a name meaning "crown mountain."

Types of Family Trees

There are not only many types of family tree layouts, but various ways of preparing them. The majority of computer software packages will produce a tree from the information input to the package. Most "drop-line" pedigrees, birth briefs and circular designs are prepared in this way, and using various colors they can also look very attractive.

Many family historians also like to draw out their own tree, allowing for their own designs, crests, heraldry symbols and photographs to be mounted on the finished item, and then have them framed. As this is a document which you will want to keep in your family for many years, it is as well to use good quality materials. Look for strong paper which will absorb the ink but will not spread; also a material which has an attractive appearance, so consider a hand-made paper instead of a machine-made one. The traditional surface for documents—of parchment and vellum—is still produced, but the cost is very high, so use it only when you are confident in its use; it is not for the inexperienced person.

Draft out your tree on rough paper first, checking your measurements and layout. The use of different color pens leads to a more attractive design. Use black for names and red for dates and place names, but experiment first.

The use of circles and semi-circles for family trees is very popular, but will only include the parents of each descendant—there is no room to include brothers and sisters. There are trees for a direct line of descent, also a narrow-line descent, when the husband and wife are produced in a line, one above each other. Spaces can be filled in with photographs and crests.

There are many pre-printed designs on the market today. Some are just a basic "drop-line" chart, others are ornate tree-shaped and pictorial designs. The masterpiece will always be that stitched family tree on the wall, to show to your friends for years to come.

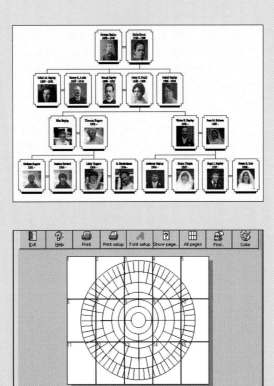

Above: Many genealogy software packages provide ready-to-use family tree charts which allow you to drop in your own family details to print out.

PRESERVING YOUR DOCUMENTS
AND PHOTOGRAPHS

THE NEED to save and preserve your family memorabilia should be a high priority on your list. Don't take notes and put the original documents to one side to look at again later because they will become very damaged. Start by making copies of all the documents. Color photocopies are ideal for most of your certificates (reduce certificates to A4 size in order to keep them in a working folder) and photographs. General documents, such as wills, copies of pages from Bibles and autograph albums can be copied on a cheaper black and white copier. By using the copies in your working files, you will save and preserve your original documents.

Frith Historic Photographs CD

Contains the vintage photographs of the famous Frances Frith Topographical Collection. Can be copied to the clipboard and pasted into generation charts. The dates range from 1880 to the 1950s.

• Available from S & N Genealogy Supplies: http://www.genealogy.demon.co.uk

Photographs are the most precious items in your collection and should be well looked after —don't forget to put the name and dates on the back (in pencil on a matt paper, in a special permanent ink if gloss). If you insist on having photographs on the wall in frames, have professional copies made by a photographer, who can even produce a sepia finish if you wish. Use these copies in the frames and then put the originals away. Whether your original quality material are prints, transparencies, negatives or glass plates, and whether black and white or color, they should all be looked after in the same way:

• Don't handle them directly, use researcher's gloves or a pair of soft cotton gloves so that the oils from your skin will not mark the originals; don't try to polish or clean smears.

• Never use spray or liquid cleaning products because most contain harmful chemical abrasives that could scratch and, even worse, discolor the surface.

• Don't reuse photographic paper-print boxes to rehouse your prints, transparencies, etc. Even if you have used archival-quality storage enclosures, practically all the boxes sold today contain very high acid, lignin, and sulphur, that will, even with short-term contact, lead to image fading, tone loss, surface deterioration and discoloration. Look for special archival-quality photographic storage boxes, that are not only acid-free, but also free of lignin and sulphur. Look for boxes that are chemically buffered externally, but have a non-buffered interior and

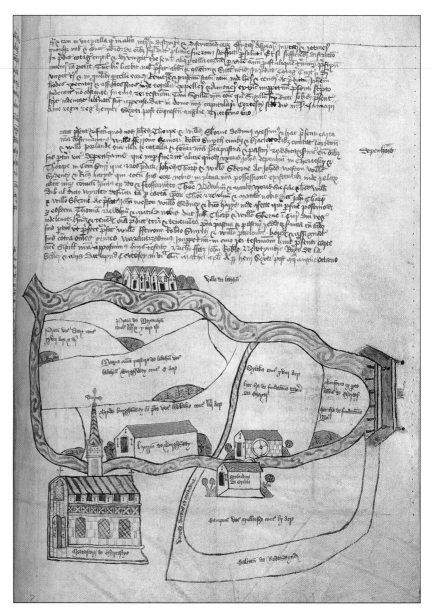

Above: Make copies of all of your documents and store the valuable originals carefully.

Crouch, Croucher—one who lived near a cross, from the Old English word of "cruc." Also a local of the river in Essex of the same name.
Cuckold—a nickname "the cuckold" for a man with a false and untrue wife. The surname did not last long.
Curtis—this is a nickname for a man who was courteous or of a good education. It is also known as a Huguenot surname.
Da Costa—a known Jewish name. Also Cost or Coste from "the son of Constantine." Constantine was formerly a popular name in Cornwall.
Dalby, Dalbey—a local of Dalby, a parish in the North Riding of Yorkshire, also a parish in Lincoln. Dalbey is an American variant of the surname, but it did exist in the UK in the seventeenth century.
Davie, Davies, Davis, Davison—baptismal name, "the son of David" in Hebrew. David came from a lullaby word for "darling" or "friend."
Dengler—(German) meaning one who repairs blades by hammering them.

are separated from each other by an inert polyester lining, not polythene. The chemical buffering will be calcium carbonate and the level should be no more than 2–3 per cent.
• Transparencies, negatives, and glass plates should be stored in an upright position; photographs and print material should, wherever possible, be stored flat in one or two storage boxes. Do take the necessary steps to ensure your images are preserved for the future.

DOCUMENTS AND CERTIFICATES

Your certificates must also be stored flat, and on the market are various sized binders, many of which will take up to forty certificates, placing them back-to-back. Special "inert" acid-free wallets are designed to fit in the binders. When buying pockets or wallets for your binders ask what they are made of. If you are not satisfied with the answer you get, or the salesperson hasn't a clue what you are talking about, don't buy. The value of your collection is always greater than the price of any kind of storage pocket. Check the sizes of the certificates before you purchase the binder and wallet.

When looking at storage pockets and folders, if it is plastic, don't use it. When it comes to looking after paper in their care, museums and record offices use only what they know to be made of archive-quality materials. They know that all material, pockets, and boxes they use are proven through chemical analysis to be inert,

pure or neutral. Use these to protect your letters, press cuttings, books, and documents. If unsure at any time, visit the local museum and ask their advice, they will be only too happy to help. (Also, if you have a damaged book or papers, see if they can advise you on someone to help with the repairs.)

The following are details on types of storage pocket materials:
• PVC (polyvinyl chloride). This is probably the most common for pockets and usually attractive due to its cheapness. It contains plasticizers for flexibility which migrate into your paper and the solvent affects whatever is stored in the pocket. It causes ink and color loss and rapid deterioration of the paper. As it is so harmful, it should not be used even for a short time.
• Cellulose acetates are initially clear, but go yellow, brittle, and shrink with age. When they have been treated with plastic to stop them going brittle, the same problems will arise as with PVC.
• Polyethelene is chemically inert in its pure form, but is visually cloudy. It is difficult to tell apart from PVC and like polythene can have added plasticizers. It has a greasy feel, and although dealers claim it is safe, it deteriorates in humid conditions.
• Polyester is the material approved by the major archives for long-term storage and protection as being 100 per cent archival safe. If in doubt ask an expert.

ABBREVIATIONS EXPLAINED

WHEN LAYING out a family tree, abbreviations are used. The straight lines, showing the descent of a family line, tell us that the children are legitimate and come from married parents. An = sign between the parents also denotes they are married. An x between the parents shows us they were not married and the child is illegitimate, the descent line for which is a squiggle. If the parents of the child marry at a later date, the x becomes = but the descent line is now a squiggle and then a straight line.

Right: Killed in action (kia); graves of fallen US soldiers in a military cemetery.

A list of useful abbreviations

=	indicates married to	dau	daughter	lab	laborer
x	unmarried parents of an	div	divorced	LDS	Church of Jesus Christ of Latter-day
	illegitimate child	ER	Examination of Removal Order		Saints (the Mormon Church)
		Exam	Examination	Lic lic	Licence
Admon	Letters of Administration	Fa	father	m mar	married
Ae Aet	aged	fam	family	Meth	Methodist
Ag lab	Agricultural laborer	F of f	Fleet of fines	MIs	Monumental Inscriptions
AGRA	Association of Genealogists and	FFHS	Federation of Family History	mss	manuscript
	Record Agents (UK)		Societies	NA	National Archives
App Appr	Apprentice	fie	son	née	surname at birth
b bn brn	born	fil et hr	son and heir	*NGD*	*National Genealogical Directory*
BALH	British Association of Local History	fo	folio	notp	not of this parish
bap bapt	baptize(d)	FS	Female servant	ob obit	died
Bapt	Baptist	GHL	Guildhall Library	OPRs	Old Parochial Registers (pre-1855
bas Bas	Bastard	GLRO	Greater London Record Office		parish registers in Scotland)
b b	Base-born (illegitimate)	GOONS	Guild of One-Name Studies	otp	of this parish
B B	Bastardy Bond	GPC	Genealogical Publishing Company	par	parish
bd bu bur	buried	*GRD*	*Genealogical Research Directory*	P Meth	Primitive Methodist
BMD	Births, Marriages, Deaths	GSU	Genealogical Society of Utah	PRO	Public Record Office (UK)
BNL	British Newspaper Library	gt	great	PR	Parish Registers
bns	Banns	he ap	heir apparent	QS	Quarters Sessions
botp	both of this parish	hse	house	Qtr	quarter
Br	Brother	Ind	of independent means	rel relict	widow
B Ts	Bishop's Transcripts	IGI	International Genealogical Index	SA	State Archives
c ca	*circa* (at about that date)	illeg	illegitimate	SOG	Society of Genealogists (UK)
c chr	christened	Inf	Infant	sic	so written
Cal	Calendar	Inv	Inventory	Spin Spr	spinster
C of E	Church of England	IRC	International Reply Coupon	TS	Typescript
cent	century	ISBN	International Standard Book	ux	wife
cert	certificate		Number	VIV	was then living
Con Cong	Congregational	ISBGFH	International Society for British	wid	widow (ed) (er)
CRO	County Record Office (UK)		Genealogy and Family History	wit	witness
Ct	Court	JP	Justice of the Peace (UK)	yeo	yeoman
d dd	died	kia	killed in action		

A couple on a family tree could look like this:

Hannah Kettle = George Spitty

When a person marries more then once, then the order of the marriage is marked (1) or (2). A male descendant who has had two wives will appear as follows:

(1) Eliza Such = George Harvey (2) Elizabeth Bannister

Under the names would be such abbreviations as: bn (for born), bapt (for baptized), m (for married), ob (for died), bur (for buried). Therefore, a descendant on a tree would appear as:

Lilla Edith Harvey
bn Jan 27, 1890, Chelmsford
m June 5, 1915, Minster Abbey Church
   Isle of Sheppey
ob July 15, 1969, Sittingbourne
bur July 22, 1969, Charing

GLOSSARY OF TERMS

The following is a glossary of terms commonly used in family history:

Abstract—A summary of the essential details from a document

Affidavit—Written declaration on oath

Allegation—Statement made on oath

Badgeman—A person responsible for ensuring that all paupers receiving parish relief wore badges to identify them

Blanket search—A search through a set of records looking for a specific reference, e.g. a surname, a trade

Brewster Sessions—Annual sessions held to license victuallers from 1729

Calendar—A précis full enough to replace an original document for most purposes. It is also commonly used for a list of names which is only alphabetical by the first letter of each surname

Chattels—Personal goods

Diocese—Area of a bishop's jurisdiction

Foundling—Abandoned infant, often left in a public place

Hundred—Administrative division of a county

Husbandman—A small farmer, usually a tenant farmer

Incumbent—Holding the office of parson, vicar, rector or perpetual curate

Palaeography—The study of old handwriting and inscriptions

Ragged School—A school for poor children, provided free of charge in cases of extreme poverty

Stray—A person found referred to in a place other than his or her place of birth or settlement

Terrier—Record giving details of land holding

Vagrant—Person of no fixed abode

Below: A Ragged School. These were schools which often provided free education for the poorest children.

Dexter—an occupational name "the dighester," a "dydter" or dyer. There are six Dexters to one Dyster in the *London Directory*.

Diaz, Dias—a descendant of Diego or Jacob. Possibly a Jewish and/or Spanish name.

Dillon—from the early German word "Dillo," possibly connected with the word for "destroy." The name was taken to Ireland in the twelfth century, and is now commonly considered to be of Irish origin.

Diprose—a local of de Prèaux, in Normandy. In France there are seven places called Prèaux.

Dive, Dives—a local of "de Dive," possibly from a local place name in Normandy, France.

PROBLEMS OF SPELLING, NAME CHANGING, AND DATES

IN DOCUMENTS from early periods it is quite common to find a variety of different spellings of a surname. Names can often appear with a phonetic spelling; as mentioned earlier, a person's dialect might affect a spelling, and because most people in centuries gone by were unable to read or write, they were unable to check how their name had been written down in official records.

Spelling gradually became more standardized during the seventeenth and eighteenth centuries, and literacy improved as time went on.

Other problems could occur if a name contained silent letters. Some letters sound the same or may have been transcribed incorrectly, "p" as "b", and "m" as "n", or vice versa. Look at the surname of Filby, Filbey, Filbee, Philby, Philbey and Philbee with the "F" as "Ph", or vice versa. Another example is the spelling of Humphry, Humphrey, Humfrey; if the "H" is dropped in pronunciation, as is the case in some English counties, the surname become Umfrey, Unfrey—note also the changing of the "m" and "n." Another surname which is easily changed in spelling but the pronunciation is the same is Rolfe, Rolf, Rolph, Rolof, Rollf, Rolhlf.

Although curates and registrars were sufficiently educated enough to do their job, it doesn't necessarily mean they could spell, any more than it does today.

Three other ways surnames changed were: deed polls, a widow remarrying (in a second marriage she would have had three different surnames), or simply because someone just wanted to change their name—it is recognized by English common law that a person may assume a new surname provided he or she does not do so for any fraudulent purpose. The absence of a formal record can be very inconvenient to the family historian when trying to find that elusive ancestor.

Additional problems can occur with relationships: women get recorded as daughter, mother or sister and could be a daughter-in-law, mother-in-law, sister-in-law, or stepdaughter, stepmother, stepsister. The same can happen with the men.

Below: Handwriting can often cause problems when searching for names.

HANDWRITING

Handwriting and language will also give problems when looking for surnames, or just in the transcribing of a document. When reading a difficult document write down the words you recognize and from this build up an alphabet of letters. Then start to read the document and when you have a section you cannot read, check on the letters you do know, and build the word from them. Any abbreviations should be copied just as they are in the record. Also in a small notebook, build up a list of the common Latin words. (Have a good dictionary by you to check the meanings of words.)

PLACE NAMES

Place names can prove a problem. In the English county of Northumberland, for example, there are two places called Wark, one near the River Tyne and the other near the River Tweed. In records they may just quote Wark, then you have to work out which one; in this case, Wark-on-Tyne is a reasonably sized market town with its own church and shops, while Wark-on-Tweed is a small hamlet without a church, no shops and very few houses. Which one would you choose, especially with a very common surname for the county? We all think of

Above: This example of a church covenant shows the probems often encountered when transcribing documents.

Index of Place Names on CD-ROM

An electronic gazetteer linking 60,000 places in England and Wales to their local government administrative areas. Produced by the National Statistics Office.

• Available from ONS Sales Desk, zone B1/06, Office of National Statistics, 1 Drummond Gate, London SW1V 2QQ.

Gibraltar as being on the tip of southern Spain, but there are Gibraltars in Kent, Suffolk, Lincolnshire, and Bedfordshire in England. The Europeans who traveled to Australia, Canada, and the United States named new towns after places they knew in the old country: Huntingdon, London, Richmond, Lincoln, Dover, and hundreds more. There are, for example, places called Liverpool in England, New York, and even Australia.

CALENDARS

The main problem with dates can occur with the use of the two calendars, the Julian calendar used from 1190 to December 31, 1751, and then the Gregorian calendar which has been used from January 1, 1752, to the present. By the sixteenth century the Julian calendar differed by ten days from the solar year, that is the time that the Earth takes to orbit the sun. The changeover resulted in the loss of eleven days between September 2, 1752, and September 14, 1752. Special charts are available that can help to discover the actual day when an event took place. Peter Wotton wrote an article entitled "That will be the day!" in *Family Tree Magazine* in February 1998. In it he gives the tables by which to work out the day of the week for both the Julian and Gregorian calendars.

Left: MacDonald is a common name in the Scottish Highlands, but it is likely to be found as Donald in the Scottish Lowlands and English borders.

Dominey, Dominy, Dominick—baptismal name "the son of Dominic," possibly from Spain. Quite rare in England, but found in London and New York.

Donald, Donalds, Donaldson—baptismal name "the son of Donald." The Scottish equivalent would be MacDonald, but in the Lowlands of Scotland and borders of England it would be found in its form of Donald.

Drew, Drewe, Druce—"the son of Drew" or "Dru," known as "Drogo" in the Domesday Book. It is also a known Huguenot name.

Dunton—a local name for someone living near the settlement of Dunton in Essex. From the Old English of "dun" (hill) and "tun" (enclosure or settlement).

Durand, Durant, Durrant, Durran—baptismal name "the son of Durand or Durant" found in the Domesday Book. Durant is old French for "enduring" or "obstinate."

Duxbury, Duxbarry, Dukesbury—a local "of Duxbury," a parish town in Lancashire.

Dwight—the son of Dionisia; could be a corruption of Thwaite.

CIVIL REGISTRATION

MORE THAN 150 years ago, it was announced that in England and Wales, from July 1, 1837, civil registration of all births, marriages, and deaths was to begin. This meant that the civil authorities would record the event and a certificate would be issued to the person concerned. The country was divided into Registration Districts, based on the existing Poor Law Unions, and each district was given its own Superintendent Registrar. Within the Registration District were Sub-Districts. The original entries of births and deaths were kept at each registrar's office and copies of the entries were sent quarterly to a central office located in London.

The recording of baptisms and burials continued in the churches and chapels just as before. Marriages taking place in the officially authorized churches or chapels were still recorded by the clergy, but it was the responsibility of the clergy to send in the quarterly returns direct to the Registrar General in London.

Until the Marriage Act of 1898, English and Welsh Nonconformists wishing to marry in their local chapel would have to obtain a licence and the local registrar had to attend to take details down in his register. After 1899 the chapels were allowed to keep their own register and dispense with the registrar. The alternative for a couple wishing to marry was to attend the local Register Office for a civil wedding, for which a licence was required.

It must be remembered that many births were not recorded in the early registers because people viewed the system with a certain amount of suspicion. Up to the Birth and Deaths Registration Act of 1874, it was the duty of the registrar to search out and record all births and deaths, but it was estimated that up to 15 per cent of births went unrecorded. From 1874 the onus was placed with the persons concerned to give notification of a birth or death, within a limited time, and if they did not heed this a fine was issued.

At the same time as the recording of births was being organized, the guesswork was taken out of the cause of death: an official certificate was to be issued and signed by a qualified medical practitioner.

ENGLAND AND WALES'S GENERAL REGISTER OFFICE

Originally the indexes for births, deaths, and marriages were kept at Somerset House. They

Above: The General Register Office holds records of war deaths and military returns.

Below: Recording of a baptism in Malta.

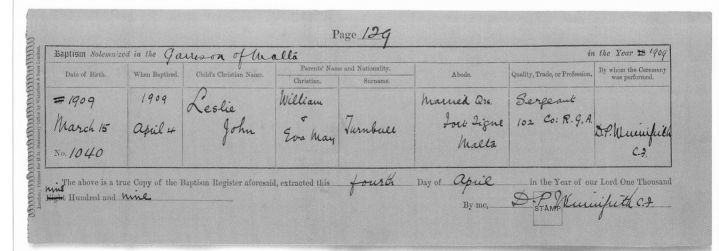

Page 129								
Baptism Solemnized in the *Garrison of Malta*							in the Year 18 1909	
Date of Birth.	When Baptized.	Child's Christian Name.	Parents' Name and Nationality.		Abode.	Quality, Trade, or Profession.	By whom the Ceremony was performed.	
			Christian.	Surname.				
1909 March 15 No. 1040	1909 April 4	Leslie John	William & Eva May	Turnbull	Married Qrs. Fort Signe Malta	Sergeant 102 Co: R.G.A.	D.P. Winnifrith C.J.	

The above is a true Copy of the Baptism Register aforesaid, extracted this _fourth_ Day of _April_ in the Year of our Lord One Thousand nine Hundred and nine

By me, _D.P. Winnifrith C.J._

Above: A certificate of marriage. Civil authorities in England and Wales have recorded all births, marriages, and deaths since July 1, 1837, and a certificate is issued as evidence of the event.

were later transferred to St Catherine's House until, in 1997, a new purpose-built location was opened, called the Family Records Centre. This building in Myddelton Street now houses the new General Register Office, the central repository for all births, deaths, and marriages in England and Wales. Included in this section are returns for birth, marriages, and deaths from British citizens abroad, war deaths, and military returns. This building also houses the census returns from 1841 to 1891.

In the Channel Islands, civil registration on Jersey started in 1842 and copies are held at St Helier, Jersey. In Guernsey and its neighboring islands, births and deaths were registered from 1840 and non-Anglican marriages from 1841. Records are held at St Peter Port, Guernsey. On the Isle of Man births and deaths were registered from 1878 and marriages from 1884; records are held at Douglas, Isle of Man.

SCOTLAND'S NEW REGISTER HOUSE

The Scottish civil registration system started on January 1, 1858, and the records for the whole of Scotland are kept at New Register House in Edinburgh. The same building also houses the Old Parochial Registers, now called Old Parish Registers, for Scotland. The advantage in Scotland is that you can view the actual statutory registers of birth, marriages, and deaths. You pay a fee to enter the building, but the copying of notes from the registers is free. You need only order and pay for the certificate

if you really need it, unlike England and Wales where you only view the indexes and to see a certificate you must order and pay for it first, then wait several days for delivery. In Scotland the indexes are also computerized, and these can be viewed on the Internet after a credit card payment. Although the information was modified on the certificates in the early years, they still hold more details than the certificates of England and Wales.

English Origins of New England Families

This Family Archive CD details over 1,500 families and references 150,000 individuals. Almost all living Americans with colonial Yankee forebears descend from several of the 1,500 immigrant families covered in this work.
• Available from Genealogical Publishing Company: http://www.genealogical.com/cdrom.htm

Above: The marriage licence of Philip Mountbatten, Duke of Edinburgh, and Queen Elizabeth II, then Elizabeth Alexandra Mary Windsor. The marriage took place in Westminster Abbey.

IRELAND'S GENERAL REGISTER OFFICE

General registration started in Ireland in 1864, although Protestant marriages were registered from 1845 onward. Records for the whole of Ireland from that date are held at the General Register Office in Dublin. Microfilmed indexes and summaries of birth certificates (1864–1867) are entered on the International Genealogical Index.

The General Register Office for Northern Ireland in Belfast holds birth and death registers for Northern Ireland from 1864, but marriages are available only from 1922.

THE USA

In the United States birth, marriage, and death indexes are available within the state archives located in the state capital city. These documents are known as Vital Records. You would generally write to the archives and request a search of these indexes for a three- to five-year period. If the correct entry is located, a certificate will then be issued, usually for a fee. Additional fees will be charged for a longer search. If the full and correct date of the event is known, the certificate can be obtained from the local town or county clerk's office (fees will vary). State registration for Vital Records differs considerably from state to state, but generally they begin in the early twentieth century, and you would need to write to the state offices to confirm these dates.

Prior to the twentieth century you will need to go beyond official state level down to county-maintained records, usually found within the county courthouses. An excellent book in which to find the addresses of these courthouses is *County Courthouse Book* by Elizabeth Petty Bentley. With marriage records, information was recorded from the start of a new county or town, so in New England this is as early as the 1600s and for counties in the South they date from the early 1700s.

OBTAINING COPIES

To obtain copies of certificates in England and Wales you may consult the indexes to births, deaths, and marriages at the Family Records Centre free of charge. Prior to visiting the center you must prepare your homework well; you may have come a long way and will not want to waste time. As you start your search, remember to be flexible with those surnames.

Within the search area the system is spit into three sections: births (indexes bound in red), marriages (indexes bound in green), and deaths (indexes bound in black). These books are arranged in quarters, ending in March, June, September and December for each year. Forty-two days are allowed to register a birth, so if the birth is not found in the quarter you think, try the next quarter. Each quarter is arranged in alphabetical order of the surname spelling. If you are unsure of the date of the event and are checking a ten-year period, make a simple chart, showing the years you are searching followed by M, J, S and D; as you check the relevant book, tick it off.

Below: A certificate of marriage. Should you wish to obtain copies of certificates in England and Wales, you can consult the indexes to births, deaths, and marriages at the Family Records Centre in London.

The birth indexes are laid out in the following order: Surname, Forename(s), Supt. Reg District, Volume, and Page. (From September 1911 the maiden name of the mother is included.) The marriage indexes follow a similar pattern; remember, it is easier to find the correct marriage if you have both names of the couple, for with the female's maiden name you can cross-reference the names and if they have the same references in the volume and page columns you can be 99 per cent sure you have the correct marriage. After March 1912 the surname of the spouse appears alongside each main entry. (Death indexes have the same information as the birth indexes.)

Once you have found the correct entry for any index, complete a form and take it to the cashier's desk and pay the statutory fee. The copy of the certificate can either be posted or you can collect the certificate, and this should be arranged when you pay the fee.

In the United States, once you have established whether what you are looking for falls within the state or county timescale, write with full details, or as much information as you can. Check the cost of search fees and the cost of

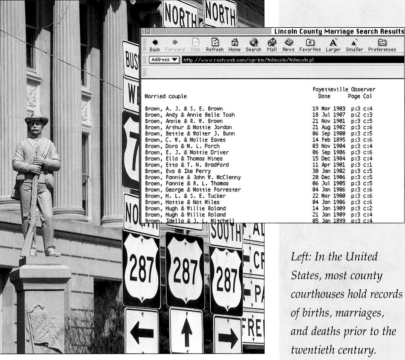

the certificate and send off to the relevant office. Allow a few weeks for them to answer. In many states you may secure the copy of the vital certificate from either the state's Vital Records office or from some local official; in other states you can get them only from the state office.

Left: In the United States, most county courthouses hold records of births, marriages, and deaths prior to the twentieth century.

Step by Step, Obtaining a Certificate

England and Wales

1. Visit the Family Records Centre (FRC) in London. Make the search in either the birth, marriage, and death indexes. When you have found the correct entry, make a note of the year and quarter which appear on the spine of the book. Note also the volume number and page number and registration sub-district—these all appear on the same line as the person you have found. Fill in the relevant form for the type of entry you require; they have different colors for a long birth certificate, a short birth certificate (there is not enough information on a short birth certificate for a family historian), a marriage and a death certificate. Fill in all the details asked for on the form, take it to the counter and pay your fee.

2. If you are unable to visit the Family Records Centre, you can make a postal application by writing to the Office for National Statistics in Merseyside. Give as many details as you can (the search made by the staff is restricted to a five-year period). In the case of the entry not being traced a proportion of your fee will be returned. It should be noted that the fees for a postal

application are a lot higher than if you decide to attend the Family Records Centre in person.

3. To obtain a certificate direct from the local superintendent registrar, you do need to know the district in which the event took place and an approximate year. You can contact the relevant registrar by post, telephone or in person. If you want to make a personal visit, remember they could be busy with their day-to-day work and therefore it is advisable to telephone beforehand for an appointment. The fee will be for the cost of obtaining the certificate.

4. Another way to receive a certificate, would be to use the services of a professional searcher or record agent. They will search and obtain a certificate for the cost of the certificate plus a fee. Their fees do vary, so check first.

United States

In the United States, records are held by the state. When you have decided the exact location of the relevant vital records, write to them giving full details and a check for the cost of the certificate, plus any fees (which vary by state).

USING RECORD OFFICES

EACH LONDON borough, metropolitan district and English county has established record offices to hold the county or district's archives and records. In addition to these the researcher needs to be aware of city and borough archives, as well as the local studies libraries.

COUNTY RECORD OFFICES

The County Record Office (CRO) will hold a vast quantity of records relevant to their area. Each CRO holds records from local courts, schools, reports from the Board of Guardians (they administered the Poor Law from 1834), electoral registers, poll books, taxation, militia records, local business records and deeds, holdings from attorneys (that is if they have not been destroyed), and assorted documents concerning property.

The CROs also act as a diocesan record office, taking in church records, such as the parish registers, vestry accounts, anything from the old parish chest, bishop's transcripts, wills, and probate prior to 1858, marriage licences, and tithe documents. The CROs hold large collections of local history, which are useful in finding out about the area in which your ancestors lived.

Most CROs will have a catalogue about the holdings and how to locate and use them, and this is worth reading before you start your research. Guides to local sources are also published by local societies. Find which indexes are available to search. Proof of identity is required at the CRO these days; also don't just turn up, telephone and book an appointment first. Pencils are a must, cameras and tape-recorders are often not permitted, but laptop computers usually are—check first. Most CROs will provide a photocopying service and some will be able to undertake research on your behalf. Details of these services and fees are available from each office.

THE GUILDHALL LIBRARY

The Guildhall Library in the City of London is an important archive for anyone with London ancestors. No reader's ticket is required and the library is open from Monday to Saturday. The collection for the City of London includes parish registers, rate books and churchwarden's books, accounts, wills, marriage licence records, maps, directories, and local history books. They also hold apprenticeship and freedom records of the City livery companies. The microfilm collection includes copies of the IGI, the 1881 census index, national indexes of wills from 1858 to 1935, Boyd's marriage index, Boyd's *London Burials*, Boyd's *Citizens of London* and far, far more. There is also a computerized catalog to their enormous printed book collection.

FAMILY RECORDS CENTRE

Although the Family Records Centre has been mentioned earlier with regard to the General Register Office (GRO) indexes to births, marriages, and deaths, it does warrant an extra section to describe the additional records that it holds. The

Below: The Family Records Centre houses the indexes for births, marriages, and deaths registered in England and Wales since July 1, 1837. In addition there are many records relating to adoptions since 1927, births and deaths at sea and many military and naval records.

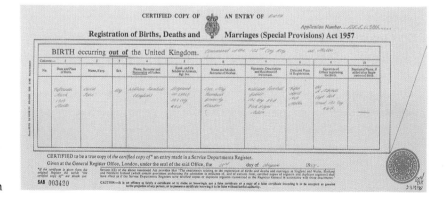

Left: The Family
Records Centre holds
many records that are
useful if you are
researching military
connections to your
family history,
including war deaths
from both world wars
and subsequent deaths
which resulted from
injuries received in
these conflicts.

Family Records Centre is run jointly by the Office for National Statistics and the Public Record Office, and it brings together for the first time under one roof some of the most important sources and indexes used by family historians.

As mentioned earlier, housed on the ground floor of the building are the indexes for births, marriages, and deaths registered in England and Wales from July 1, 1837. But also held are the adoptions registered in England and Wales since 1927; births and deaths at sea registered from July 1837 until 1965; regimental Army chaplains' returns; RAF returns of births, marriages, and deaths; Royal Navy returns; Consular returns; civil aviation returns and High Commission returns. War deaths include Natal and South Africa forces, Boer War, World War I and World War II, including deaths after the war which resulted from injuries received in the conflict.

The Scottish Link is also on the ground floor and has indexes to the births, marriages, and deaths from 1855 to date; divorce files from 1984 to date; old parish registers from 1553 to 1854; and the 1881 and 1891 census returns. These indexes are on-line and can be searched for a credit card charge.

On the first floor of the Family Records Centre are the Public Record Office records; microfilm copies of census returns from 1841 to 1891; microfilms of Death Duty registers from 1796 to 1858; wills and administrations; many Nonconformist registers; the IGI 1992 edition on microfiche; *FamilySearch* on CD-ROM; *Worldwide Genealogical Data*: Ancestral File 1993 edition of the IGI, with addenda; and the *Genealogical Research Directory 1990–1996* on CD-ROM. Access to the records is free, but photocopies may be purchased if required.

A new edition of *In and Around Record Repositories in Great Britain and Ireland*, by Jean Cole and Rosemary Church, has just been published which includes details of more than 740 record repositories in Great Britain and Ireland. Available from *Family Tree Magazine*, the book gives details such as opening times, telephone numbers, parking facilities, appointments, ordering systems, the geographic area of the records, research service, publications, and general remarks.

> **USEFUL WEBSITES:**
> **Essex County Record Office:**
> http://www.essexcc.gov.uk

Ellwood, Elwood—the "son of Aylward;" a variant of the name appears in the thirteenth century: Elward.

Elvey, Elvy—baptismal name of Allvey.

Emery—"the son of Emery" or "Amery." In the eighteenth century it was used as a boy's or girl's name. Also a known Huguenot name.

Enright—an Irish name found mainly in the United States. Could be similar to the English names ending in "wright," as in Arkwright, Cartwright.

Evans, Evanson—a Welsh personal name, from "the son of Evans."

Ewart, Youart, Ewert—an occupational name, "one who tended the ewes." There is also a parish called Ewart in Northumberland.

Ewen, Ewing, Ewan, Ewings—"the son of Ewan." Was a popular name in Scotland and in the north of England as a font name; could have come from the Welsh name of Evans.

Ey, Eye—a local name from a parish in Suffolk.

PROBLEMS OF ILLEGITIMACY AND ADOPTION

IT WOULD be very unusual to find no illegitimacy in the family as you trace your ancestors further and further back. In England, a Parliamentary Act of 1575–76 decreed that mothers and fathers of bastard children were to be punished and sent to prison by the local magistrates. A further Act in 1609 did not improve matters, stating that any lewd woman having a bastard could be sent to the House of Correction unless she gave security for good behavior.

Legislation failed, however, to stop the growth in illegitimate births from the seventeenth century through to the mid-eighteenth century, and a further Act in 1732–33 stated that a pregnant women had to declare to the Overseers of the Poor that she was pregnant and to name the father. In spite of this, parish officers dealt with illegitimacy without too much bother, often trying to force a marriage between the two parents, because a child born within a month, or a day, after marriage was still considered legitimate.

BASTARDY ORDERS

If no marriage took place, the father could be charged with the upkeep of the child. The process involved applying to the Petty Sessions for a Bastardy Order against the father; if granted, a Bastardy Bond would be issued against the father and he would make weekly payments for the child, or sometimes a one-off payment was agreed.

Many of the Bastardy Order records still exist today in the local record offices in England and Wales, and in some cases it is possible to find not only the bonds but the affiliation orders, examinations, and warrants for the arrest of the father. Even later, during the Victorian period, it was not unknown for a couple to have a child and then get married, so take it into consideration when looking for that missing marriage in the GRO indexes because looking for the birth certificate of an illegitimate child doesn't necessarily mean you will find the father's name. When the birth was registered the father's name was normally omitted.

Even in the parish registers of baptisms, it will often be stated "bastard son/daughter of ..." and only give the mother's name. Unless you can find any bonds relating to the child's birth the ancestral line is lost. There is quite a collection of names to be found found in registers beside the bastard child; examples are: Base, Base-born, By-blow, By-slip, Lovechild, Whoreson, and many more.

ADOPTION AND CHILDREN'S HOMES

Adoption is another genealogist's problem. In England and Wales the Adoption of Children Act was passed in 1926, and this made a provision for the adoption of infants. These registers are kept with the GRO indexes in the Family Records Centre. Prior to this date children, many of them abandoned, were given away to some couples, while others went to foundling hospitals and homes. Children given away would find it difficult to trace the natural parents (or to be traced), unless the details have been passed down in the family. There were many homes for unwanted children but some records do exist. The Thomas Coram Foundation for children started as a Foundling Hospital in 1739; the Muller Homes for Children

Above and below: Many illegitimate infants were offered for adoption or simply abandoned, while others went to foundling hospitals and homes. In many cases, records of these children may prove difficult to trace.

was formed in 1836; the Christian's Aid Society was formed in 1856 and amalgamated with Dr Barnardo's in 1966. Dr Barnardo must surely be the most famous name associated with homes for children throughout the English-speaking world. Not all his children were orphans: some were placed in care because the mother could not cope, and others were illegitimate. In 1870, Dr Barnardo's first children's home was founded (he had opened a successful mission in 1867) and the records for "his children" are deposited in the Archives Department of the University of Liverpool, but they are not accessible to the public.

Adoption in the United States is provided by a state adoption register and is operated through the department handling the vital records. For a fee, the departments will feed searches into their databases. If both the birth parent and the adoptee register they will help to arrange a meeting of both parties.

The Internet has also become a new medium for adopted children to look for missing parents. In the past, society was cruel to the unmarried mother and also to the child, because

illegitimacy was a social and legal stigma. To avoid humiliation, the mother would be sent away for an extended visit to a relative, deliver the child and then give him/her up for private adoption. She would then return home without her community knowing anything about it.

Above: Orphans at a Dr Barnardo's home. Left: Many Barnardo boys were sent to Australia in the 1930s to take up farm work.

Falconer—a hawker, keeper or trainer of falcons. Also could mean "worker of crane," a wooden crane used in building.
Feldmeier—(German) meaning "field farmer."
Figueroa—(Spanish) a maker of statuettes.
Filby, Filbey, Filbee—local name from the village of Filby, a parish in Norfolk. This name can also be spelt with "Ph." Earliest traced person was a Ralph de Fileby in Norfolk in 1280.
Fischer—a fisherman or from the fish trade.
Fletcher—an occupational name; an arrowmaker or seller of arrows. Name found in the Derbyshire and Nottingham area, which includes Sherwood Forest, but it is rarer in the southwest of England.

The Lost Children

Many destitute children were involuntary emigrants to North America, forced there through the actions of the Petty Session Court in England, Scotland and Wales or sent by philanthropic organizations. The children would very easily have lost contact with their natural birth parents.

Between 1617 and 1778 some 30,000 children from Christ's Hospital School, London, alone took articles and left England to serve apprenticeships, or to serve as cheap labor for pioneers. About 1,000 of these went to Virginia and other parts of the United States. Christ's was not a hospital in the contemporary sense, but was opened in 1553 for the benefit of poor, homeless and orphaned children. Provided they were legitimate children of freemen of the City of London, over four years of age and free from obvious illness, they were educated and prepared either for entrance to university or apprenticeship to a trade.

From the late seventeenth century, up to 150 children were admitted annually to the famous Bluecoat School on the recommendation of their parish. A further ninety entered under the terms of charitable endowments. The first children to take their articles in the United States were apprenticed to the Virginia Company in 1617. The "Children's Register" is housed in the manuscript department of the London Guildhall. An example of one register is: "Thomas Heath aged 4, son of Jeremy Heath, whitebaker, admitted from St Giles Cripplegate 23 March 1608; 2 May 1619 put to Lady Altome and sent to Virginia in September 1621."

Within North America itself, hundreds of children from the streets of New York were taken to the West and were found work on farms and homesteads. Many were too young to remember their own families, therefore creating a further problem for the family historian. In Britain, the Poor Law Amendment Act (1850) encouraged the emigration of pauper children and the practice continued until after World War II, the total numbers having exceeded 150,000. Many thousands of adults with families of their own in Australia, Canada and New Zealand who were shipped out as orphans in the post-war years have discovered that they have living relatives in the UK and are actively tracing their roots.

US COUNTY AND STATE RECORDS

EACH STATE in the United States has its own county-based organization; some states collect old county records into the state archives, while others leave them within the county system. It is the county records which will provide the family historian and genealogist with a goldmine of information.

County records are not cataloged; in fact some counties may keep records in different offices. If you cannot find the whereabouts of records before you arrive, ask when you get there. Most courthouse employees are willing to offer help, but as they have their own job to do, keep your time with them to a minimum.

WHAT TO LOOK FOR

The following is a list of categories grouped together which can act as a helplist when conducting a search.

• Vital Records—birth, marriage, and death records, divorce records, and filed either separately or within the marriage-record books could be marriage affidavits of minors, signed by parents or guardians.
• Records dealing with property, taxes, land records, wills, inventories, estate sales, settlements, and slave records (slaves were considered to be property).
• Court records—civil, criminal, justice of the peace, and probate. These records can include documentation, minutes, and case files. Included in the case histories would be divorces and naturalization of citizens.
• Administration records—minutes of the county commissioner, sheriff, and jail records, drivers' licences, voters' registration, and many other miscellaneous records.

Some of the records may have been microfilmed, others will be in their original form. Guardianship and orphan records are important and are found within the county probate court records. If you find the record of a guardian, don't stop looking as they will appear in court records regularly because they had to report on the income and expenditure of the child. When the child came of age, a final account was prepared.

NATURALIZATION

Naturalization records are difficult to find but keep looking—since 1906 naturalization proceedings have taken place in a federal court. Generally citizenship started with the "declaration of intention", or "first paper." As residency requirements were fulfilled, the alien went back to court, where he/she petitioned for citizenship and then took an oath of allegiance to the United States. These papers were filed in a court with the "first paper."

Among many federal land records are the homestead records. The Homestead Act of 1862 was passed to help settle the West. People submitted papers to claim their allotted 160 acres and the case files created by the claims will have valuable genealogical information. Any citizen, male or female over the age of twenty-one, could claim this "unoccupied" land.

State archives are public records and they contain thousands of records and documents from government departments and agencies. Each state archive will have its own particular finding aids to help the researcher find out what is in the collection. As well as government

Above: County record offices hold collections of many different categories of documents, including Vital Records. They are not cataloged, and some counties keep their records in different offices, so check before you visit them.

Above: A growing number of African Americans are carrying out genealogical searches to find out more about their ancestors, many of whom were originally transported to North America as slaves.

USEFUL WEBSITES:
Rhode Island State Archives:
http://archives.state.ri.us
New England Historic Genealogical Society:
http://www.nehgs.org.us
Jim Craig, Rhode Island Genealogical Resources:
http://www.ids.net/~jcraig/ri_gen.htm.us

African American:
http://www.genhomepage.com
http://www.oryxpress.com/authors/a00230.html

documents, newspapers published in the state, maps, private and business papers of citizens will be found. They also hold the state census and census substitutes. Eastern states hold colonial and Revolutionary War records and in the South there are the pension applications and other records arising from the years of the Confederacy. (A Confederate pension law was passed in May 1899 in Texas, resulting in 58,000 veterans and widows filing applications.)

State prisons, residential institutions, and hospitals sometimes maintain their own records, and you may need to declare why you require information from them. State court systems operate mainly at county level, with each state having its own court structure. As with all visits to county and state archives, you must have your facts clear and know what you are going to look for, so prepare yourself properly by writing to the office for information as to the viability and dates of their records.

Below: This inventory of 1777 shows slaves listed and valued.

African Americans

Portugal was the first European country to explore West Africa and to trade in slaves, but it was the Spanish who transported the first shiploads of African slaves into the Americas, to Hispaniola, but it was not until 1518 that large numbers of slaves began to arrive to work on the sugar plantations of Santa Domingo.

The first African slaves were imported into what is the modern-day United States in 1619 in Virginia, and in 1624 the first black child was born in Jamestown and christened in the Church of England. They were a small minority, amounting to about 2 per cent of the population by 1760. The Dutch West India Company was the largest importer of slaves and took them into New York, although the slave trade during the 1600s was centered in Boston, Massachusetts. In the seventeenth century much of the labor in the English and French colonies was supplied by indenture contracts, served mostly by nationals from those countries, but by the 1700s this was no longer cost-effective and the cheaper African slave market grew. Between 1709 and 1807, nearly 1,000 ships left Rhode Island for Africa, importing 106,544 slaves.

Slaves were traded by local chieftains off the West African Gold Coast in return for rum, and then transported to the Caribbean, and in later years to South Carolina, Georgia and Virginia where they were traded for tobacco, rice or bills of exchange. The African people thus transplanted lost touch with their established society and the different tribes were mixed on the plantations, resulting in a babel of African language, although much of the culture survived in various forms.

There are a few slave records available, and the federal census records for the period 1790 to 1870 often hold only numerical information. During 1850–1860 these records contained only first names because slaves were known to take their master's surnames. A growing number of African Americans are undertaking researches so more information is becoming available through their findings. There are many ways to discover information: state and county records, historical newspapers, shipping records, the Freedmen's Bureau, military service files, and more.

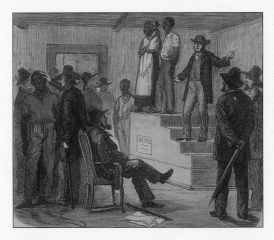

Above: A sale of African slaves in America in 1861.

Flower—there are two meanings for this name: the first is an occupational name, "the flower" being an archer, one who shot the "flo" or arrow; the second came from "the son of Flower," a natural name. It is also a known Huguenot surname.

Ford—local meaning, "at the ford." Could have been the official position in maintaining a right of way. Also could be of Jewish descent.

Fowler—from the old French word "Oiseleor" meaning a hunter or catcher of wild birds.

Fox—a nickname for a person with a cunning and sly nature.

Freeman—a freeborn man, not a serf.

Friedman—(Jewish) a descendant of "the peaceful man."

Fritz, Firths, Fritz, Frizzle, Fritzsche, Fritzius—comes from Friderizius, the Latin for Friedrich.

US NATIONAL ARCHIVES, WASHINGTON DC

THE NATIONAL Archives is the official repository for all federal government records in the United States. Its main center is in Washington DC, but it has regional archives in Atlanta, Boston, Chicago, Denver, Fort Worth, Kansas City, Los Angeles, New York, Philadelphia, San Francisco, and Seattle.

Roll of Honor: Civil War Union Soldiers

Useful source of information on American Civil War deaths.

• Available from Genealogical Publishing Company: http://www.genealogical.com/cdrom.htm

Due to the large amount of records and resources in the two primary federal depositories, the National Archives and the Library of Congress (LoC), researchers are advised to study the published guides to the collections prior to their visit.

The Library of Congress is known as the largest library in the world, and it holds massive collections of published manuscript and microfilmed works. It even has a library catalog which is accessible online through the Internet.

The National Archives hold federal records, starting with the American Revolution (1775–1783) and Continental Congress. The records are organized by department and to help the researcher through these 450 record groups, many publications have been written. Researchers can obtain copies of records in three areas of the archives: ship passenger arrivals, census records and military records (these include pension and bounty land warrant applications). Contact them for current fees.

The coverage for military records is extensive, covering the period from the Revolutionary War (in which several thousand African Americans fought) through to the early twentieth century. They detail the service records and other evidence of service for volunteer soldiers, the US Navy, and the US Marines. The information comes from muster

Above: The National Archives building in Washington DC is the main official repository for all federal government records in the United States.

Left: The Internet website for the National Archives, Washington DC can be found at www.nara.gov

Left: Interior view of the Library of Congress.

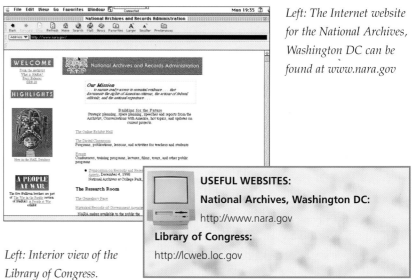

USEFUL WEBSITES:

National Archives, Washington DC:

http://www.nara.gov

Library of Congress:

http://lcweb.loc.gov

rolls, pay lists, hospital and prison records, and many other sources. The details can vary with some showing just their name, rank, and unit, while others give the birthdate, birthplace, and a description of the person. These records are arranged by war or time period, then by state and unit, with the surnames running alphabetically within each unit.

Indexes and other records can help to find a soldier's unit. There are records of volunteer soldiers who served from 1784 until 1812, records of the Indian Wars and disturbances of 1815–1858. It covers the Patriot War (1838–1839), the Mexican War (1846–1848) and the records of volunteer Union soldiers who served during the American Civil War (1861–1865). Many of the Confederate records were lost in the final days of the civil war, although some service records have been compiled from the surviving Confederate and state records, and the Union prison and parole records.

The federal census for the United States is stored in the National Archives and it includes those of 1840 Pensioners and 1890 Union Veterans. The census was taken for a number of reasons, but the most basic was purely to count the population every ten years to determine representation to the House of Representatives. From 1790 to 1840 only the heads of the household were named, and the remainder of the family listed in age brackets. From 1850 every person was named with full details.

Immigration and naturalization records are also found here, a great source from which to find when and where your ancestors came from. Except for some odd documents, few actual passenger lists were kept, until, that is, federal law required it from 1819 onward. The largest ports of entry for many years were Baltimore, Boston, New York, Philadelphia, and New Orleans. Passenger lists are not indexed and many are incomplete, and they are therefore very tedious to read. These lists are not always

The Civil War CD-ROM II: The Navy

All thirty-one volumes of the US Navy from 1861 to 1865, including despatches and reports of naval engagements of both Confederate and Federal navies. (Windows and Macintosh.)
• Available from the Guild Press of Indiana, Inc: http://www.guildpress.com/cdroms.htm#civilwar

centralized but their publication has made them accessible to researchers. One other genealogical resource which should be mentioned here is the Rhode Island State Archives in the state capital of Providence. Rhode Island is one of the smallest states in the United States, but it has a treasure chest of information for the family historian and the genealogist. This was mainly due to the high value placed on early events by its founding fathers. Beginning in 1853, state law required that all births, marriages, and deaths should be recorded. There is a 100-year ruling on births and marriages and a fifty-year ruling on deaths. The tax and land records, state and national census details, military records, and town meeting records are kept in the archives. The staff are always willing to help with research on request, but try to limit each inquiry to three names, providing as much information as you can each time.

The New England Historic Genealogical Society library is less than one hour's drive north from Providence. The library is supported by 17,000 members, has more than 150,000 volumes, and 10,000 rolls of microfilm. The quantity of sources it offers will surely keep any researcher going for weeks.

Confederate Military History

Includes a series of twelve volumes written by "men of unchallenged devotion to the Confederate cause". Each volume focuses on a particular state, set of states or subject. It also contains excellent engravings from the original hard copy. (Windows and Macintosh.)
• Available from the Guild Press of Indiana, Inc. Website: http://www.guildpress.com/cdroms.htm#civilwar

Fuller—an occupational name for a fuller of cloth. The raw cloth was scoured and thickened by beating with water. This was achieved by men tramping on the cloth in a trough.

Galbraith—this is Scots Gaelic for a stranger or a Briton who had settled among the Scots.

Gallyon, Gallon, Gellion—the son of Juliana, or Gillian. Gallyon is a known name of Huguenot descent.

Garrard, Gerard, Garratt, Garrud, Garret—baptized from "the son of Gerard." Old English from Garret, Germ and Jarratt. A known Huguenot name; also traveled into Ireland, becoming Fitz-gerald and Fitz-garrett.

Gaskin—a native of Gascony from the southwest of France.

Giddings, Gidden—a local "of Gidding" a parish near Stilton in Huntingdonshire; also a parish near Stowmarket in Suffolk. Listed as of Huguenot descent.

Gideon—"the son of Gideon." No early indication of its origin; it is of Jewish descent and was imported into England as late as 1700.

Left: The National Archives hold extensive collections of records relating to military subjects, including those of volunteer Union soldiers who served in the American Civil War (1861–1865).

MICROFILM IN THE NATIONAL ARCHIVES
AND THE SOUNDEX CODE

MANY RECORDS in the National Archives in the United States have been microfilmed to give improved access for users. As well as being available for use in their main Washington DC offices, they are also available from their eleven-office strong National Archives Regional Archives System (see page 54), as well as other repositories. A booklet entitled "Regional Branches of the National Archives No 22" gives more details.

The American Indian CD-ROM

Includes *Schoolcraft Encyclopedia, American State Papers* (through 1820), *The American Indian as Slaveholder and Secessionist*, and many more.
• Available from the Guild Press of Indiana, Inc:
http://www.guildpress.com/cdroms.htm#civilwar

THE SOUNDEX CODE

To help with your search for names in the archives, the phonetic soundex code is used. Instructions are at the front of most archives which use the system. To enable you to have your soundex code ready, follow this guide:

Soundex Coding Key

Number	Letter Equivalent
1	B P F V
2	C S K G J Q X Z
3	D T
4	L
5	M N
6	R

The letters A, E, I, O, U, W, Y, and H are disregarded. Now follow the next step:

• Use the first letter of the surname you are searching to begin the code.
• Cross out the vowels and the letters W, Y, and H in the surname.
• Using the table, assign an equivalent number to the first three letters left in the surname.
• Disregard any of the remaining letters in the surname.

If the surname has less than three letters left, assign zeros in those places, thus two Ts will be 3, not 33. Two or more letters with the same code number that appear in sequence in a surname are assigned one number, thus CK in Dickson is coded as 2, not 22, the surname of Shrubsall thus becomes S612.

MICROFILM AND MICROFICHE ARCHIVES

In 1820 the United States Congress took a census of manufacturers who made more than $500 a year. These are microfilmed in the National Archives series M279.

In 1885 the federal government offered to help pay for a census for any state that wanted to take one between the decennial census. The states which took part were Colorado, the Dakotas, Florida, Nebraska, and New Mexico. Films are available for purchase from the National Archives.

The 1890 Union Veterans was a special census giving details of each man's service during the American Civil War, and includes widow's details. This is available on 118 rolls of microfilm, series M123.

Above: Although Native Americans have lived there for millennia, their written history is short and families are hard to trace.

Left: The National Archives in Washington DC. Many records have been microfilmed to give greater access for family historians.

To find out the full resources which the National Archives has on microfilm or microfiche write to them for copies of the following publications:

National Archives Microfilm Resources for Research: A Comprehensive Catalog, Washington DC, and Genealogical and Biographical Research: A Select Catalog of National Archives Microfilm Publications, Washington DC.

As well as the microfilm and microfiche available through the Church of Jesus Christ of Latter-day Saints' Family History Centers (see pages 98–99), it is possible to rent films and fiche from the American Genealogical Lending Library which has more than 250,000 titles. There is also the National Archives Microfilm

Southern Historical Society Papers

This CD contains fifty-two volumes of the Confederate version of the war, as compiled by the Southern Historical Society, including letters and records of citizens as well as military officials of the southern states. (Windows and Macintosh.)
• Available from the Guild Press of Indiana, Inc: http://www.guildpress.com/cdroms.htm#civilwar

Rental Program; the titles include the "Federal Census 1790–1920," "American Revolutionary War Service Records," and "Pension and Bounty-Land Warrant Application Files." *The Genealogist's Address Book* by Elizabeth Petty Bentley is full of addresses for archive repositories (both national and state), special resources, and indexes to periodicals, and newsletters.

Goddard—"the son of Godard;" it has been known in England since 1273. It could be a variation of the German name of Gotthard. It is also said to be of Jewish descent.
Goss—"the son of Goce;" listed as a known Huguenot name.
Goehmann—dweller on the Goe.
Goldberg, Goldenberg, Goldberger—(German) meaning "from a gold mountain;" there are several places in Germany of this name.
Goldstein—(German) meaning a goldstone or topas, or a descendant of a goldsmith (below).

Grainger—a person who kept a grange or barn for corn or granary; also known as a farm bailiff.
Graver—occupational name for one who digs graves or dikes. Also Graveson, a nickname of Grayson.
Green—a person who lived at the village green or common. It could also mean "young and immature."

Left: The National Archives at Fort Worth hold records of the "Five Civilized Tribes."

Native Americans

It is possible to trace Native Americans back several generations, but, as with any ethnic group, it helps to learn more about them, their historical background, and customs. Find out where they lived and the kinship system of the various tribes. Federal records divide Native Americans into two divisions, those who participated in the government programs and supervision (Reservation Indians) and those who did not.

Although Native Americans have lived in North America for thousands of years, their written history is short. The main early records are a result of contact with armies, governments, and missions. Among the best known of the tribes are the Cherokee, Creek, Choctaw, Chickasaw, and Seminole, often called the Five Civilized Tribes. They lived in the southeast before their forced removal to the area known as Indian Territory, where they were a self-governing nation until 1906, just prior to Oklahoma gaining its statehood.

Among the largest collections of archives of these five tribes are those kept at the regional branch of the National Archives at Fort Worth in Texas, the Oklahoma Historical Society and the Western History Collection at the University of Oklahoma.

There are numerous other records related to the Indian reservations and their people. From 1830 onward, church (including schools), mission, and land records offer a source with which to trace Native Americans. As the federal government started to force the Indians onto reservations between 1850 and 1887 census records are also helpful in tracing individuals. The National Archives have records relating to those groups which kept their tribal status, arranged by tribe for the period 1830 to 1940 and the Bureau of Indian Affairs at the Department of the Interior (created in 1947 from the Office of Indian Affairs at the War Department) holds many relevant files.

CENSUS

*T*HE HISTORY of the census or the counting of people goes back a long way, back to before the Bible in which it is recorded that at the time Jesus was born a census was taking place. In 1086 the Normans carried out their own census, or survey, of England; this was the Domesday Book. Centuries later, as the population, wealth, and power of England grew, it was deemed necessary to count every person, not just the landowners and tenants. A Parliamentary bill was put forward in 1753 but failed because of opposition by the government.

LISTS AND SURVEYS

For centuries the government, Crown, or state has been interested in where people live, their ages, occupations, and places of birth. This is much the same information that present-day governments collect, but this time to place new transport links, schools, hospitals, and housing.

Other lists have been compiled over the years for a number of reasons; for example, in wartime volunteers were needed in the various forces and lists were made of those fit enough to fight or capable of bearing arms. In England and Wales, these muster lists were compiled parish by parish of men between the ages of fifteen or sixteen and fifty or sixty, depending on the conflict. Similarly, lists were made of families who were opposed to the Established Church and those not attending the parish church, who could be Roman Catholics, Quakers, or Jews. Sometimes these lists were used to impose extra taxes on those with different religious convictions.

Surveys were conducted on some manors and landed estates to establish who was living on which land or property, how much rent was paid and so on. Many of these surveys and lists survive in the Public Record Office at Kew under such titles as "the Hearth Tax 1662–1688," "the Window Tax 1696–1851," and the "Poll Tax from 1377." It sometimes seems to us today as if any reason was dreamed up to impose more and more taxes on the population.

THE CENSUS ACT

The 1800 Census Act was called "An Act for taking an Account of the Population of Great Britain, and the increase or diminution thereof."

It was followed by the first official census in 1801 of the whole of Britain, but excepted Ireland. It was taken by the local overseers, who carried out the counting of the people within their own parish. The government only required to know the number of people, their age and sex, and the numbers of inhabited and uninhabited houses within the parish. These were sent to London, to be analyzed and then destroyed, as were the censuses of 1811, 1821, and 1831. Some parishes kept a copy of the census for their own use, and some even entered the names; those which have survived

Left: A detail from a page of the Domesday Book. This famous book was a survey of England which the Normans carried out in 1086, and was effectively a census of landowners and tenants.

Left: An example of an early census return. The first official census took place in 1801 for the whole of the British Isles, except Ireland.

World War II, when, instead, national registration took place and everyone was issued with a national identity card. The returns for 1931 were completely destroyed by enemy bombing in the subsequent war.

In 1841 the census forms were distributed by the enumerators to each household, just as happens today. The enumerator, or some other responsible person, would help to fill in these forms for those who could not read or write. The forms were collected, entered into a printed book, and the original forms destroyed.

The census returns at present available to the public, with their Public Record Office class reference, are:

HO 107	June 6, 1841
HO 107	March 30, 1851
RG 9	April 7, 1861
RG 10	April 2, 1871
RG11	April 3, 1881
RG12	April 5, 1891

(HO = Home Office; RG = Registrar General)

Each census included all persons staying in a house, hospital, barracks, or institution at midnight on these dates. So the 1841 census on June 6 covers midnight on June 6/7.

There is a 100-year ruling on the census, and the census for the year 1901 should be released to the public in about 2002.

Below: This picture shows women at work on hand punching machines which printed, stamped, and sorted the census cards following the census in April 1931.

can now be found in the relevant local county record offices around the country, but it is only a very low percentage. The statistical tables were published as Parliamentary papers and these are still available in the larger reference libraries.

The statistics show that the population in England and Wales in 1801 was just under nine million, but by 1851 it had increased to nearly 18 million (possibly due to improved living accommodation). During this fifty-year period many of the population moved from the countryside to the cities and towns. In 1801, 75 per cent lived in the country, but by 1851 only 54 per cent still lived there, and by 1901 there was only 30 per cent of the population still living in the countryside.

With the changes in the structure of local and central government after the 1832 Reform Act, new methods of administration were developed. The Poor Law Amendment Act of 1834 created the Union as a general unit for the Poor Law administration and the Birth and Death Registration and Marriage Acts of 1836 provided for the civil registration of births, marriage, and deaths. This created a new system which was to be the basis of census-taking from 1841 onward.

Since 1801 there has been a national UK census every ten years, except in 1941 due to

ENGLAND AND WALES
CENSUS SEARCH PROCEDURE

THE FIRST of the censuses to be of any use to the family historian is the 1841 returns, as these are the first to give the names of each person who was staying in the abode at the time. Remember, however, that some returns are missing and some are damaged; the London returns for Kensington and Paddington in 1841, for example, are known to be among those lost. The following details are found on the 1841 returns:

FTM: Census Index : Colonial America 1634–1790

Each record on this CD consists of the head of household, township, county, and state of the head of household. It also includes each surname's soundex code.
• Available from Appleton's Online:
http://www.appletons.com/genealogy/genebbcd.html

• Place (street name, house number or house name, pub name).
• Whether inhabited or uninhabited.
• Names of each person, with surname and forename.
• Age and sex of each person, males in one column, females in the other. Ages up to fifteen years are given precisely in years. Over fifteen years the ages were reduced to the nearest five years: for example, forty-three years would show as forty years and twenty-nine years would show as twenty-five years.
• Profession, trade, employment or of independent means.
• Where born. Column to be marked Y, for Yes, if born in the county, or N, for No. In the next column the following letters would be entered where appropriate: S, born in Scotland; I, born in Ireland; F, born in foreign parts.
• The end of a building is indicated by the use of two oblique strokes://
• The end of each household within the building is indicated by the use of one oblique stroke:/

In the 1841 census, relationship to the head of household is not given, but the 1851, 1861, 1871, 1881, and 1891 censuses give much more information:

1851 CENSUS
• Number of schedule.
• Name of street, place or road with name or number of the house.
• Forename and surname of each person who was residing in the house at midnight on March 30/31.
• Relationship to head of family—including servants, lodgers, etc.

• Condition—whether married, unmarried, widow or widower.
• Age and sex. Actual age at the time of the census.
• Rank, profession or occupation.
• Place of birth.
• Whether blind, deaf or dumb.

Over the years, additional questions were added or changed; to the last category (above) they asked also if an imbecile, idiot or lunatic lived there, and in the 1881 census the question was asked "age next birthday". You must remember that some people lied about their age, or maybe did not remember how old they were. Some could not even remember their place of birth, this is because they spent their childhood in a different area to their birthplace. It is always wise to keep an open mind and be a little sceptical about things you read.

The complete census returns of England and Wales can be found on microfilm at the Family

Below: This example of a completed census schedule for the Wrangham family records the information that was required from each person on the night of Sunday April 2, 1871.

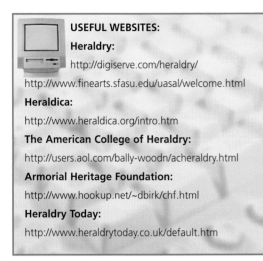

Records Centre at Myddelton Street, London (see pages 44–45 and 48–49). The center does issue free leaflets on how to find and use the census, and these are a very good search aid. The returns are arranged by enumeration district, and if you are searching a village or small town it is worthwhile making a note of all the people with the same surname as the one you are seeking. They might possibly be family and it will save time later, as you will not have to research that particular piece of film again. Photocopies can be made of any sections of the returns that you want, and these you can add to your family history documentation. When making a search, don't forget to look at nearby workhouses, prisons, military barracks, hospitals, and asylums. If your ancestors lived near a river or by the sea, then check the ships; also, up to 1851 the prison hulks would have had prisoners aboard waiting to be transported.

Above: Even prisoners on hulks awaiting transportation would have been recorded on a census return.

Gross—from the nickname "the gross," meaning large, fat, or heavy. It could be of either French or Jewish descent.

Hadley, Hadleigh—a local name of Hadleigh in Essex, derived from the Old English "hae" (heath) and "leah" (wood or clearing).

Haliwell—a local of "holy well or spring," Old English. A place in Middlesex, also a parish in Dean, Lancashire.

Hall—a local who worked at the hall or manor house and could be resident there.

Haliva—a name of Jewish descent.

Harding—a brave man, a warrior or a hero.

Visitations of the Heralds

The heralds are responsible for granting and confirming arms in England under the controlling body of the College of Arms, created by King Richard III in about 1483. Heralds worked mainly at tournaments, where they were employed by kings and lords to announce the entry of their masters and act as a director of ceremonies. In the thirteenth century coats of arms, like surnames, were becoming hereditary. About 1,500 families were entitled to hold a coat of arms, so to prevent duplication the heralds were required to check the lineage of the families.

The sixteenth century saw the start of the minimum property requirements. A person had to have land worth £100 per year or moveable goods to the value of £360, they could then be granted a coat of arms. The King of Arms made journeys up and down the country to check gentleman's claims, taking into account the visitation made by previous heralds, personal knowledge and family traditions, and either confirmed or disallowed the claim.

The books are preserved in the College of Arms as official records of the state. If your family holds a coat of arms these books are a means of obtaining more information about previous generations. To be entitled to arms by inheritance, a family of today needs to prove a direct male line of descent from an ancestor who is recorded in the official records held at the college.

The official registers of the college include thousands of family trees for English and Welsh families. The address is: The College of Arms, Queen Victoria Street, London EC4. The college is open daily with an Officer of Arms always in attendance to deal with inquires.

Left: In London examples of heraldry are commonplace, and may even adorn buildings.

COMMON PROBLEMS

When searching in the larger towns and cities, it obviously helps to have some idea of the address. There are street indexes to the larger places, which generally means that there was a population of more than 40,000. If you have no idea what the address was you will patiently have to work through the whole census returns for that area. The censuses are a valuable aid to where an ancestor was born and it also gathers a family around them; firstly, when living with parents, it will show brothers and sisters; and after marrying the census will give the sons and daughters and these could be names that you didn't know about. Some family historians, because of an unusual surname, carry out one-name studies and this involves searching the census for that name and its variants.

It is possible to narrow down the period when looking for the death of a person. For example, if they appear in the 1861 census but you are unable to find them in the 1871 one then they could have died. You would then check the civil registration death indexes for a death after April 8, 1861, up to the end of March 1871. As these indexes are in the same building, such clues can be followed up quickly. You can also use the age of the eldest child on the census return as a guide to a start date for the marriage indexes. If your ancestor is on the census, this will give an age—sometimes not a true age—but an age which gives you another starting point with the birth indexes. Men would give the wrong age so that they did not appear

USEFUL WEBSITES:

England, local:

http://www.midas.ac.uk/genuki

http://www.gensource.com

http://www.3w.co.uk/familyhistoryfairs

Federation of Family History Societies

http://www.ffhs.org.uk

Genealogy sources for Yorkshire:

http://www.jeack.com.au/~treaclbk/relatively/speaking.htm

Norfolk Family History Society:

http://www.uea.ac.uk/,s300genuki/NFK/organisations/nfhs/

Above: Census returns may help you to trace individuals on other indexes. For example, you may be able to use the age of the eldest child on a census return as a guide to a start date for the marriage indexes.

Left: If your ancestors were sailors they may have been at sea when the census was recorded, as were the officers and crew of the vessel Peace *whose completed schedule is shown here.*

	NAME and SURNAME	CONDITION	AGE [Last Birthday] of — Males	AGE — Females	RANK or OCCUPATION	WHERE BORN	If (1) Deaf-and-Dumb (2) Blind (3) Imbecile or Idiot (4) Lunatic
1	Henry Bennett	Married	57		Captain	Ramsgate Kent	
2	Henry Scott	Unmarried	22		Mate	London Middlesex	
3	William Gould	"	19		Fisherman	London Middlesex	
4	John Richard Millett	"	19		Fisherman	London Middlesex	
5	Henry Walker	"	15		Boy	Hull Yorkshire	
6							
7							
8							
9							
10							
11							
12							
13							
14							
15							

LIST of OFFICERS, CREW, and OTHERS on BOARD of the SHIP or VESSEL named the *Peace* on the NIGHT of SUNDAY, APRIL 2nd, 1871.   134

I declare the foregoing to be a true Return, according to the best of my knowledge and belief.

Witness my Hand,   (Signature)   Henry X Bennett   his mark

Left: Taking the census in the Adelphi arches, London. It is likely that many homeless people were never recorded, or that names and ages were incorrectly given.

Harris—"son of Harry;" family name of the earls of Malmesbury. Harry was the regular pronunciation of Henry in the Middle Ages, but is rarely found in documents, where the name is usually in the Latin form of Henricus.
Harvey, Harvie—"son of Harvey." This name can be found in every county in England and every state in the United States.
Hassell—a local name "of Hassell," a place in Oxfordshire. Also "at the hazel," from a residence beside the hazel tree.
Heiser—a surname of Jewish descent.
Herr, Herre, Herrn—(German) for "hoary," "senior," or "master."
Hess, Hesse, Hessian, Hermann—a German-American name
Hoffman, Hoffmann—a name meaning "courtier," "manager of a cloister farm," or "farm worker."

younger then their wives, and women would want to appear younger; and it was also not unknown to perhaps put a son down as fifteen when he was twelve so that he earned a better rate of pay.

You may have problems with reading some census returns because the microfilms are just copies of the manuscript and the enumerator's handwriting could be difficult to read, but it just takes time—that said, it is best to have short breaks as it can be quite tiring on the eyes.

When you have found your family, either take a photocopy or record every detail, also note the registration district, the sub-district, name of city, town, village and parish, the number of the enumeration district, the folio, and page number. Write down servants, lodgers, and any visitors. If you found your family in one of the census years, search the other years

in the same area; are they in the same house? Was the house in which they lived their business premises—a shop, a baker's, a pub?

If you are unable to travel to London, the census can also be viewed in the county record offices. Each office will hold part, or all, of its own county's returns. Not all of these offices have reader-printers, so you will have to write the details down. You may find the returns in larger county libraries or local studies libraries, but write or telephone to check first. Also you will need to book a microfilm reader. No booking, however, is required at the Family Records Centre. There are also books published by the Federation of Family History Societies (see pages 134–137) which list the holdings of record offices and libraries. These are an ideal source of reference for the genealogist.

Many family history societies have indexed various returns of their area, some as a full transcript and others as just a surname index, but all are useful search aids (visit some of the sites listed). The 1881 census has been transcribed and indexed for the whole of England and Wales. Although at the moment it is in county form, there are plans by the Church of Jesus Christ of Latter-day Saints to produce this as a CD-ROM with a complete index. This would be a major aid when it comes to finding that missing ancestor.

USEFUL WEBSITES:
Genealogy sources for Kent:
http://home.thezone.net/~mrawson/
Northants Family History Society:
http://ourworld.compuserve.com/homepages/
NORTHAMPTONSHIRE-FHS
Kent Family History website:
http://www.centrenet.co.uk/~cna49/kfhs.htm
http://www.ftech.net/~kcm/ap/index.htm

Farmer.

CENSUS—SCOTLAND AND IRELAND

THE SCOTTISH and Irish censuses are broadly similar, almost exactly so in fact to those conducted in England and Wales. In Ireland's case, however, much of this documentation was subsequently destroyed during military action at the Four Courts building in Dublin early in the twentieth century.

Right: In 1861 the Scots noted how many rooms which were occupied had one or more windows.

SCOTLAND

As in England and Wales the most used censuses are those covering the period from 1841 to 1891. These are public records and held by the Registrar General in Scotland. There is a daily pass fee which also includes access to the census.

The only differences between the Scottish records and those in England is that in 1861 the Scots also noted how many rooms which were occupied by the householder had one or more windows, and they also required to know if any persons were employers and how many people they employed. The 1881 census index can also be viewed in New Register House and at Mormon Family History Centers. A few census listings before the 1841 census also survive, but as with the English ones, they do not contain individual names.

The Scottish census is also laid out in a similar way to that of England and Wales. The Society of Genealogists in London hold some of the census indexes, but check which ones are available before you visit.

IRELAND

In Ireland the first census was taken in 1821, but unfortunately this census plus the 1831, 1841, and 1851 ones were destroyed by fire in 1922 at the Four Courts in Dublin. A few fragments survived and some transcripts were made. To find which are in print refer to *Irish Genealogy: A*

New Irish Records CD

Land Records—index to *Griffith's Valuation of Ireland 1848–1864.* An excellent tool for hunting Irish ancestors. It can be used as a census substitute for the years before, during and after the Great Famine (1845–1850).
• Available from S & N Genealogy Supplies:
http://www.genealogy.demon.co.uk
• Also from Heritage World, 26 Market Square, Dungannon, Co Tyrone, Northern Ireland BT70:
http://www.iol.ie/irishworld

Record Finder by D. F. Begley (1987). The government ordered that the 1861 and 1871 censuses were to be destroyed and no census was taken in 1881 and 1891, so the earliest returns for the whole country are for 1901. The 1901 and the 1911 census returns can be viewed at the National Archives in Dublin and the Public Record Office of Northern Ireland in Belfast. The 1911 census asked married women to state how long they had been married, the number of children born to them, and how many were still living.

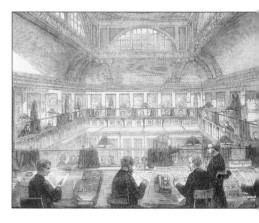

GRIFFITH'S VALUATION

The *Griffith's Valuation* has survived, which is some compensation to the researcher in Ireland. This survey of land and property existed in order that tax could be calculated for the upkeep of the poor. It is arranged by county and lists names of tenants and landowners between 1846 and 1865, including the extent and value of their property. The valuation can be viewed at

Above: An engraving showing the indexing of the 1861 census.

USEFUL WEBSITES:
Scotland research:
http://www.angus.gov.uk/history/history.htm
Scottish clans and tartans:
http://www.sgiandhu.com/clans/online/index.html
Glasgow and West Scotland FHS:
http://users.colloquium.co.uk/~alistair/GWSFHS/ GWSFHS.HTM

the National Archives, Dublin. Tithe applotments compiled between 1824 and 1828 and arranged by parish give the occupier's names, land, and amounts paid. These are also at the National Archives, Dublin, and Public Record Office, Belfast.

IRISH CENSUS SUBSTITUTES

Ireland, like England, has several records for the seventeenth century which can be used as census substitutes. These include the muster rolls, a census of landowners from 1659, subsidy rolls, poll tax rolls, books of survey, and hearth money rolls. Details of these are given in leaflet number 14 in a series produced by the Public Record Office of Northern Ireland, under the title "17th-Century Census Substitutes."

CENSUSES FOR THE CHANNEL ISLANDS AND THE ISLE OF MAN

Censuses for Guernsey, Jersey, Alderney, Sark, and the Isle of Man all appear at the end of the class of records that make up the census returns for England and Wales. The Channel Islands Family History Society have published *The 1891 Census of Jersey: An All-Island Listing.*

Left: Taking the census in a middle-class home. The 1901 and the 1911 census returns can be viewed at the National Archives in Dublin.

Holme, Holmes—a local name for "at the holm," a small island in a river or flat land partly surrounded by water.

Hood—"the son of Richard" from the nickname of "Hud" or "Hood." There are many references to the name Hud in records and old rolls. Many refer to Robin Hood, one quote is "A Lytell Geste of Robin Hode." It has also been referred to as a Huguenot name.

Hoover—tenant with a "hide" of land, approximately 120 acres. German name of Huber.

Howard, Hayward—(German) meaning "heart/mind" or "high/chief warden." Hayward is an occupational name for a keeper or bailiff of the "ewe-herd."

Hubert, Hubbard, Hobart—"son of Hubert." The patron saint of hunters is St Hubert. Hubert is also of Huguenot descent.

Hughes, Hugh—the "son of Hugh." Thousands of people owe their nominal existence to these names in the diminutive forms of Hewett, Howitt, Hewlett, Hewling, Hutchins, and many more. Hugh is found in great numbers in the Domesday Book.

Censuses in Europe

Sources of records vary, of course, from country to country, and it is always a very good idea to read up about the archives of any country that your ancestors came from. France and Spain took early colonial censuses in North and South America but the information in them varies. To trace any foreign ancestor start with the mother country's census. Although other censuses were taken in the Scandinavian countries, very few national indexes exist and you will need to know where your family were living to locate the appropriate archive center.

To trace back American-Italians, first check the 1900, 1910, and 1920 censuses for the United States. These will provide a date of immigration for residents born overseas and will indicate if the resident had been naturalized. Earlier censuses do not give this information, but the majority of Italians did not arrive in the United States until the late 1800s or early 1900s. By checking the naturalization records and the ships' passenger lists, these will help you to continue your research back to Italy. In Italy, the Italians do not have to search to learn about their grandparents and ancestors, they know where and how they lived for they tended to remain in the area of their birth for several generations, this is due to a strong attachment to the *famiglia*.

In France there were various censuses taken before and after the French Revolution and these could be quite worthwhile exploring. From 1836 onward a census was taken every five years, in the years ending in one and six. The 1871 census took place in 1872, and there were no census recordings done in 1916 and 1941 due to the world wars. For various reasons many of the returns have been lost but those which have survived will be in the archives departments.

USEFUL WEBSITES:

Italian surname search:

http://www.icom.it/nobilitas/

German research:

http://www.geocities.com/Colosseum/1959/index.html

Odessa (German-Russian):

http://pixel.cs.vt.edu/library/odessa.html

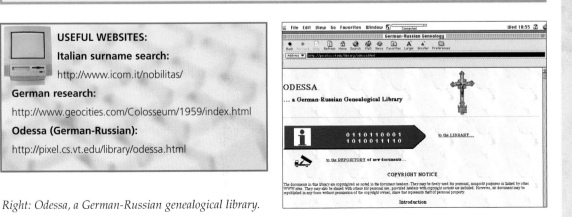

Right: Odessa, a German-Russian genealogical library.

FEDERAL CENSUS—USA FROM 1790

THE PRIMARY purpose of the federal census in the United States was to count the population every ten years to determine representation in the House of Representatives. In the early censuses from 1790 to 1840 only the heads of the household were named, the remainder of the family were just listed in age brackets. From 1850 onward, every person was named, together with their age, sex, race, birthplace, and occupation. Because these censuses are a useful tool in genealogy, they should be the next records to be used after the family sources. Much can be learned about the extended family in this way, therefore helping you to find out more about your direct ancestors. But like all sources of research, census records can contain errors and omissions and you must always use caution. The most convenient way to view the censuses is through the Census Microfilm Rental Program.

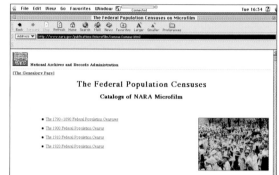

Above: Details of US federal population censuses are available from the National Archives at their website: http://www.nara.gov

In the census year, one day was given over as census day and the information available should be that which was correct for that day; people who died the day after the census should therefore be included but babies born after census day will not. As the returns might not be completed for several days, these instructions might not have been followed, but it does show that the family were resident on that day.

The following is a record of the days in which the census from 1790 to 1960 was taken:

1790, 1800, 1810, 1820: First Monday in August
1830, 1840, 1850, 1860, 1870, 1880, 1890, 1900: June 1

1880 Indian Schedule: October 1
1910: April 15
1920: January 1
1930, 1940, 1950, 1960: April 1

The most significant change to the United States census came in 1850 when the entire format was changed. Lemuel Shattuck of Massachusetts, America's great crusader in vital registration and the public health movement, was chiefly responsible for this. The 1845 census in Boston prepared by Shattuck had so impressed federal officials that they invited him to Washington DC, in 1849 to assist with the planning of the 1850 US census. The most important alteration was the naming of the

Left: Perhaps your ancestors looked similar to these characters recreating the lives of early settlers in North America. In the censuses from 1790 to 1840 only the head of the household was named and the rest of the family were just listed in age brackets.

complete family, so rather than the one line per family of the previous censuses, it changed to one line per person. The census was also used to collect data such as births, marriages, and deaths, and a series of questions combined with a special morality schedule sought to discover the reason for any deaths within the twelve months prior to the census. This method of collecting vital statistics was eventually abandoned in 1910 when the first census by a census bureau which was a permanent government agency was conducted.

WHAT THE CENSUS TELLS US

Some of the details found in the 1790–1840 censuses are: name of head of family only; number of free white males under sixteen and the number over; number of free white females, with an age breakdown; number of all other free persons, including colored people; civil division of place of residence; number of people employed in the various occupations; and the total living in the household. The census content from 1850 to 1910 was more comprehensive, naming every person in the household, the full address of the residence, the age and sex of every person, their race, occupation, the value of the real estate owned by the person, the place of birth of each person, the place of birth of each person's mother and father, if the person was a convict or a pauper, their length of time in the United States, whether they spoke English, and many other minor questions. Quite an interesting picture of the family can emerge from the answers.

Atlas of the Official Records of the Civil War

This was prepared originally in the 1890s. The electronic format allows you to digitally zoom in and print from 175 full-color plates. Contains 800 maps and hundreds of drawings and engravings. (Windows.)

• Available from the Guild Press of Indiana, Inc: http://www.guildpress.com/cdroms.htm#civilwar

---

Ibbett, Ibbetson, Ibbitt, Ibbot, Ibbotson—the "son of Isabel." From Yorkshire down to Cornwall this was the favorite nurse-name of Isabel. Ibbotson is particularly widespread in Yorkshire.

Illingworth, Illingsworth—a local name "of Illingworth," a chapelry in the parish of Halifax in the West Riding of Yorkshire. The American form is generally Illingsworth.

Ince—local for an "island" or "river meadow." Local name from Cheshire, Lancashire and Cornwall.

Inch—local "of Inch" or "of the Inch," a Scottish surname, "inch" meaning island or level ground next to a river.

Inger, Ingerson—the "son of Ingvar," derived from a Scandinavian personal name.

Innes—(Celtic) "dweller on an island."

Irish—a nickname from "the Irish," an Irishman.

WHERE TO FIND THEM

Much of the 1790 census has been indexed and published, and copies can be found in many libraries throughout the United States. They have been reprinted by both the Reprint Company in South Carolina and by the Genealogical Publishing Company. A project to transcribe and index the 1850 census was undertaken by the National Genealogical Society in Washington DC, but the project was abandoned in 1968 because of the cost. All of the censuses from 1800 to 1880, 1900, and 1910 are available for personal search at the National Archives in Washington DC, (in some case copies have replaced the damaged originals). The Bureau of the Census has microfilmed the schedules of 1840–1880 and retired the originals; it has also filmed the 1900–1940 census, but due to a seventy-two year closure restriction period these are not all available for public viewing.

Population censuses are available on microfilm at the LDS Family History Library, and others in selected libraries, genealogical societies and agencies throughout the United States. All available censuses from 1790 to 1910 are accessible through inter-library loan or direct from the National Archive Microfilm Rental Program. Many libraries hold the schedules for their own state.

PROBLEMS FOR THE RESEARCHER

Many problems have occurred which have resulted in missing schedules, mostly a result of material being transferred between jurisdictions and bureaucracies. Under the provisions of the Census Acts, from 1790 to 1820 the schedules were placed in the District Courts, but on May 28, 1830, a resolution was passed which requested that the District Clerks forward the schedules for the first four censuses to the US Secretary of State. Later, in 1849, the responsibility for the census was moved from

the State Department to the Interior Department and all records were transferred to the new department. No inventories of the transferred material were compiled, or have been found at least, and when comparing inventories made in 1865 and 1870 with later ones it was discovered that many were missing, including seventeen volumes of the 1790–1820 census lost prior to 1895. In early times, census schedules were often lent between the State and Interior departments and this could also have resulted in schedules being lost. In addition, as a result of a fire in the Commerce Department in 1921, many of the 1890 schedules were destroyed, and the others were so badly damaged that Congress authorized their disposal.

Information can be obtained from the restricted population schedules by the Bureau of the Census—these are the schedules that are less than seventy-two years old—but can only be released to the person to whom it relates. If the record sought relates to a dead person, a death certificate or any other evidence of death must be shown. Even then it can only be filed by one of the following:

- A blood relative, parent, child, brother or sister.
- The spouse of the deceased.
- A direct bloodline descendant.
- A beneficiary with legal proof.
- Their minimum age must be eighteen years.

There is a street index for the 1910 census to thirty-nine of the United States' largest cities. This was to aid the Bureau of the Census in finding data requested by government agencies. This index has now been filmed and is available on microfiche from the Federation of Genealogical Societies.

CIVIL WAR VETERANS

The 1840 census includes information about Revolutionary War pensioners of the federal government and the 1890 census includes Union Army veterans of the American Civil War and widows of deceased veterans. There is an index and publication for the 1840 census of pensioners called *A Census of Pensioners for Revolutionary or Military Services*. Both the list and index have been published by the Genealogical Publishing Company.

As in the United Kingdom, the United States

Above: Census records are very useful in tracing Native American families after they were transferred to the reservations between 1850 and 1887.

also has additional censuses. A few of these were taken during the colonial period and some states, for various reasons, have taken their own censuses. A US government pamphlet by Henry J. Dubester was produced in 1948 called "State Censuses; an Annotated Bibliography of Censuses of Population Taken After the Year 1790 by States and Territories in the United States." Although now out of print, it is available in libraries and government depositories. An updated listing is in a catalogue called "US and Special Censuses" by Ancestry Publishing, Salt Lake City.

With the transferring of the Indians to the reservations between 1850 and 1887, the census records are a very useful and important tool. It will be possible to find a tribe and families within the tribe in one place and by name.

The Civil War CD-ROM

Contains all 127 volumes of the *Official Records of the Civil War*, *Fox's Regimental Losses*, Dyer's *Compendium and Guide Index to the Offical Records* by the National Archives historians, and *The User's Guide to the Official Records* by Alan and Barbara Aimone. (Windows and Macintosh.)

• Available from the Guild Press of Indiana, Inc: http://www.guildpress.com/cdroms.htm#civilwar

---

The American Civil War

The American Civil War, fought from 1861 to 1865 between two blocs of states with two very different ideas about how to shape society, was a truly tragic episode in the history of the continent and a young, dynamic nation. Its causes are complicated and much debated and do not concern us here. The scale of the death and suffering, however, was on a massive scale. With five million soldiers participating, over 600,000 killed, and many more wounded and maimed, it touched the overwhelming majority of families in one way or another. (More Americans died than in all the other American wars pre-Vietnam combined; some 2,000 died for every 100,000 of the population—the comparable figure for World War II is 241.)

It should not be forgotten that, historically speaking, it is a fairly recent event. Many participants lived on well into this century and therefore for many families one need not go back many generations at all. It is also one of the most written about and investigated episodes in the nation's history. There are dedicated museums and dozens of expert organizations. Today, the battlefields are lovingly preserved and well visited, and many families are interested in tracing their ancestors' participation in the war.

There are various means of finding out more information. The overall records are extensive, but in the National Archives are some of the more readily accessible ones, albeit unindexed and arranged by state. All can be looked at on site or purchased. They include all the volunteer soldiers who fought for the Union and Confederacy, although many of the latter's records were destroyed at the end of the war and have had to be compiled from surviving sources. There are records relating to black troops, Indians, units by state, navy and marine personnel, POWs, and more. Also, details from the General Index to Pension Files found at the National Archives, can give a description of the soldier, his occupation, unit, where enlisted, and when pensioned. There is an on-going project to provide an index of the soldiers who served in the war, with the end aim of a CD-ROM to hold the database, making it available to the public and to libraries.

Irving—a "green/fresh river." A location in Ayrshire and Dumfriesshire, Scotland.

Isaac, Isaacs, Isaacson—meaning of "He (God) may laugh," or smile upon you. Hebrew for the son of Abraham. A well-known personal name, but no more confined to the Jews than Adam or Abel. Many people in whom no Jewish blood flows bear one or other of these surnames.

Isham—local meaning of "a homestead on the River Ise." The name Ise meaning "water."

Ison, Izon, Izen—baptismal name meaning "the son of Isan," probably a Welsh personal name. Found in modern times in Liverpool within the Welsh population of the area.

Jackman—an occupation "the man of Jack," a servant of Jack. Also of possible Huguenot descent.

Jacob, Jacobs—although there is evidence to show this name was used in medieval times, the modern name is certainly Jewish. The Hebrew meaning is "he supplanted," a possible reference to his treatment of his elder brother Esau.

Left: The National Archives are a good starting point for records relating to the American Civil War.

PARISH RECORDS

ENGLISH PARISH registers date from early in the sixteenth century, when Thomas Cromwell, Vicar General to Henry VIII, ordered the clergy in 1538 to keep written records of baptisms, marriages, and burials. The response, however, was slow and an injunction in 1597 reinforced the original mandate. It gave instructions for the existing registers to be copied onto parchment in order to preserve them. Where both records have survived, extra information may be gained by one having more details than the other, but always check both when copying anything over because mistakes could have been made. From 1598 onward, the incumbent of the parish was to send copies annually to the bishop, and these are known as bishop's transcripts (BTs).

The parishes in England and Wales varied in size from a few hundred acres to thousands of acres, and at one time there were about 11,000 ancient parishes. The parish registers have survived well; indeed, much better than the bishop's transcripts. During the nineteenth century the growth of the towns and cities meant many small parishes were absorbed into urban areas and many new ones were created.

The majority of parish registers are kept within the county record office; only a small number are still kept in the parish church. With the very small village parishes, it will take longer to fill the register and it will still be in use in the church. Contact the vicar to make an appointment to view these registers; most vicars are only too willing to assist you, but don't forget to make a small donation to the church fund (it helps if you require a second visit). To view the parish registers in the county record office, check whether you can view the original or if it is on microfilm.

BAPTISM REGISTERS
Early entries can be disappointing, a record of baptism may give just the date, the name of the child, and the father; marriages give the date and names of the young couple; burials give the date and name. It was not until later that more information was introduced. In early registers, you may be confused by the dates because the custom was to start the year not on January 1,

but on Lady Day, March 25, a method that ceased in January 1752 when Britain fell in line with the rest of Europe.

The baptism registers were not a record of the birth, but of the church ceremonies. It was usual to have the baptism three days after the birth, but it can be found in some registers that the parents had whole families baptized and the children all vary in age. Some clergy will write the date of birth in the margin or give an age.

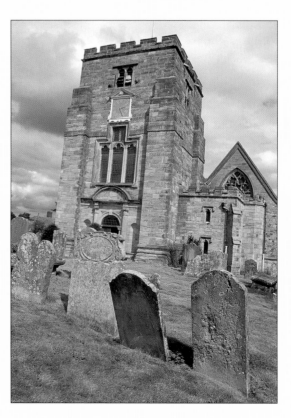

Left: English parish registers date from 1538 when the clergy were required to keep a written record of all baptisms, marriages, and burials. From 1598 onward, copies of these records were sent annually to the bishop, and these are known as bishop's transcripts. Most parish records are now held within each county record office, and only a small number may still be found in parish churches.

BANNS BOOKS AND MARRIAGE REGISTERS

Marriages were performed in the parish church following the calling of the banns, and in many cases the banns book has also survived, giving a clue as to whether the couple lived in that parish or another. Some couples would marry under the grant of a licence, and these licences may have survived too. Early records just give a date and a name, while later ones in addition provide details of age and abode.

Registers were finally standardized by an Act of 1812, following which the registers became bound books of pre-printed forms. The marriage register underwent a few changes but was finally brought into line with the onset of civil registration, when the register was given the same format as the marriage certificate, thus giving a lot more information then previously.

A number of parish registers have been published, transcribed, and/or indexed, some privately and others by family history societies. To find dates of parishes and where they are kept, there is a series of volumes called *The National Index of Parish Registers*, published by Phillimore. Also remember that the Church of Jesus Christ of Latter-day Saints used the baptism and marriage registers as their main sources of information for the International Genealogical Index (IGI).

In Scotland the system of parish registration goes back to 1552, when the Church of Scotland ordered baptisms and banns of marriage to be entered into a register. This was extended to burials in 1565. In Ireland, early records for nearly 1,000 parishes were destroyed by fire but some transcripts did survive. Microfilms of most Roman Catholic registers are available in the National Library of Ireland.

THE UNITED STATES

The role of organized religion and churches in the United States is very different from Britain with its Established Church, closely identified with the state. Nevertheless, the same principles

of valuable record-keeping apply and, while they may not be as old and venerable as their European counterparts, American churches do hold a great many genealogically valuable records relating to baptisms, confirmations, marriages, and burials (see also page 76). Many individual churches look after their own, while others have been microfilmed and placed in various collections. It is worth approaching denominational universities at a regional level and local or state historical societies or archives for further information.

Above: Many American churches hold a wealth of genealogically valuable records relating to baptisms, confirmations, marriages, and burials.

Below: The National Library of Ireland has microfilms of most Roman Catholic registers which are available for viewing.

> **Tri County Pack**
>
> Contains photographs of churches, maps, and details of the English counties of Warwickshire, Devon, and Norfolk. Includes a free CD of the complete 1851 census for these three counties.
>
> • Produced by LDS. Available from S & N Genealogy Supplies: http://www.genealogy.demon.co.uk

THE POOR LAW AND THE WORKHOUSE

ENGLAND'S POOR Law dates back to the reigns of King Henry VIII and of Queen Elizabeth I, when parishes were required by law to provide money from the rates for the relief of the poor. Because of the burden placed on the rates of a township due to the migration of poor people, an Act of Settlement was passed in 1662 by which township officers could remove a stranger within forty days of arrival unless the person occupied a property worth £10 per year.

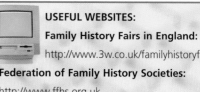

USEFUL WEBSITES:

Family History Fairs in England:
http://www.3w.co.uk/familyhistoryfairs/

Federation of Family History Societies:
http://www.ffhs.org.uk

In 1697 a further Act was passed which allowed the officers to issue a certificate to a person who wished to look for employment elsewhere. The certificate gave the township's promise to accept him/her back if it was necessary. This Act gave authorities elsewhere the right to return a poor person to the parish where they were last legally settled. The parish of settlement was the place where a person was born, or if work had moved them to another parish and they were there for more than a year, that became their settlement parish. When a woman was married, she became the responsibility of her husband's parish and for this reason the overseers were always keen to marry a young girl to someone in another parish, because this passed the responsibility away from them.

The job of finding homes for poor orphans fell to the overseer, the Acts of 1598–1601 having given him the power to bind children as apprentices and pay their premiums from the parish rates. This could also happen to children whose parents were in receipt of poor relief. Children could be taken as soon as they were able to work, which meant quite young by today's standards.

THE WORKHOUSE

In the early 1800s the Poor Law was changed so that recipients were paid in kind rather than money. The 1834 Poor Law Amendment Act stated that all poor, able-bodied people should be relieved in a workhouse. As workhouse conditions were intended to be very unpleasant, it was supposed to make people work harder to stay in their own homes rather than face going into the workhouse. As soon as this Act was passed, many Poor Law Unions started to build their own workhouses. The main records of the Union concerned the day-to-day running of the workhouse, and where these records have survived they are to be found in the county record office. These records offer one of the most underused sources to the historian and family historian. They include registers of the inmates, recording births and deaths, and parishes whence they came; minutes of the Board of Guardians (sometimes with a list of inmates); committees for boarding-out (with lists of children); and accounts ledgers, petty cash books, poor rate returns, loans granted to paupers, and admission and discharge books. A series of four books called *Poor Law Union Records* by Jeremy Gibson, Cliff Webb and Colin Rogers is available from the Federation of Family History Societies. These books are split into areas of England and Wales and list the records and where they can be viewed.

Below: The workhouse of St James' Parish, London, 1809. Poor Law Unions began to record details concerning the day-to-day running of the workhouse together with a register of inmates.

THE PARISH CHEST

The Poor Law of 1552 directed the officers of each parish to provide a strong lockable chest, with three keys, to hold the alms for the poor of the parish. From the early sixteenth century separate legislation decreed that every parish register should also be held in a locked chest. In most cases one chest was used for both purposes. Church chests, however, date back to long before the Tudor injunctions, because in most cases the church's treasures as well as its records were kept there. Chests were mentioned in churchwarden's accounts and the lack of one would be recorded in the visitation articles of the heralds.

The records which were kept in the parish chest will have been placed in the safety of the county record office, where they are readily available for viewing. The churchwarden in every parish was chosen by the joint consent of the religious minister and the parishioners. If they could not agree, they would have two churchwardens, one chosen by the minister and one chosen by the parishioners. Among the churchwarden's accounts can be found such things as: payments to the poor, churchwarden's expenses, church rates, payments for the bread and wine for communion, Michaelmas or Easter, and repairs to the church. In the latter case the accounts may name the person from whom timber was purchased, or the leather for the bells, the carpenters and masons who had done work on the church, maintained the clock and so on. This is a good source to see if your ancestors were employed in a trade.

Other items kept in the parish chest would have been the charity accounts and records. Some parishes would have had several charities, which were administered by the parish church. Also there were the glebe terriers (surveys of Church possessions in the parish), tithe records (sums due to the Church from landowners, a form of tax for the Church's upkeep) and appointments, and other ecclesiastical records.

Civil records were kept too: the vestry minutes and agreements, petty constable accounts, records of the Poor Law administration, records of highway maintenance and of open-field agriculture enclosure. Not all these will have survived in every parish, but it is certainly worth checking, for these are the type of records which will put the leaves on your family tree.

Above: American evangelist Dwight Lymon Moody with a group of orphans at one of his Chicago missions, c. 1870.

Above: An early document showing assessments for church lands in parts of Kesteven, in the county of Lincolnshire, England, in the year 1200 when the rate of 3 shillings was levied per plough.

Jackson—from "the son of John" from the popular nickname of Jake or Jack.

James—a form of Jacob made popular by the two apostles. Also Janeson, Jami(e)son, meaning "son of James." Very common in Scotland.

Jarvis—"the son of Gervase." The name of Gervas still exists and is of Huguenot descent.

Jasper—"the son of Jasper." The French for this name is Gaspard, also known to be of Huguenot descent.

Jay—nickname of "the jay," a chatterer, or a gaily-dressed person. A local "of Jay," a town in Hereford. Also of Huguenot descent.

Jerome, Jerram, Jarrom—a name of Jewish descent, first found in England is about 1612.

NONCONFORMIST RECORDS

T HE TERM Nonconformist describes those people belonging to English Protestant denominations other than those of the established Church of England; they were also sometimes called Dissenters. In 1662 an Act of Uniformity was passed which required all English and Welsh clergy to consent to the entire contents of the Book of Common Prayer. Nearly 2,000 clergyman failed to comply and were ejected, continuing to preach for a time in unauthorized places or employed as private chaplains by gentry families, until in 1689 they were allowed to licence their meeting houses for public worship. (The Church of Scotland retained its separate Presbyterian beliefs and organization.)

Nonconformism consisted of different groups with different beliefs, ranging from Quaker and Baptist to Presbyterian and Independent (Congregationalist). Their early registers were mainly for records of baptism, because for marriages and burials the Dissenters used the Church of England (and sometimes a baptism can be found in both).

During the eighteenth and nineteenth centuries Britain experienced an evangelical revival which some of the older Nonconformists were slow to respond to, although the Congregationalist (Independent) and Baptist denominations were eventually transformed by it. This period also saw the growth of the Methodist movements, with the Wesleyan, the Primitive, New Connection and others. The Methodists outgrew the other groups and soon began to rival the Church of England: a national census of religious attendance on Sunday March 29, 1851, revealed that the Nonconformist denominations accounted for half of the church-going population. A great deal of building of new chapels and renovation of old ones took place in the Victorian period, replacing the plain, square boxes with more imposing buildings.

PURITANS

To which Nonconformist group did your ancestors belong? Puritan was a general term for what later became the Presbyterian, the Independent, and Baptist churches. The Puritan parent would often give their children Old Testament forenames. The Puritans mainly adopted the creed of Presbyterians, a group which followed in the footsteps of Thomas

Cartwright (1535–1603) and many of their registers have survived, the earliest from 1650.

PRESBYTERIANS

The Presbyterians were happy to work for change from within the Anglican Church, but the Separatist faction rejected the close connection between the Church and the state on scriptural grounds and developed into the Independents. One famous Independent was Oliver Cromwell, less well known were the London contingent of Independents who were passengers aboard the *Mayflower* when she sailed to America. The Independents later became known as Congregationalists and in 1972 the United Reformed Church was founded as a successor to the Presbyterian and Congregational churches.

BAPTISTS

The Baptists preferred adult baptism, and therefore rejected infant baptism. The Baptist religion can be traced back to 1611, but a small group adopted the Calvinistic doctrines of predestination in 1633.

QUAKERS

The Quakers, also known as the Society of Friends, was formed in 1647 by George Fox (1624–1691). The Society of Friends in London started to keep their own records from the 1650s, and they are known as the most conscientious of record keepers. They were

Above: The Mayflower *was among many ships which brought families of different beliefs to North America where they continued to strengthen their Nonconformist religions.*

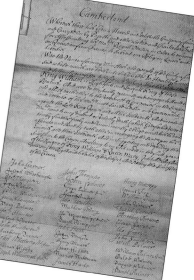

Above: An Association Oath of Loyalty to William III by Nonconformists of Cumberland, England, dated 1696.

exempt from Hardwicke's Marriage Act of 1753 and allowed to marry according to the terms of their faith, whereby a couple would pledge themselves to each other in front of witnesses. Their original records are held in the Public Record Office and copies are also held in the library at Friends' House in London.

METHODISTS

The Methodist movement originated through the dedicated activities of John and Charles Wesley, and their churches could be found throughout England and Wales. As with other Nonconformist religions they split into various other factions: Wesleyan, Bible Christian, Primitive, New Connection, and Tent Methodists. The Countess of Huntingdon founded the Calvinistic Methodists who were known as the Countess of Huntingdon's Connection. Her Christian name of Selina was often used by the Methodists when they named their daughters.

OTHER NONCONFORMISTS

There were other Nonconformist sects. The Moravian missionaries came from Europe, and at one time both John and Charles Wesley were members; the Salvation Army, founded by William Booth, still exists today; the Plymouth Brethren; and also the Church of Jesus Christ of Latter-day Saints who recruited from the United Kingdom and took many of their converts back to the United States. Wales is a strong

Nonconformist community, but today many of their chapels have long been closed, have changed their use, or have been pulled down.

Some of the Nonconformist groups kept registers for births, baptisms, marriages, burials, or deaths from the late seventeenth century, while others founded then or later either did not make any registers or they have not survived. The Non-Parochial Register Act of 1840 requested all Nonconformist groups, except the Jews, to hand registers to the Registrar General containing entries prior to 1837; many failed to comply, particularly Roman Catholics. Those surrendered, however, are now held in the Public Record Office in classes RG4 to 6. A further collection was made in 1857, and these are in classes RG4 to 8. All these records, some 9,000 registers, are available on microfilm at the PRO search room at the Family Records Centre and many of them are entered on the International Genealogical Index (IGI), although not the Quaker or Roman Catholic registers.

Above: Puritan families going to church. An engraving by George Barry, 1883.

Jefferson, Jeffreson—"the son of Geoffrey."
Jenkins—a double diminutive of John, probably from Janekyn meaning "young John."
Johnson, Johns, Johnes—the "son of John," originally pronounced and spelled Jone.
Jones—"son of John," from Ioan, the Welsh for the first name of John.
Jergen, Juergen—(German) translation of the name George.

Jungst—(German) the youngest in the family or group.
Junior—nickname "the junior," the younger of two men bearing the same surname, the older becoming senior. It was common for two or three brothers to have the same Christian name, and this needed a mark of distinction.

German Emigration

The two exit ports for Germany were at Bremen and Hamburg in the north of the country, and from here millions of Germans and other Europeans left to settle in Ireland, Britain, and North America. For the period from 1850 to 1914 there are complete passenger lists surviving from the port of Hamburg; unfortunately this has not happened for Bremen. The surviving records have been microfilmed and are found in the Historic Emigration Office in Hamburg.

Civil registration began in Germany on January 1, 1876, and from this date births, marriages, and deaths have been registered with the local registrar (very similar to the system in England and Wales). Records for what was East Germany are available at the West Berlin State Archives. Church registers are the main sources for records from the sixteenth to the nineteenth century. The three main churches in Germany are the Roman Catholic, the Lutheran, and the Presbyterian.

Lists of all citizens in the larger towns can be found and are known as Town Rolls (*Burgerbucher*). These town rolls are taken instead of a census and some date back to the sixteenth century.

Tracing your ancestors can be a relatively easy task in Germany, as in centuries gone by ordinary people were unable to move from place to place without permission. German-related family history societies offer an ideal way to get help and advice with any German research.

HUGUENOTS AND JEWS

The Huguenots fled to England from France as a result of religious persecution at home, the name being applied to French Protestants who had adopted the Calvinistic form of the reformed religion. Although small numbers had arrived steadily prior to the 1680s, at that point they came in force and settled into the English community, Anglicizing their surnames. Not all French immigrants, of course, were Huguenots, some came over as a result of the French Revolution and The Terror. (Many useful and interesting records are published by the Huguenot Society.)

In 1290 Jews were banished from England, and only started to return from 1655 onward. Many Jews fled from the Russian Empire during the period 1881–1914, emigrating to the United Kingdom and the United States, and more went to the United Kingdom in the 1930s to escape from Nazi Germany. As with the Huguenots, the Jews have made a large contribution to British life and culture over the centuries. Jewish records are still with the synagogues or deposited in the county record offices.

RELIGIOUS GROUPS IN THE NEW WORLD

The earliest organized religion in the New World was Roman Catholicism, the official Church of all the Spanish, Portuguese, and French colonies. The Catholic Church had a continuous presence in the New World from the time that the Franciscan missionaries accompanied Columbus on his second voyage. The first Roman Catholic settlements were in Florida in 1565 and Mexico in 1598. Maryland was the only English colony to allow Roman Catholicism, although even there it was banned from 1649 to 1657.

In the United States, many of the thirteen original colonies had their own Established Church, the most popular of which was the Congregational Church. As more and more immigrants arrived in the United States, many seeking religious freedom, they brought with them their own religious preferences. Many faiths took root but record-keeping and preservation, alas, were not always as meticulous as they might have been, although good material has survived. The Quaker records or minutes, however, are excellent and these have been microfilmed by the Church of Jesus Christ of Latter-day Saints and are available

USEFUL WEBSITES:
Jewish research:
http://www.jewishgen.org
French research:
http://www.world-address.com/francetres

through its family history centers. An excellent article on the church records and the different religious sects has been written by Lesley Klippel; it is called "Genealogical Research: Utilizing Church Records" and is from *PAFinder Newsletter 1998*, Silicon Valley PAF Users Group, Volume 9, Number 7.

Of the denominations which took root, the Moravian and the Lutheran were two of the most widespread. The Moravian Church was founded in Moravia in 1457 and was first established in the New World in Georgia in 1734, before moving its headquarters to Bethlehem, Pennsylvania, in 1741. The Moravians sent missionaries to the Virgin

Above: A crowded Jewish cemetery in Prague. Many Jews fled from the Russian Empire between 1881 and 1914, emigrating to the UK and USA. Others escaped from Nazi Germany in the 1930s. Jewish records may be found in local synagogues or in county record offices.

Below: Denominations of Nonconformist groups that established themselves in the United States included Moravian, Lutheran, and Methodist churches. A black Methodist congregation is shown worshipping in Cincinnati in 1852.

Islands in 1732, New York in 1752, and Wachovia in North Carolina in 1753. The Lutheran Church was founded in 1517 and held its first service in Hudson Bay in 1619. A Lutheran congregation was organized in New York City in 1648, and then in 1709 the Palatine Germans founded Germantown in New York. The Lutheran Church was made official in North America in 1748.

The Huguenots fled from their homes in the northern part of France, not only to England but also to exile in Germany, The Netherlands, and Switzerland. In 1562 Huguenots settled in Florida, but their settlement was destroyed by the Spanish. They eventually established themselves in New Amsterdam, Virginia, New York, Massachusetts, Rhode Island, and North Carolina.

Other religions of Americans included the Anglican Church (later the Episcopal), the Congregational Church, the Presbyterian, Reformed Dutch, Baptist, Dunkards (Church of the Brethren) Methodist, and Judaism. (These and many others are given in full in the *Genealogical Encyclopaedia of the Colonial Americas* by Christina K. Schaefer published by the Genealogical Publishing Company.)

Left: From a page of a Moravian baptism register of 1755.

Left: English Quaker prison reformer Elizabeth Fry (1780–1845) reading the Bible to a group of prisoners at Newgate prison, c. 1810.

Kachler, Kachner—(German) for "tile-maker" or "potter."

Kaufman—(German) descendant of a merchant or tradesman.

Keegan—(German) meaning "heart" or "mind," a popular name after the Norman Conquest. It is also an Irish corruption of McEgan, "son of Egan."

Keen, Kean, Keene—a nickname for a person who was keen, sharp, or eager, also a brave man.

Keller—"the keller" or "kilner," a worker of the lime kiln or furnace.

Keer—(Celtic) "dweller by the marsh."

Kemp, Kempe, Kempson—an official or occupational name, meaning "the kemp," a knight, a soldier, or a champion. The name of Kemp is also considered to be of Jewish descent.

Pennsylvania German Church Records 1729–1870

This CD contains images of the pages of all three volumes of Pennsylvania German Church Records originally published by GPC. The records include births, marriages, and burials, and identify approximately 91,000 individuals and their relationships to one another.
• Available from Genealogical Publishing Company: http://www.genealogical.com/cdrom.htm

BANNS BOOKS, MARRIAGE LICENCES, AND VESTRY MINUTES

THE BANNS of marriage was the proclamation in church of a couple's intention to marry, and the banns would be called in both the parish church of the bride and of the bridegroom on three successive Sundays. It was done to find out if there was a reason that they could not wed. From March 1754 onward, following Hardwicke's Marriage Act of 1753, all marriages in England and Wales had to be held either by banns or licence, and a banns register was to be kept. Named after the first Earl of Hardwicke, the full title was an Act for the Better Preventing of Clandestine Marriages, and it was as a result of this legislation that marriages by process of affirmation before witnesses were no longer recognized by law.

If during researches you have problems finding a marriage in the marriage register, see if a banns book has survived. The banns register gives the date the banns were called and the parish where the wedding took place (remember that weddings were often held in the parish of the bride). The requirement to register banns continued until 1812.

The wording would be something like this: "Banns published between William Turnbull, bachelor of the parish of Kirknewton, and Isabella Scott spinster of this parish. 7th January 1800, 14th January, 21st January." If the marriage was due to take place in some other parish, the clergyman might have written, "The marriage took place at Kirknewton on the 28th January 1800."

Between 1653 and 1660, during Cromwell's Protectorate when marriages were civil contracts under the authority of the Justice of the Peace, banns were also called in the local marketplace, on three successive market days, and this record may be found with the name of the market, in a book which is separate to the marriage book.

LICENCES

The procedure of the banns being called could be avoided by applying for a marriage licence. Since there was no need to wait for the banns to be called, a marriage could take place on the day the licence was issued or promptly thereafter. It cost to have a licence issued, but

Above: A page from The Catholic Encyclopedia *which gives information relating to the history of the religious act of marriage and explains the purpose of reading banns prior to a marriage.*

Below: The certificate of the marriage of William Turnbull and Eva May Rossiter at Milton Parish Church, Kent, England on August 3, 1901.

No.	When Married.	Name and Surname.	Age.	Condition.	Rank or Profession.	Residence at the time of Marriage.	Father's Name and Surname.	Rank or Profession of Father.
389	Aug. 3 1901	William Turnbull	32	Bachelor	Bombardier	Sheerness	John Turnbull	Labourer
		Eva May Rossiter	19	Spinster		3. Cranbrook Villas, Chalkwell Rd.	George Thomas Rossiter	Fitter

Page 195

Marriage solemnized at the Parish Church in the Parish of Milton next Sittingbourne in the County of Kent

Married in the Parish Church according to the Rites and Ceremonies of the Established Church, after Banns, by me, Stephen Chapman

This Marriage was solemnized between us, William Turnbull / Eva May Rossiter

in the presence of us, George Thomas Rossiter / Grace Maud Rossiter

I Certify, that the foregoing is a true Extract from the Register of Marriages belonging to the Parish Church in the Parish of Milton n. Sittingbourne. Witness my hand this 3rd day of August 1901. Stephen Chapman Designation Assistant Curate.

* Note.—Strike out that which does not apply.

there were various reasons why one might be preferred to banns: the couple could be living away from home, they might wish to marry quickly, the young husband could have been called for military duty abroad, or, of course, the bride could have been pregnant.

There were two types of marriage licence. The first was special, granted by the Archbishop of Canterbury or his officials, which allowed the marriage to take place anywhere. Examples are very rare because not many have survived down the years. The second type was quite common and would name one or two parishes where the marriage could take place; it was issued by either the archbishop, the bishop, or, in some parishes, archdeacons or ministers.

A marriage licence was presented to the couple and while many have been lost, some may still be among the family documentation, and others will have found their way to the county record office. The licence itself has very little information on it: the couple's names and the place and date of the wedding. However, it was usual for the groom to apply for the licence by submitting an allegation or sworn statement that there was no impediment to the marriage taking place. This allegation would give names, ages, occupations, and places of residence of the couple, whether they were single or widowed, and where the marriage would take place. If either was a minor, the parent or guardian consenting to the marriage was also named. Again, if these have survived they will be in the county record office.

Kennedy—Irish and Scots Gaelic nickname for "ugly head."
Kessler—(German) for a "kettle-maker," or tinker

Tea kettle

Kettel, Kettles, Kettell, Cetel, Citel—the variants of this name are many. "Kittle" is an old Norse word for "bowl" or "cooking pot;" a "Kittle Flickara" is a kettle-maker, a tinsmith, or a smith. It could also mean a sacrifical cauldron relating to northern mythology.
Kilby—a location name for a farm of young nobles or a gentleman. There are places with this name found in Leicestershire and Lincolnshire, in England.

VESTRY MINUTES

The governing body of the parish was named after the room in the church where the meetings took place, and its members were the incumbent, as chairman, the churchwardens, and respected householders of the parish. The householders were either elected onto the committee by the existing members or by the parishioners themselves. The size of this committee varied; in a small parish there might only be ten or twelve, whereas in a city it could increase to forty.

During the sixteenth and seventeenth centuries, these meetings slowly took over the functions of the manor court. The committee were responsible for the appointments of the Constable, the Overseer of the Poor, and the Surveyor of the Highways, all subject to the approval of the Justice of the Peace. It was not until the Local Government Act of 1894 that the various civil functions were transferred from the parish church to the parish council. Minutes of the committee meetings were kept and might still be with the incumbent or, alternatively, in the county record office. These records will shed more light on the lives of our forebears, the history of the parish, and may well mention names. There will also be account books of the various appointees.

King

King—a nickname given to a person appearing in village festivals or tournaments as a king or emperor.
Kirkkomäki—Finnish name which was changed to Churchill.

Above: A seventeenth-century hand-colored woodcut depicting a priest performing a marriage ceremony.

FTM: Marriage Records

A range of marriage index CDs for selected US states.

• Available from Appleton's Online:
http://www.appletons.com/genealogy/genebbcd.html

QUARTER SESSIONS

THE QUARTER Sessions was a type of court which had jurisdiction over an English county and the system operated from the fourteenth century until 1971, meeting four times a year, hence their title of "quarter sessions." It was presided over by a Justice of the Peace, also known as a magistrate, who was appointed by the commissions of the peace from the king. Although their power and jurisdiction increased over the years, they dealt with less serious crimes than those handled by the higher Assize Courts, but the Quarter Sessions could still hand out severe sentences such as death or transportation.

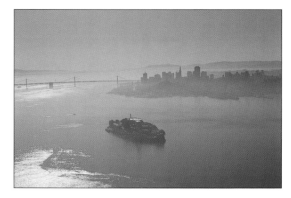

The workload of the Quarter Sessions included such crimes as theft, assault, riot, poaching, and murder but not civil cases, treason, or forgery. They also supervised the Poor Law, which included settlements and bastardy examinations; issued licences to certain traders, such as an alehouse keeper; saw that craftsmen were qualified by guild membership, or by having served an apprenticeship; and supervised the administration of taxes, the upkeep of the highway, and also local defense.

As the workload became greater and greater, from the sixteenth century the Justices of the Peace were empowered to meet between Quarter Sessions but this was to deal only with very minor matters. An Act of Parliament in 1541 required the Justices to meet in divisions, six weeks before the Quarter Sessions to make inquiries into vagabonds. In 1605 an Order in Council requested the Justices meet to discuss alehouses. These sorts of meetings became known as Petty Sessions.

Justices were empowered to levy a county rate from householders with which to cover the expenditure and upkeep of houses of correction, the courthouse, and lunatic asylums. They also had to finance the movement of prisoners from gaols and court. Accounts would be kept for all of these rates together with the names of the individual ratepayers.

THE CLERK OF THE PEACE

The records of the Justice's work were kept by the Clerk of the Peace, who was also a lawyer. The Clerk of the Peace was the officer appointed to assist the Justices at the Quarter Sessions and to keep the county records. The post was abolished in 1971–72 and the records were transferred to the county record office or the city or borough archives. Other documents kept by the Clerk of the Peace included poll books, electoral registers, enclosure awards, lists of freemen, tax returns (these could be window taxes, servants taxes, and taxes for dogs or horses), alehouse licences, and land tax records. All useful documentation for the researcher.

Some of the Quarter Sessions would have been published and contemporary calendars were made of them. Even if you find an entry in these published works it might not be the full transcript; always turn to the original record at the county record office for a complete version of the documents. A book by J. S. W. Gibson called *Quarter Sessions Records for Family Historians* is published by the Federation of Family History Societies. It lists, county by county, the holdings of the record offices, and Wales is also included (using the old Welsh county names).

Above: Some convicted British criminals were placed on the hulls of redundant ships, known as hulks. A more modern equivalent would be the well known prison island of Alcatraz, near San Fransisco, California.

Below: This engraving of the interior of a courthouse illustrates a murder trial held in April 1849 in London, England. Convicted murderers were often sentenced to transportation for life and shipped to the British colonies in the West Indies and North America.

Left: The surname Knight is to be found in many parts of Europe and the USA.

Kisch—a name of Jewish descent.

Knapp, Knappe—(German) a "page boy" or a "miner."

Knight—nickname for a youth, a soldier, a warrior, or knight; also used to describe a person serving in a knight's household.

Kofman—a name of Jewish descent.

Kramer, Kramar, Kreamer—an occupational name, meaning "a creamer." Krammer is of Jewish descent. Kramer is an American variant, meaning a traveling trader.

Kreisel, Kreisler—(German) translated as a "spinning top."

Kruger—(USA) descendant of an innkeeper, possibly of German origin.

The Transported

From the late 1500s some British criminals who had been sentenced to death had their sentence changed to transportation for life and, until 1782, many thousands were sent to the British colonies in the West Indies and North America, mainly to Virginia and Maryland. After the American War of Independence, this stopped. In addition to ordinary criminals, others transported included people involved in rebellion (Duke of Monmouth's in 1685 and Highland risings in 1715 and 1745) and early trade unionism. Prisoners were placed in the hulls of redundant ships, known as hulks, which were anchored in the River Thames and off the coasts of Chatham, Sheerness, Portsmouth, and Plymouth in the south of England. The conditions aboard these hulks was appalling: the food was inedible and the sanitary provisions non-existent. Punishments included close confinement and whipping. The convicts were also employed at hard labour in the dockyards.

Transportation to Australia was recommended in 1787 by the British government as a means of reducing the number of convicts held in the hulks and the prisons. The first fleet set sail on May 13, 1787, and arrived in January of the following year. It was made up of 586 male and 192 female convicts, together with sailors and free settlers, making the total 1,493. During the voyage forty-five people died and seven children were born. On January 26, 1788, New South Wales was declared a British colony. Between this date and 1868, when transportation ceased, some 160,000 people were shipped to Australia from England, Scotland, and Ireland, only 15 per cent of them female.

After a few years, the convicts would be granted a "ticket of leave" which gave them limited access to free movement in the area. When the convict had proved himself reliable once more, he was granted his conditional pardon. This meant he was a free man in the colony but could never return to the United Kingdom. Many generations of people in former British territories have kept the information quiet that their ancestors were convicts.

Right: Convicts in striped uniforms building roads near Atlanta, Georgia, USA, in 1870. Many British criminals were transported to North America from the late 1500s until the American War of Independence (or Revolutionary War), whereupon prisoners were sent to Australia instead.

MAPS, BOOKS, LAND REGISTRY, AND PROPERTY

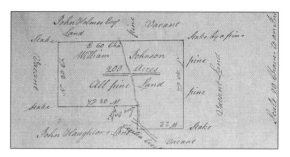

THE EARLIEST known map of England was drawn in 1250 by Matthew Paris, a Benedictine monk in St Albans. As time passed and map-making progressed, it became sufficiently advanced for cartographers to accompany local surveys in the fifteenth century. The earliest map held by the Public Record Office is of Inclesmoor, in Yorkshire, made in 1406–7. During the 1570s, Christopher Saxton, a servant to Thomas Secford, master of the Court of Requests, made maps of all the counties in England and Wales.

It is important to know the land and parishes around where your ancestors lived. Where was the nearest market town? By studying maps it is possible to find out possible reasons why the family moved around. The Institute of Heraldic and Genealogical Studies in Canterbury has produced some excellent maps showing the parish boundaries and the date of the earliest parish registers. These are also reproduced in a book by Cecil Humphrey-Smith, *Atlas & Index of Parish Registers*.

ENCLOSURE MAPS

The enclosure maps date from around the middle of the eighteenth century to the middle of the nineteenth. These maps accompanied an enclosure award and came with a schedule which listed details of ownership of the land. Early maps show the boundaries of ancient parishes. These enclosure awards and maps were lodged at the Quarter Sessions and should be held in the county record office.

TITHE MAPS

The parish tithe map, produced between 1838 and 1854, was very similar to the enclosure map. The tithes were a type of annual local taxation, made in kind, by the farmers and landowners. A large-scale map was drawn up of the parish, showing every field, building, and home. Schedules were made up of ownership, and in some cases also showing the tenants. By using the censuses of 1841 and 1851 it is possible to pinpoint the exact residence of an ancestor. This legislation did not apply to Scotland or Ireland, but Wales was very well covered. Even if the map is missing, there may well still be a copy of the schedule. Three copies were made of the tithe maps and they can be found in the county record office, the Public Record Office or the diocese archives.

ESTATE MAPS

Estate maps were commissioned by large landowners who would hire a surveyor to map their property and estate. The earliest estate maps are from the sixteenth century, and although the level of detail varies greatly, it is generally good. Tenants were listed with their names, the acreage occupied, and the terms of their lease. A large estate could cover several parishes and it was the appearance of the large-scale ordnance survey maps in the 1870s that put a stop to these private estate maps. Check the county record office for their holdings, as well as the Royal Commission on Historical Manuscripts which has an index to a large number of estate papers and collections.

STREET MAPS

Although many of the above maps relate to the county areas, there are numerous street maps

Above: Part of a plan showing land in Florida, granted to William Johnson in 1772.

Above: A cottage in Williamsburg, Virginia. Land and property records are a rich source of information for the family historian.

Below: Maps and land registry documents exist from the early European settlement of America.

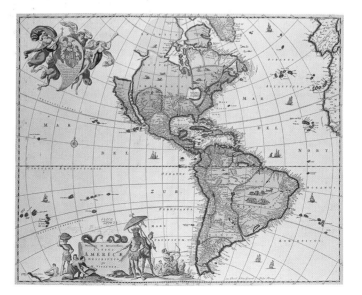

for the towns and cities. These should not be missed out and can provide fascinating detail. One book series of particular interest is *Tallis's London Street Views 1838–1840* (all the volumes of which are in the British Library Lending Division), whose maps don't give the usual aerial view of a city but are viewed as if looking directly at a building. The roads are all named and the houses numbered, in some cases with the names of the owners of the building and shops. Honwood's map of London shows it as an aerial view, and these maps were revised in 1813 by Faden.

Do not forget to use the maps produced by the Ordnance Survey, as well as fire insurance plans and public utility maps and plans. Check the large holding of maps in both the county record office and the Public Record Office in Kew.

US GEOLOGICAL SURVEY

In the United States an agency of the federal government has produced a series of maps that covers the entire country and shows most towns and cities. These are most useful to the genealogist, helping to locate cemeteries and sites where your ancestors lived. These topographic maps were made from aerial photographs taken by the United States Geological Survey (USGS). The maps can be purchased direct from them or from commercial map-sellers around the country. These maps do not name individual residences or landowners.

Land ownership maps can also be accessed in many research libraries and archives. The Library of Congress has a checklist of all such maps from the nineteenth century, and the Post Office produced and/or collected many useful maps and diagrams which are now available in the National Archives.

LAND RECORDS

For many hundreds of years ownership of land was proved by documents known as title deeds,

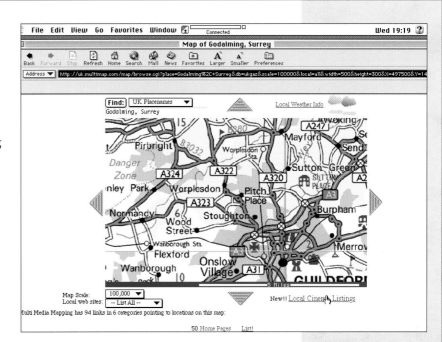

such as wills and trust deeds. Many of these have survived in the county record offices and other collections. Old title deeds of property are still mainly held by families, usually if the land is unregistered, and the deeds are proof that the property belongs to you. Many older records have been destroyed, but many remain and these are in the county offices.

Different types of land records are available to the family historian in Britain; they are:

- **Abstract of title**—a condensed history of the title to a section of real estate. It should contain a summary of every conveyance of the property. It will often include maps and other aids. Although not a complete record it will serve as an index to the original records.
- **Acknowledgement**—a formal statement at the end of a deed, after the signature of the person who executed it.
- **Affidavit**—a written statement of facts, made voluntarily and affirmed by oath of the party making it.
- **Bill of sale**—this is a statement showing a transfer of ownership by sale.

You will find these records and many others in various locations, including county courthouses. Some states even require the filing of final records of probate with the custodian of local land records so they are recorded as proof of title. Many of your early American ancestors would have acquired land, and land ownership records do exist from the early European settlement of the continent.

Above: A page from the website of Multimap: http://uk.multimap.com/

Lamb—a nickname for a person of a mild inoffensive character or one who tends the lambs.

Lang—a nickname meaning "long" or "tall," used as a prefix in place names like Langford and Langridge.

Lassey—a local "of Lacy," possibly a place in France. The name is of Huguenot descent.

Lawrence—a post-Conquest first name of Lawrence; very common in the south of England.

Levi, Levy—a name of Jewish descent.

Lewis, Lewison, Levison—"the son of Louis or Lewis." Lewis is used by the Welsh as an Anglicization of Llewellyn.

Lipman—a name of Jewish descent.

Lloyd—Welsh for "grey" or "hoary;" a location from Llwyd in Denbigh.

LATIN AND EARLY HANDWRITING

ATTEMPTING TO read documents which are less then 200 years old should not give anyone any problems. Words would have been spelled the same as today, and the letters also formed the same. The only problem could be the condition of the documents, with the ink having faded.

Following the Norman Conquest of England, most official documents were written in Latin and various forms of abbreviation were also used. The most common types of handwriting between the twelfth and sixteenth centuries was known as Court Hand; although the use of abbreviations continued, by the late 1600s it was more like a squiggle at the end of a word, for example "ing" became a meaningless flourish.

LATIN

Latin was still used for most documents, and for the family historian who has not studied it this will present obvious problems. Luckily there is help available, because with a list of the most used Latin words to hand it is possible to read the parish registers quite easily. A book by C. T. Martin, called *The Record Interpreter*, gives a medieval word list and a list of abbreviations. Try to form your own list on a small card, listing things like: both—*ambo*, bachelor—*coelebs*, were married—*copulati sunt*, of this parish—*de hac parochia*, his or hers—*ejus*, were joined in matrimony—*n matrimonia juncti sunt*, died—*obiit*, by banns—*per bannos*, by licence—*per licentiam*. Some of the Latin words do look similar to the English words.

SECRETARY AND ITALIC HAND

A great many sixteenth- and seventeenth-century documents were written in Secretary Hand, but by the late seventeenth century the Italic Hand was more widely used by scholars and the abbreviations disappeared. A very common example is the double s when a long f is used beside one s.

By just practicing the reading and writing of the various hands you will soon become quite accomplished in reading old documents. If you do have problems, respond to one of the many adverts in various magazines, who for a small charge will translate your document for you.

CALENDARS

Until 1752 the English used what is called the Julian calendar, and this meant the year started on Lady Day, March 25. This can prove a major headache when checking parish registers, for a child born on January 31, 1743, in the Julian calendar is born on January 31, 1744, in the Gregorian calendar. There are several ways to record this in your notes: 1743 OS (old style) or 1744 NS (new style); the usual way would be to write it as 1743–44 while some people just update it and call it 1744.

By an Act of Parliament, known as Lord Chesterfield's Act of 1751–52, the Julian calendar was abandoned in favor of the Gregorian calendar. The Act meant the year started on January 1, 1752, and would finish on December 31, 1752. The only problem was that the year had to be adjusted and September 2 was immediately followed by September 14, thus losing eleven days. Scotland had adopted the new calendar in 1600, 152 years before England. So if you have both English and Scottish ancestry, take care.

Above: A depiction of Eadwine the scribe, from the "Eadwine Psalter" c. 1150. (Trinity College, Cambridge, England.)

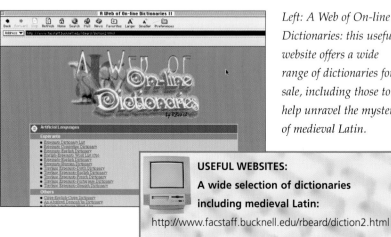

Left: A Web of On-line Dictionaries: this useful website offers a wide range of dictionaries for sale, including those to help unravel the mysteries of medieval Latin.

The Domesday Book

More than 900 years ago, in 1086, one of the most extraordinary historical records in the world was created. The name given to this document in the twelfth century was the Domesday Book. It was called by various names, The Book of Winchester, The Great Survey, The Inquisition, The Great Description of England, but we still know it as the Domesday Book.

The incredible thing was that this book was transcribed and written up by one man. Although it was to be prepared for a foreign lord, the Norman William the Conqueror, the work was done by a native Englishman. The parchment made of sheepskin is still supple and as creamy yellow today as it was all those years ago. The writing is clear, a stylish Latin Hand, with a touch of flamboyance in the long descenders. No other country in the world has such a detailed record from so far back giving us an account of the courts, the people, the land, the industry—even the weather.

It gives details such as herring fishermen in Great Yarmouth in Norfolk, the iron smelters of Corby in Northamptonshire, the slaves in the West Country and the freemen in East Anglia. One description of a local property is that of "an excellent house with good wines." It shows that rents were paid in a variety of ways: wheat, barley, 480 hens, 32 hogs of bacon, 240 fleeces, and so many more.

This record includes details of land, property, and the people. It might be your aim to trace your ancestors back to the Domesday Book; many already claim to have done this, but it is in fact very difficult to get beyond the earliest parish registers. In the early 1980s, the book was published as more manageable county editions, and reproduced with a copy of the original page on one side with a fascinating modern-day translation on the facing page.

Lobley—a local of Lobley in Lancashire; also from Lobley Gate in Basildon in Essex.

Lombardo, Lombard, Lumbard—possibly a nickname "the Lombard;" one who came from Lombardy. Some evidence shows that this name could be Jewish. Lumbard also shows evidence of a Huguenot descent.

Lopez—(Spanish) descendant of Lope or Lupe, meaning the "wolf-like man." Also a known Jewish name.

Lucas, Luke—a surname from the Midlands and Southwest of England. Could also be from the local place of Lucca in Italy or from Luick (Liege) in Belgium.

Lynch—a hilly location, a bank or boundary for dividing land. Found in the UK mainly in Devon, Somerset, and Sussex. Many of the Lynches in New York are of Irish parentage.

LOCATION OF IRISH AND SCOTTISH RECORDS

THE TREATY of Union of 1707 gave England and Scotland the same British government and parliament (they had had the same monarch since 1603), but Scotland retained its law and administration, and therefore its record-keeping. The later Act of Union of 1801 formally united Ireland and Great Britain into a United Kingdom. In 1922, Ireland was partitioned and six counties in the north remained part of the United Kingdom and became known as Northern Ireland, while the remaining twenty-six counties formed the Irish Free State, later renamed the Republic of Ireland. The relationship between Britain and Ireland has long been a troubled one, complicated by religious antagonisms, and it would be a good idea for the family historian to read up on some history of the two countries.

Above: The Church of Scotland has over 900 ancient parishes whose registers are archived on microfilm.

LOSS OF IRISH RECORDS

Research in Ireland will always be difficult due to the loss of many of its records in the fire of 1922 at the Four Courts in Dublin, which was the location of the Irish Public Record Office. Even so, there are still many sources available for the researcher. Because the administration in Ireland was British up until 1922, many of the Irish records are very similar to those in England and Wales. Many records have been kept in Britain at the Public Record Office (PRO) in Kew, and these are described in guides produced by the PRO Current Guide. Of particular interest are the records of the Irish army regiments and the militia, navy, and merchant seamen. Prerogative Court of Canterbury (PCC) wills and administration, death duty registers, and crown estates are all types of records to consider when visiting the PRO. There are important collections relating to Irish genealogy at the British and Bodleian libraries (see an article by C.R. Humphrey-Smith in *Family Tree Magazine*, April 1990).

CIVIL REGISTRATION

Civil registration began on April 1, 1845, for Protestant marriages and on January 1, 1864, for all births, marriages, and deaths. The registration districts follow the Poor Law Unions, the same as in England and Wales. These indexes are held by the Registrar General at Joyce House in Dublin, and after 1922 the Northern Ireland records have been kept by the Registrar General in Belfast.

Very few census returns survived the Four Courts' fire. Those lost covered the period from 1821 to 1851 and the government destroyed the

returns for 1861 to 1891. There are books available which list the few surviving returns.

The majority of Irish people were Roman Catholics, but the Anglican Church of Ireland was the official church until 1869. Its ministers were required to record only baptisms and burials from 1634 and the surviving register only starts in the late eighteenth century. Once again the majority of these records were destroyed in the 1922 fire.

WILLS AND PROBATE

Most wills and other probate records were also lost in the fire of 1922. Wills proved since 1922 are available and calendars of wills and admons since 1858 are at the National Archive. The National Archive has tried to replace some of the missing probate records by collecting them from solicitors and families.

Above: The grave of Rob Roy MacGregor, near Inversnaid, Scotland.

Below: South Pass City, Wyoming, USA, a ghost town which was deserted when settlers moved on.

To help with your Irish family history, consider joining a family history society. The Irish Family History Society publishes *Irish Family History* and the Irish Genealogical Research Society publishes *The Irish Genealogist*. A quarterly journal, *Irish Roots*, is available through the PRO and the Society of Genealogists (SoG).

SCOTLAND

As with Ireland, a little reading on Scottish history will help, mainly for the sixteenth and seventeenth centuries. There are a lot of published family histories, so check with the family history societies and libraries. With surnames, families in the Highlands would take the clan name, while the families in the Lowlands developed in a similar way to the English.

Civil registration commenced on January 1, 1855, but was a far superior system to that existing in England and Wales. Copies of births, marriages, and deaths are held by the Registrar General at New Register House. A fee is charged, but there is access to the census returns and parish registers. There is a computerized index to enable you to find the correct entry, and when this is found you can view the registers on microfilm. The birth indexes from 1929 and the death indexes from 1974 give the mother's maiden name. From 1868 onward the death indexes give the age at death and, from 1969, the date of birth. As you are viewing the registers, details can be written down and the certificate only ordered if it is really needed.

As in England, the census was taken every ten years from 1841 to 1891. These are held by the Registrar General and they have a similar layout to the census in England.

PARISH REGISTERS

The Church of Scotland has more than 900 ancient parishes whose registers are held by the Registrar General and are available on microfilm. Some copies of these registers are in the SoG and the Scottish Genealogy Society's library, and don't forget to check the Scottish regional record offices. A mother's maiden name is shown on a baptism record and this can assist in finding further siblings and the marriage of the parents. In Scotland there is no banns book, but a proclamation of marriage is given, although these were not always recorded. In Scotland it was possible to marry without a church service. These were the irregular border

The Complete Book of Emigrants 1607–1776

With approximately 140,000 recorded names, this CD is a comprehensive list of emigrants from Britain to America.

• Available from the Genealogical Publishing Company: http://www.genealogical.com/cdrom.htm

marriages and they took place all along the border between Scotland and England, the most famous being the Gretna Green marriages. The Church of Jesus Christ of Latter-day Saints have microfilmed the Scottish parish registers and they can be viewed at any family history center in the world.

Until 1868 land and buildings were always left to the eldest surviving son; only if there were no sons was the property left, equally, to any daughters, or to the spouse. Only moveable property, money, furniture, or livestock, could be left to anyone. From 1868 onward, the property could be willed to whomever. These records are available in the Scottish Record Office, and the SoG also has a large collection.

AMERICAN SETTLERS

About 150,000 Scots emigrated to America prior to the Revolutionary War, settling in English, Dutch, and French colonies, so there are many millions of North Americans alive today with Scottish ancestors, many of whom continue to hold Highland Games and other traditional events annually.

Mahoney—(Irish) "a descendant of the bear."
Male, Mayle—referred to as a Huguenot name.
Manley—a brave, upright and independent person. An Old English term for "communal wood clearing."
Marcus—the son of Mark, possibly a name of Jewish descent.
Mark, Marks, Marx—the son of Mark. Variants of Marcus.
Marsh—local name for a person living on or near a marsh.

Below: Many Irish and Scottish emigrants flocked to America in search of work. Taken in 1905, this picture shows European settlers on the Oregon Trail after a river crossing.

INDEXES

*A*S THE need for more and more information on our ancestors grows, then so do the numbers of booklets and indexes. As researchers pinpoint a certain interest—be it a surname, an occupation, or a location—then they will want to advertise it in family history or genealogical magazines. They may be requesting more information or publishing their findings in print form, microfiche, or, increasingly, on the Internet via their own webpages. As more people search record and archive offices, so a greater number and diversity of records are found.

Use the workhouse records, the school and university records, the lists of prisoners, and check the local history of the area—so much is available to search, but when you find new records, let the rest of the world know, don't hide them again.

AMERICAN LIBRARIES
In the United States there are several libraries devoted just to genealogical research and records. These include the New England Historic Genealogical Society in Boston, the Daughters of the American Revolution Society Headquarters in Washington DC, the Newberry Library in Chicago, and the New York Genealogical and Biographical Society. The LDS Family History Library in Salt Lake City in Utah is classed as the largest genealogy library in the world, but its records are available throughout the world, wherever there is a family history library.

THE LIBRARY OF CONGRESS
The United States' greatest general library is the Library of Congress. Their card index of books is computerized, so to view this just visit a nearby university or large public library. To demonstrate a copyright, the publisher must give the Library of Congress copies of the book, so it obtains copies of newly published material. The same thing happens in England: when copies are given to the British Library, the copyright is recorded on any published material.

Microfiche, which is also a published work, will have copyright; you can work with the microfiche but you cannot publish it again without being in breach of copyright. Many professional researchers purchase these fiche to help with their work.

Below: There are always articles on how to use library indexes and news about using the Internet for genealogy in a range of magazines. Published monthly or quarterly, they will keep you up to date with the latest technology to help you with your search.

USEFUL WEBSITES:

British Library:
http://blaiseweb.bl.uk/
http://www.bl.uk

**Indexed details of British Library services
(800 pages):** http://portico.bl.uk

Every state in the United States also sponsors a major library devoted to historical books and records within their state. They are found in the state capital, but there are also branch libraries elsewhere. The university libraries and major libraries have genealogy and family history sections. Libraries do produce guides to the records available; the National Archives publishes a booklet called "Using Records in the National Archives for Genealogical Research."

THE BRITISH LIBRARY

In the UK, the British Library has moved to a new purpose-built structure in London's St Pancras. The library's catalogs and indexes are available on its website. In addition to the British Library, the Bodleian Library in Oxford is also entitled to receive a free copy of all published works in Britain. It is attached to the university at Oxford and is the second largest public library in Britain. It holds approximately six million books and many thousands of manuscripts, including family archives, county histories, parish registers, and Army and Royal Navy lists. Other large libraries are Cambridge University Library, the National Library of Wales, the Scottish National Library, and the Library of Trinity College in Dublin.

THE CITY OF LONDON

Anyone who has London ancestors should go to the Guildhall Library in the City of London. Their holdings for the City of London include parish registers, rate books, churchwardens' accounts, wills, marriage licence records, maps, plans, directories, and local history information. The records of the City livery companies are held there, and they include apprenticeship and freedom records. The library produces several booklets which list its holdings.

The archives of the City of London's governing bodies are in the Corporation of London Record Office (CLRO) at the Guildhall. These are records which date back to medieval

times and they include the records for the 500,000 freemen of the City of London. Many British cities and boroughs have their own archives, all of which are listed in an HMSO booklet.

OTHER ARCHIVES

The Borthwick Institute of Historical Research is located in York. It holds the records of the Archbishop of York, which include wills, marriage licence records, parish registers, and bishops' transcripts. Other places to visit are specialist museums such as the Imperial War Museum, the National Maritime Museum, and the National Army Museum.

Above: The new purpose-built structure which now houses The British Library, London.

Below: The United States' greatest general library, the Library of Congress, is known as the largest library in the world. A library catalog is accessible on-line, through the Internet: http://lcweb.loc.gov

BRITISH CENSUS INDEXES

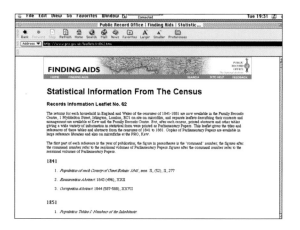

D URING THE 1970s a project to transcribe and index the 1851 census returns was started, mainly by the family history societies. The project is still going on. Some counties which took part have finished and published their indexes, both as books and also on microfiche. To view any microfiche you purchase, you can either go to your local library or look for a small second-hand fiche reader (they can be obtained for quite a reasonable price). Larger counties obviously take longer to compile, so write to the relevant family history societies for details of their publications and inquire if the 1851 census has been transcribed for their county. There is the possibility that a private company has published it for them.

OTHER CENSUSES

Other family history societies may have transcribed and indexed other census returns as part of their general project work. For example, the East of London FHS has worked on the "1861 Census Index Series", published in booklet form; Huntingdonshire FHS has transcribed the 1841 census returns and are due to publish on microfiche in 1999; Nottingham FHS has indexed the 1841 to 1891 census returns, and these are published on fiche; Lincolnshire FHS also has census surname indexes for the 1851–1871 and 1891 returns, again available on microfiche; and Buckingham FHS has a transcript of the 1851 census returns on computer and will make a surname search, for a small fee. Two publications worth reading are *Marriage, Census and other Indexes for Family Historians*, by Jeremy Gibson and Elizabeth Hampson, and *Current Publications on Microfiche by Member Societies*—both are available from the Federation of Family History Societies.

Collections of most census indexes are held by the Public Record Office, the Society of Genealogists, the Guildhall Library, county record offices, and some libraries. The important thing to remember is to check what their holdings are before you visit. Indexes may only contain the surname, then the piece and folio number of the census returns, while other indexes contain full details. Once you have found your family among these indexes, go back to the original returns, find your family and then have a copy made for your documents file.

THE 1881 INDEX

In the 1980s another project was started on the 1881 census returns, between the Genealogical Society of Utah, the Society of the Church of Jesus Christ of Latter-day Saints, and the British Federation of Family History Societies. As a result of this work, the whole of the British Isles has been indexed onto microfiche. Included in this are England, Wales, Scotland, the Isle of Man, the Channel Islands, and the Royal Navy returns. At the moment this is published by county, but the Genealogical Society will soon make available a complete nationwide index on CD-ROM. This will help in tracing those lost ancestors, as it will list each person alphabetically by surname.

Above: A page from the Public Record Office website, which offers visitors plenty of useful census information.

Below: A Master's schedule for his ship "Spanker" of Hull, Yorkshire, for the England and Wales census of 1871. The document clearly sets out how the details of each individual aboard the ship must be recorded at sea at midnight on April 2, 1871, and gives a few examples for reference.

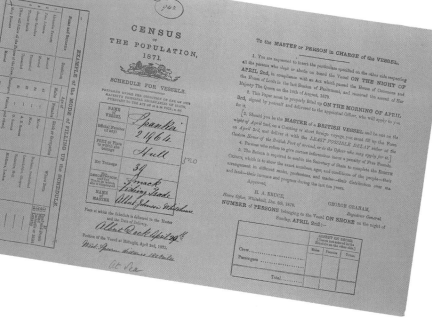

The 1881 index by county is divided into several sections, each section of a fiche is colour coded:
• 1: yellow—as enumerated
• 2: pink—surname index
• 3: orange—census place index
• 4: green—birthplace index
• 5: brown—miscellaneous and various notes
• 6: brown—list of vessels/ships
• 6: brown—list of institutions

The reference numbers relate to the Genealogical Society of Utah, and this is the reference to use when ordering films from the family history census. The "as enumerated" section is a transcript of the returns and gives the PRO piece, folio, and page number. This allows you to check the original returns. The surname index lists all people who were in the county on the night of the census, these are in alphabetical order and show forename, age, sex, relationship to the head of household, marital condition, census place, occupation, name of head of household, where born (county and parish), notes, PRO references, and the LDS film reference number. This is an ideal index to use for finding that missing ancestor if they moved about within the county. By using the birthplace index, it is possible to find brothers, sisters, and other family members who were born in the same village or town and then moved away.

These indexes can be viewed via the family history societies, which may offer a research service, but not all societies have the facilities to send print-outs. There are copies in the Family Records Centre, the Society of Genealogists, the Public Record Office, and (LDS) family history centers. The indexes are also available from the Federation of Family History Societies.

The 1891 census is available on microfiche for purchase from the Reprographic Ordering Department of the PRO at Kew. You do need to have a reference number as the census is available on 15,000 fiche, each containing 100 census pages. Once you know the piece number, the department will let you know how many fiche cover the piece and the cost. Street indexes of the London registration districts in the 1891 census are also available to buy.

Mill to grind Flower

Marshall—alongside Smith and Faber, the name of one who treats or tends horses. Early examples refer to high officers of state.

Martin, Martins, Martinson—"the son of Martin." This once popular Christian name, coming as it did in the hereditary surname period, has filled directories from the nineteenth century.

Mason—an occupational name for a stonemason or a woodmason.

Mayhew, Mayow, Mayhow—"the son of Matthew." Also a Huguenot descendant.

Miller—an occupational name for one who grinds the corn to make flour. This surname can be found in every county of England.

Montgomery—Montgomerie is near Lisieux in Normandy. This family name was given to the county and town of Montgomery in Wales.

Left: A cartoon by George Cruikshank, which was published in The Comic Almanack, *depicting the 1851 census. Work to transcribe the 1851 census began in the 1970s, and although not all counties have completed the task, many have now published the information as both books and microfiche.*

AMERICAN INDEXES

IN THE United States there is a mass of indexes on microfilm and microfiche as well as printed booklets, but the latest boom is in the publishing of indexes on the Internet. This is now the modern way forward, so spend some time searching for all the available indexes.

Mortality Index: United States 1850–1880

• Available from Appleton's Online:
http://www.appletons.com/genealogy/genebbcd.html

CENSUSES AND SOCIETIES
Most of the federal censuses are indexed, but not all, so you do need to check the index first before checking the census. Every census from 1790 to 1850 has state-wide indexes. These indexes are available either as a printed book or on microfilm or fiche; local genealogists and librarians will also have prepared indexes.

Indexers of the 1880, 1900, 1910, and 1920 censuses used a "Soundex" system (see page 56). This is a phonetic index and puts together names that sound the same rather than in alphabetical order. Apply the Soundex code to your surnames before you visit a repository and you will save time.

Family history and genealogical societies also publish journals. If you have just joined, see if there is an index to back issues of the journal because other people may have written in with surnames the same as yours. This is a useful way to find others researching your family.

MARRIAGE, LIFE, AND DEATH
There are several other indexes which will help the family history researcher. Find out where the marriage records are kept; if you cannot look at the actual records, there may be a separate index for the grooms and brides. Once you have checked in the index, note the book and page number which allows the archivist to find your entry. Some city or town directories have a reverse listing by street address, known as the householder's index, making it possible to check their neighbors and look for other members of the family. While looking at these indexes look at the businesses—was your ancestor a grocer or butcher? Examine the business listings. Do the local newspapers have an index for birth, marriages, and death announcements? As well as looking for death indexes, check for obituaries for they will give a lot of information on the family, who attended the funeral and details of the person's life:

occupation, offspring, age, and even place of birth could be recorded.

CONSOLIDATED INDEXES
A consolidated index is an index which combines several indexes together as one. A census index from 1850 to 1900 could be consolidated to one index, for example. Another known index is the *Compiled Military Service Records* which incorporates the Revolutionary War, the War of 1812, various Indian wars and disturbances, the Mexican War, and the American Civil War. These indexes are on microfilm, but the original records are not. Copies are available at the National Archives' branches. The *Index of Revolutionary War Pension Application in the National Archives* is widely available in book form, the microfilm is not. By consulting this index you can find your ancestor in the applicant's list and note their file designation, then search the repository with the microfilm of the actual pension film.

Indexes are an important aspect of family history. They are a quick method of checking to see if your ancestors are listed, rather then spending fruitless hours looking at the original records.

Above: The Compiled Military Service Records *index incorporates the Revolutionary War, the War of 1812, the American Civil War, and many other disturbances. The picture shows American Civil War Colonel John Mosley and men of Baltimore.*

Left: A consolidated index may contain details of the archives of various wars including events concerning Native Americans. This engraving by Catlin shows the Mandan tribe during archery practice.

Irish Emigration

The Irish emigrated in great numbers during the 1800s, mainly due to the potato famine and religious troubles. They traveled to Britain and across the seas to the United States, Canada, and Australia, forming large Irish population groups. Once they had decided to emigrate, a sailing ticket was acquired from the local agent of a shipping line, often a shopkeeper in the nearest town. Following a long hard walk, they would then have to wait several weeks for a place to become available on a ship. In 1855 the cost to go to North America from Ireland was £24 for a family of eight. The master of each ship was to provide daily allowances of water and food, while the passengers provided their own bedding and utensils. The voyages could last from between fifty to eighty days and many did not survive the trip. It was not just individual families which traveled out together, but whole communities often went on the same ship and reformed a new community when they reached their destination.

Between 1823 and 1825 more than 2,000 people sailed from County Cork to Canada. The ships' papers are found in the library of Peterboro in Ontario and they contain the original lists of emigrants' names. There are no official records of the emigrants leaving Ireland, but their entry to the United States can be found in the vast records held in the National Archives in Washington, DC.

Below: Irish emigrants at Cork embarking on their journey to America in 1820.

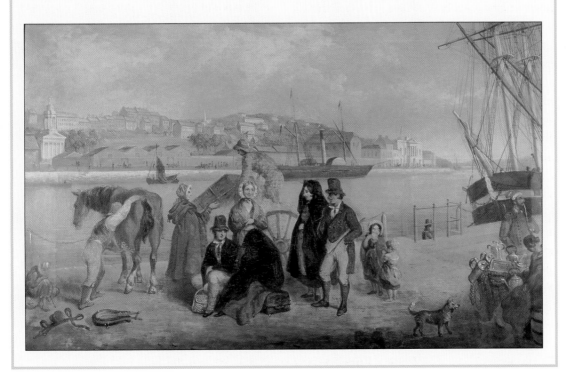

Moore—the moore, old French Maur from the Latin Maurus, name of a sixth-century saint. As a nickname meaning "dark," "swarthy" or a resident near the moor, marsh, or fen.

Morales—(Spanish) meaning "mulberry tree" or descendants of Moral. Also names of places in Spain.

Morris—meaning "moorish," "dark as a moor;" also Morrison "a son of Morris."

Murphy—a descendant of the Sea Warrior, an Irish name. This is among the commonest names in Ireland.

Murray—a name from the province of Moray in Scotland, a seaboard settlement.

Nale, Nail, Naile—local meaning of "at the ale house."

Nash, Naish, Nayshe—a local name "at the ash tree," from a residence beside the ash tree. Esh is still popular for ash in Furness, north Lancashire. This surname is found throughout the English-speaking world.

BOYD'S AND PALLOT'S MARRIAGE INDEXES

BETWEEN 1925 and 1955 Percival Boyd complied an index of marriage entries for sixteen counties in England, mainly from printed parish registers. They start from the beginning of registration in 1538 and go up to 1837 when civil registration started. The coverage is incomplete. The counties included in the index are as follows (the figure in brackets relates to the number of parishes covered within that county): Cambridgeshire (169), Cornwall (202), Cumberland (34), Derbyshire (80), Devon (169), Durham (72), Essex (374), Gloucestershire (121), Lancashire (101), London and Middlesex (160), Norfolk (146), Northumberland (84), Shropshire (125), Somerset (120), Suffolk (489), and Yorkshire (174). Also included are two miscellaneous series. The collection amounts to more than six million marriage register entries. It offers a useful aid if the marriage did not take place in the parish in which you expected— parental disapproval or pregnancy could be the reason for this. The index records both the names of the bride and groom, the name of the parish, and the year of the marriage.

USEFUL WEBSITES:

WorldGenWeb Project:
http://www.worldgenweb.org/

Familia:
http://www.earl.org.uk/familia

Genealogy Gateway to the Web:
http://www.gengateway.com

Genealogy SiteFinder:
http://www.familytreemaker.com/links/index.html

THE WORK OF BOYD

The Society of Genealogists holds the 534 original transcript volumes and it has published *A Key to Boyd's Marriage Index*. The index itself is on microfiche and is available for viewing at the Guildhall Library. It is also available in the archives of the sixteen relevant counties.

Boyd also published *Inhabitants of London* (or *Citizens of London*) which consists of 238 volumes of entries, recording about 60,000 London residents from the fifteenth to nineteenth centuries. There are a further twenty-seven volumes constituting the indexes. The original volumes are in the Society of Genealogists, with a microfilm copy held in the Guildhall. The information in the index comprises the name of the person; the date of baptism or birth, burial or death; the parents; the livery company; and details of the marriage and children.

PALLOT & CO

An index was begun in 1818 by a firm of record agents who specialized in chancery work and intestacy cases and whose successors included Messrs Pallot & Co. Much of the index was destroyed during World War II, but the surviving part covers 98 per cent of marriages

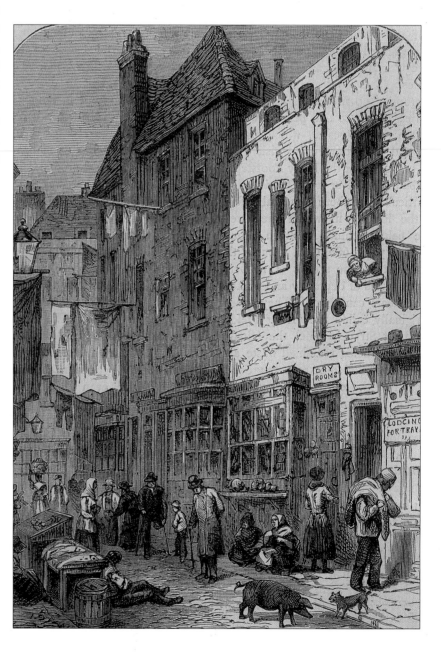

Above: The birth, marriage, and death details of certain sections of London's population were very difficult to record. This illustration by an unnamed artist shows the "Rookery" of St Giles, near Seven Dials, London, where even the police were at risk. This was drawn around the time of the 1851 census.

from 101 of the 103 ancient parishes of London and many Middlesex parishes for the period 1780–1837, with a smaller number from elsewhere, together with 30,000 baptisms from a number of London and provincial registers. The index is now cataloged and held by the Institute of Heraldic and Genealogical Studies in Canterbury. A catalog is available which lists the parishes included.

These indexes can give clues to where a family came from. Women's details are more helpful than the details of the groom as the marriage tends to take place in the bride's parish. Any marriage found in an index should, of course, be checked back to the original register.

SMALLER GEMS

Gentleman Magazine, which was published from 1731 to 1868, was a monthly magazine which contained a mine of miscellaneous information, so much so that it was also known as the *Monthly Intelligencer*. The topographical descriptions of the towns and villages are of particular interest. The general items in each month's issue were deaths, casualties, promotions, marriages, bankrupts, and accidents. Observations were made on gardening, foreign affairs, books published, the price of grain, and stocks.

G.L. Gomme edited this material for a series of county books published at the turn of the twentieth century. There are two indexes for it which cover the period 1731–1810, and there is an index of marriages for 1731–1768 and indexes for obituaries and biographies for 1731–1780 have also been published. The obituaries hold valuable information for the family historian, while the death and marriage indexes would need to be checked back to the original magazines because not all the information was taken into the index. The complete series is held in the British Library and the Public Record Office. The collection held in the Society of Genealogists is incomplete.

Many of the family history societies have also compiled and published marriage indexes, some of which will carry out a search, if requested by non-members, for a small fee. There are two publications from the Federation of Family History Societies: "Marriage Indexes," a booklet on how to find, use and compile them, and the book *Marriage, Census and other Indexes for Family Historians*, a book by Jeremy Gibson and Elizabeth Hampson.

Left: The bride signs the register at her wedding, c. 1880. For marriage entries prior to 1837, when civil registration began, the indexes compiled by Percival Boyd and Pallot & Co are available for viewing on microfiche.

FAMILY HISTORY SOCIETY INDEXES

THE AIMS of the family history societies are to aid the public study of family history, genealogy, heraldry, and local history in their own county. Societies hold monthly meetings and publish a journal perhaps two, three, or four times a year. They may have extensive libraries, and work toward producing transcripts, indexes, and other projects for their own county. At the monthly meeting they arrange for a wide selection of speakers on many different subjects. All this and more for just a small annual fee. The family history societies are usually run and organized by local members, not all of whom are researching their ancestors locally, but realize it is useful to attend talks and to use knowledge gleaned from others. Out-of-county members can also receive help with their research. The best advice is to join a local society, and the societies in the counties you are researching.

Many family history societies from all over the world are members of the Federation of Family History Societies (FFHS). This was formed in 1874 to join the various societies together. The FFHS publishes a large number of specialist books and a twice-yearly journal, *Family History News and Digest*, which contains reports of the societies and a list of the secretaries, as well as book reviews, news of new books, and a listing of key articles which have appeared in member societies' journals. There is an Association of Family History Societies for Wales and a Scottish Association of Family History Societies.

AMERICAN FAMILY HISTORY SOCIETIES

In the United States there are hundreds of genealogical societies, with all nationalities and creeds represented. To make contact with a society consult directories of societies and associations in the reference section of your public library. Further information about societies are in the *Meyer's Directory of Genealogical Societies in the USA and Canada* written by Mary Keysor Meyer. Consult the list

of societies and libraries in Everton's *The Genealogical Helper*, printed annually each summer; also *Genealogical Sources in the United States of America* compiled by M.E. MacSorley.

THE SOCIETY OF GENEALOGISTS

The first meetings of the Society of Genealogists (SoG) were held in a small room in London's Fleet Street in 1911. Its collection of genealogical material has grown over the years, and it now owns the largest collection of genealogical books and material in the UK. The SoG is situated in Goswell Road, only ten minutes walk from the

Above: US settlers who were born in the UK may be traced through family history societies who help the general public in the study of family history. The picture shows Granary burying ground, in Boston, Massachusetts.

Below: Family history societies deal with local history in their own county.

The Open University

The Open University offers project reports on Family and Community History. CDR0008 contains the 1994 reports and CDR0015 contains the 1995 reports.
• Available from Faculty Office, Faculty of Social Sciences, Open University, Milton Keynes, MK7 6AA, UK

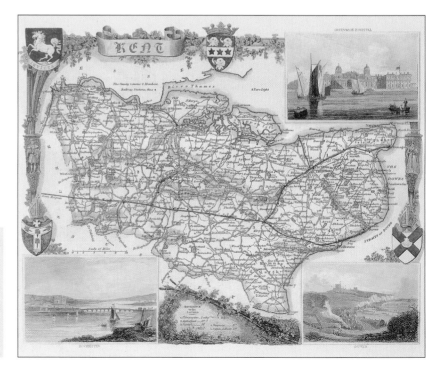

Barbican Underground station. As well as Boyd's marriage index, there is also the "Great Card Index" with more than three million names. Each county has its own section in their library and the society is in the process of the mammoth task of computerizing its complete inventory of material. There is a quarterly journal for its members and for a fee non-members are able to use the facilities. The society offers a wide range of books from their own publications, as well as books and leaflets from other publishers.

CANTERBURY

The Institute of Heraldic and Genealogical Studies in Canterbury is dedicated to the study of family history, genealogy, and heraldry. It arranges day and residential courses and an excellent correspondence course, supported by qualified tutors. It has a large collection of research material in its library and its publications include the series of county maps for genealogists and its own journal, *Family History*. The institute has recently purchased the Lang family registers from Gretna Green.

INDEX PROJECTS

Most of these organizations and societies are busy compiling and maintaining indexes and ongoing projects. Some work as individuals while others work in groups. These people are trying to put back something into their hobby, ready for the new researchers to come along,

and they also hope that this is being done in their counties of research. As well as their own projects, they are also working collectively on two further indexes. The Strays Index is organized by the Federation of Family History Societies. As items in parish registers, censuses, and others are found of a person or persons living in one county but coming from another, these "strays" are collected and sent to the strays co-ordinator. It is another way to find those wandering ancestors. The second project is the National Burial Index Project (NBI), again run by the FFHS for England, Wales, Ireland, and Scotland. The NBI database will include the name of the deceased, age, date of burial, parish, county, and a source code. To find out the various ongoing projects and indexes, write to the societies for details, but always enclose a stamped self-addressed envelope.

Above left and left: US historical societies re-enact everyday scenes from the past and offer an informative and entertaining way to discover more about the way your ancestors may have lived and how early American towns would have looked.

CHURCH OF JESUS CHRIST OF LATTER-DAY SAINTS AND THEIR FAMILY HISTORY CENTERS

CHURCH OF Jesus Christ of Latter-day Saints is the full and correct title for the Mormon Church, sometimes known as the LDS. Members are known as Mormons from the *Book of Mormon* on which the beliefs of their Church are based.

USEFUL WEBSITES:

The Church of Jesus Christ of Latter-day Saints: http://www.lds.org/Main.html

The Church was founded in 1830 by Joseph Smith in New York, but the persecution of their members led to them traveling west across America until they came to the Great Salt Lake in modern-day Utah. There they settled and formed their new community.

The Church has a special interest in encouraging family history studies, not only because of the great emphasis that is placed on the importance of family life but because it is obligatory for its members to trace their ancestors in order to give them salvation by proxy.

THE RECORDING SYSTEM

The Genealogical Society of Utah was started in 1894 "to gather records that help people trace their ancestry." It opened its first library in Salt Lake—the precursor to the Family History Library system which is now run worldwide. In 1938 they began the microfilming of records, and today they have 250 camera operators who are working in more than fifty countries. Their microfilms include records such as birth, marriage, death, wills, immigration, and many more. Each year they record and catalogue approximately 100 million new pages of records on microfilms, microfiche, and in books. Most of the records cover the period from 1550 to 1920 and so do not include many living people.

It is possible to research your family wherever you live. In the United States, to be able to travel to places like Washington DC, or Salt Lake City has its advantages, but to live in or near is not essential. Help may be required

Below: Mormon immigrants at a camp during the journey to the Great Salt Lake in 1847. The detailed family records of the Genealogical Society of Utah were started in 1894 and are now freely accessible through nearly 3,000 family history centers all over the USA and the UK.

Lager der Mormonen in der Wüste.

from a professional genealogist at some time and the Family History Library in Salt Lake City has a program for freelance genealogists, with those who pass the tests placed on a recommended listing.

Left: Researchers use the extensive records of baptism to trace their family history.

Below: The Church of Jesus Christ of Latter-day Saints built the impressive Mormon Temple, Salt Lake City, Utah, in 1893.

A system of freely accessible family history centers was established in 1964 to widen the scope of the library's resources. There are now nearly 3,000 of these libraries worldwide, with about 2,500 in America and approximately ninety in the British Isles. The library is usually attached to a local Latter-day Saints church and they are staffed by volunteers. When planning a visit, you should always phone and check their opening hours and whether you are required to book a seat for a microfiche reader or a computer seat.

THE FAMILYSEARCH CENTER

In Salt Lake City, the FamilySearch Center in the Joseph Smith Memorial Building is an excellent place to discover about family history. The center is fully equipped with about 200 computers, loaded with *FamilySearch* for free public use. This is a powerful computer system that will help researchers find and organize their own information.

The LDS produces a "Family History Library Catalog," which is available at all their centers; it is found on microfiche and CD-ROM as part of the *FamilySearch* program. It offers a full listing of all the library's holdings and lists all microfilm, microfiche, and book references; you can look under location or surname. These references allow you to order the records you require (there is a small postage and handling fee for this service). The location section is arranged by country or state. If, for example, you look under England, or for wider coverage Great Britain, you will find that it is split into counties. The surname section covers family histories and biographies—the CD-ROM version does not include the author-title section, and this is another reason to check both versions of the catalog, fiche, and CD-ROM. The CD-ROM version is updated at six-monthly to yearly intervals and should be consulted regularly to check for new updates.

There are nearly two million rolls of microfilmed records and over half a million microfiche available for use at the Family History Library. The US is covered by about a quarter of these records, with every state represented, including approximately 160,000 rolls of federal records. The records come from more than 2,500 county courthouses, plus many other archives and repositories. They include census returns from 1790 to 1920, military and pension records and indexes, passenger arrival lists, probate, taxation records, as well as a large collection of church records.

GREAT BRITAIN

For Great Britain all the census records from 1841 to 1891 are on microfilm, and just under half of all parish registers. Other records are probate material, GRO indexes (civil registration from 1837), Nonconformist records and military records from the Public Record Office at Kew.

The Family History Library has a collection of more than a quarter of a million books, of which about half are on microfilm or microfiche. The actual books are not circulated to family history centers and only the film and fiche copies can be borrowed. Since the libraries do not charge a fee, other than postal and handling charges, they do ask that you share your family history in return, to disseminate the information and preserve it for future generations.

Olsen, Olson—(American) a descendant of Olaf or "ancestor."

Opie—a descendant of Osbert.

Oppenheimer—(German/Jewish) meaning "open hamlet."

Osborne—a Pagan name meaning "God-bear" or "warrior," possibly of Scandinavian origin. Although found in England before the Norman Conquest it was also a common name in Normandy.

Ostendorf—(German) meaning "east village."

Otterbach—(German) a "swamp" or "brook."

Owen, Ewan—at one time a first name, from St Owen, after whom many churches were named. Owen is very common in Wales and in the USA.

INTERNATIONAL GENEALOGICAL INDEX

THE INTERNATIONAL Genealogical Index, often shortened to and known as the IGI, has been produced by the Church of Jesus Christ of Latter-day Saints (or LDS, better known as the Mormons) and was at one time known as the Computer File Index, or CFI. This index lists names found in the Genealogical Department of the Mormon Church, but only contains the names of deceased people. It is not limited to members of the Church and their ancestors.

Cemetery Records: Salt Lake City 1848–1992

Many of the Mormon pioneers and their descendants were buried in this cemetery. The information on this CD includes details of births, deaths, and burials.

• Available from Appleton's Online:
www.appletons.com/genealogy/genebbcd.html

AN ARTICLE OF FAITH

It is part of the Mormon religion to join families together as one unit and church members trace their ancestors and then baptize them into the Mormon faith. To help them with this task, members of the Church have traveled to record repositories all over the world to copy parish register entries. At first there was a lot of opposition to this from churches and chapels, and in some instances Mormons were not allowed access. Over the years this problem has receded, as many authorities realize the benefits of the Mormon Church's work of recording, and therefore preserving, records.

Many years ago the LDS Church created vaults by blasting a number of huge caverns within the granite hillside of the Wasach Mountains in Little Cottonwood Canyon, Utah. These are now used as storage halls for the original films containing the family history details that the Church has collected from all over the world. The caverns are temperature- and humidity-controlled to protect the condition of the records. The International Genealogical

Below: Mormon families on their trek westward in 1847. As part of the Mormon task is to join all families together as one unit, the indexes of the International Genealogical Index have been compiled from information transcribed from parish registers all over the world.

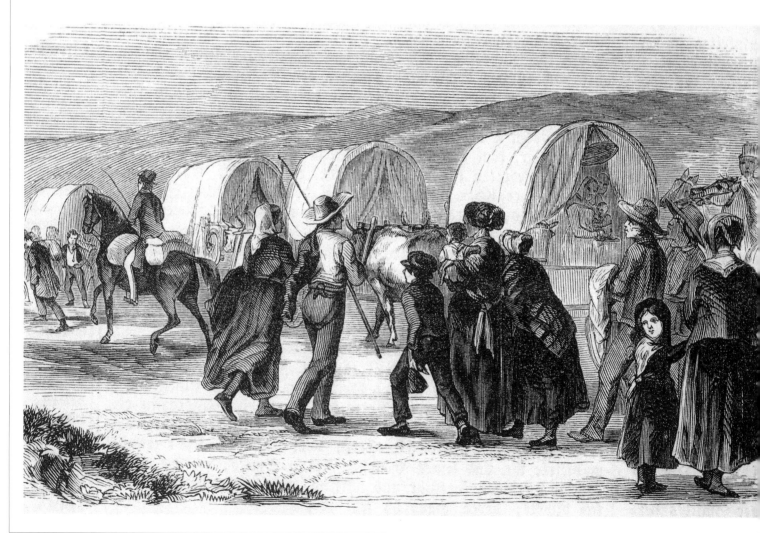

Index is a worldwide index and it must be remembered that Americans have ancestry not only from the UK but also from most of the non-English speaking countries of the world. The IGI is divided into countries, then counties or states.

USING THE INDEX

The index, which is available on microfiche or CD-ROM, contains entries for more than 240 million people from Great Britain, Ireland, the United States, and more than seventy other countries. It is one of the most popular indexes and offers a useful starting point for the family historian. However, do remember that it is only a research aid; there could easily be mistakes and additional information which was not recorded in the index so you should always check back to the original records.

The index can be used in three ways:
• To find genealogical information and also to check sources.
• To avoid duplication of research. Someone else could be researching the same family line and the input source may give a name and address.
• For LDS Church members to determine the dates the temple ordinances were performed for the deceased family members—these could have been performed during their lifetime or by proxy after their death. The records of living LDS members are kept by the Church Member and Statistical Records Division.

Page—a young or personal male servant in a noble's house.
Pais—a name of Jewish descendant.
Paley—a local "of Paley" a place in the West Riding of Yorkshire. Also a name of Huguenot origin.
Parker—an occupational name meaning "the parker," a park keeper or custodian of the park, found in every early register all over the UK.
Pepper—an occupational name for a dealer in pepper and spices.
Perez—a descendant of Pedro or Peter.

The Trek and the Mormon Religion

By April 6, 1830, Joseph Smith's vision had led to the formation of the Mormon Church in Fayette, New York. Persecuted by others who resented their success and wealth, the Mormons wanted a place where they could settle and practice their religion in peace; first they moved to Ohio, Missouri, and in spring 1839 to Nauvoo in Illinois. But on June 27, 1844, in Carthage, Illinois, Joseph Smith and his brother Hyrum were taken from jail and shot by a hostile mob.

As persecution of Smith's followers persisted, they decided to travel west to unclaimed territory, to set up their own community. In spring 1846, led by a new leader, Brigham Young, the first wagons left Nauvoo and crossed the Mississippi River on their route westward. The long journey was nearly ended on April 5, 1847, when Brigham Young entered the valley of the Great Salt Lake. On July 24, 1847, at the top of Big Mountain Pass, Brigham Young lifted himself from his sick bed in his wagon to view the valley, and after a few moments of deep thought he uttered the prophetic words, "It is enough. This is the right place. Drive on."

The next twenty years would see about 70,000 Mormons traveling west by wagon and cart to this valley. The transcontinental railroad was completed in 1869, making the journey for future emigrants far more comfortable.

The 1,300-mile route is now a part of a National Trails System and commemorates the 1846–47 journey.

Salt Lake City is the world headquarters of the Church of Jesus Christ of Latter-day Saints. In the center of the city stands the massive Mormon Temple, built between 1853 and 1893. The Mormon Tabernacle was built in 1867, and the city finally became the state capital in 1896.

The Mormons, as part of their religion, are encouraged to trace their ancestors, and due to their hard work and dedication they now house, in Salt Lake City, the largest library of its kind in the world. It is said that the trail really began in Liverpool, when Brigham Young and others recruited converts from all over England and Wales, and today more than half the people in Utah can trace their ancestors back to the United Kingdom.

Left: Joseph Smith (1805–1844).

Below: Brigham Young.

CONTENTS OF THE INDEX

The IGI covers the period from early 1500 to 1900. It lists primarily baptisms and marriages; there are no burials included. Most of the entries in the English section are from parish registers, although also included are the Nonconformist registers and other sources such as bishop's transcripts and printed registers. Within the Baptist religion the baptism is of an adult, therefore you will find birthdates recorded. The IGI should only be used as a finding aid, because, like most indexes produced by human hand, errors can creep in and it is not a complete index of every living person.

As people migrated from parish to parish, the IGI will enable you to find that elusive ancestor who moved every few years and seems to have had a child in every home. People moved mainly to where work was available and the family which stayed in one parish for more than 100 years was an exception. As each country is split into counties or states, the names of individuals are in alphabetical order within that county or state, making it easier to search for that missing ancestor.

The coverage of different countries varies considerably, as does that of counties and states. For example, in the 1988 issue only 100 out of 482 parishes in Somerset, England, were covered; in Northumberland 97 per cent of the county was covered; but in Northampton the coverage was only 5 per cent, a very low figure. You can check which parishes are covered, and what periods, by looking at the "Parish and Vital Records List" (PVRL) which appears as a fiche within the IGI. Also *Atlas & Index of Parish Registers* by Cecil Humphrey-Smith notes the parishes covered. The type of document used to record the entries will also be shown in the PVRL.

THE MICROFICHE

The IGI is divided into a series of microfiche for the different countries of the world and each fiche can contain approximately 16,000 to 17,000 names. There is also a fiche for births at sea, and also nearly thirty headed "England/County Unknown." The IGI is an ideal tool to trace a surname and the variants of that surname, as the compilers have placed together all those names that sound similar, rather than in strict alphabetical order. Each fiche consists of about 460 pages, with about sixty entries per page.

The layout of the IGI is as follows: the surname; the forename of the person indexed; then either the parents (if it is a baptism) or the spouse (if it is a marriage); the sex of the person; whether it is a christening (C), a marriage (M) or a birth (B) (other codes are shown at the bottom of the page); the date of the event (if the year is shown as <1800>, this tells you the year is estimated); the town and parish. The next three columns headed B, E, and S, record the Mormon ceremonies; the last two columns will note the batch or film number and the serial sheet number, and this will direct you to the source material which is held by the LDS.

Copies of the 1992 IGI can be purchased by the general public for a minimal cost, and if you have local access or own a microfiche reader you can save yourself time in searching. Copies of the PVRL and the batch number index are also included with your order. Further details

Below: A service in the Mormon Tabernacle, Salt Lake City, Utah, 1871. Using the extensive records held in Salt Lake City, today more than half the people who live in Utah can trace their ancestors back to the United Kingdom where the Mormon movement is said to have begun.

can be obtained from the Family History Department in Utah.

The IGI is included in *FamilySearch*, a Mormon CD-ROM package which includes genealogical programs and data files. From the CD-ROM version, information can be sorted in different ways and also downloaded onto a computer disk to use at home. The IGI has been made widely available for public use at family history centers, public and county record offices, public libraries, family history societies, the Society of Genealogists in London, and in record repositories all over the world.

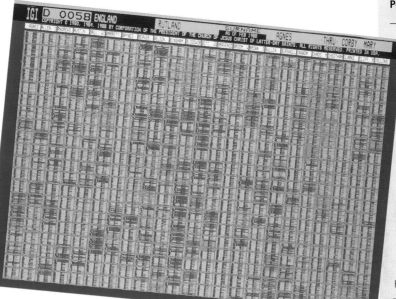

Above: Microfiche—records saved on film—are microphotographs of printed text or documents and are viewed using a special microfiche reader.

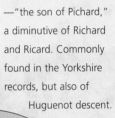

Above: Elvis Presley.

Peterson, Peter, Peters—"the son of Peter," this name has been the basic form of many variations such as Parkin, Perkin, Peterman, etc.

Pettit, Pitit, Pettet—a nickname for "le petit," the French for "little." A Huguenot name.

Peyton—a local name "of Peyton," a parish in Devon. Also a known Huguenot name.

Phillips, Philip, Philps—a name meaning "the son of Philip."

Picard, Pickard, Pitcher—"the son of Pichard," a diminutive of Richard and Ricard. Commonly found in the Yorkshire records, but also of Huguenot descent.

Presley—could be a variant of Pressland, a local name meaning "the land belonging to the parson," or "at the priest-land."

OTHER SOURCES OF
INFORMATION

NEWSPAPERS ARE a highly useful source from which you can find not only references to your ancestors, but information about what their life must have been like. There are large collections of newspapers in various places, especially county and state archives, but one of the largest collections in the world is housed at the Newspaper Library, Colindale, North London. This section of the British Library houses British and Irish newspapers from the eighteenth century to the present day, together with British Empire and Commonwealth newspapers and selected foreign newspapers, periodicals, magazines, the Thomason Tracts (English Civil War and other seventeenth-century newsbooks and newspapers), and the Burney collection of manuscripts (700 volumes of newspapers from the 1602–1818 period). There are published indexes to *The Times* and the *New York Times*, and a number of other newspapers, on the reference shelves.

BRITISH LIBRARY MANUSCRIPTS

Another section of the British Library is the Department of Manuscripts, situated in the new building at St Pancras. The collection contains handwritten material offering outstandingly important research from classical times to the present day. Historical, political, topographical, medieval, and illuminated manuscripts are well represented in the collection.

NATIONAL MONUMENTS RECORD

In the United Kingdom, the National Monuments Record is now situated in Swindon, Wiltshire. The library contains an extensive reference collection on archaeology and architecture, together with smaller sections on maritime studies, industrial archaeology, archive preservation and management, aerial photography, and place-name studies. The aerial photographs give a unique angle on any site, allowing you to see what a place is really like (or was like). The National Monuments Record has a large holding of Ordnance Survey maps and can also offer a postal service if you are unable to visit in person.

POST OFFICE ARCHIVES

The Post Office Archives in London house records which fill almost two miles of shelving, reflecting the variety of operations and services provided by the Post Office, or Royal Mail, since it was created more than 350 years ago. The material is organized into classes according to type: financial records, files and other working documents, newspapers, magazines, and reports.

The Post Office has long been one of the largest employers in the United Kingdom and its records include registers of appointments, pensions and gratuities, salary lists, and establishment books. The pension records can often provide information about name, date of birth, years of service, wages, cause of

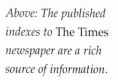

Above: The published indexes to The Times *newspaper are a rich source of information.*

retirement, positions held, and details of any absences. There is a public search room with photocopying facilities, but no postal research can be conducted. Various information sheets are available free of charge from the search room or by post.

GREATER LONDON RECORD OFFICE

The Greater London Record Office and History Library are part of the London Metropolitan Archives in Northampton Road, London. Greater London covers an administrative area of 610 square miles with a population of more than six and half million. It came into being in 1965 as a result of the London Government Act 1963, which abolished the administrative counties of London and Middlesex and established the Greater London Council. The collection is very large and very varied, containing the records of the London County Council from 1570 and the Middlesex County Council from 1549. These include Middlesex Sessions records (starting in 1549), the records of gaol delivery of Newgate for the county of Middlesex (Old Bailey Records) (1549–1834), and the Westminster Sessions records (1620–1844)—these total more than 10,000 volumes, 6,000 rolls or bundles, and thousands of separate documents.

As a Diocesan Record Office, the Greater London Record Office receives records from 300-plus parishes, Nonconformist records for more than sixty churches, and manorial, family, estate, business, and other private records. The History Library contains a large collection of books on London, but also has books on charities, poor law, crime, education, hospitals, transport, and many other useful subjects. The library is open to all members of the public, but it is for reference only.

SCHOOLS AND UNIVERSITIES

Another subject that should not be overlooked is education. The records of schools and universities can include genealogical information; if you find your ancestor's records it could confirm their date of birth, their parents, and place of origin. Your ancestor could have been a schoolmaster or schoolmistress. To find out which schools your ancestors may have attended check a commercial directory for the relevant area and time period and it will show the schools in the locality. When you have found your schools, go to the county record office and find out what

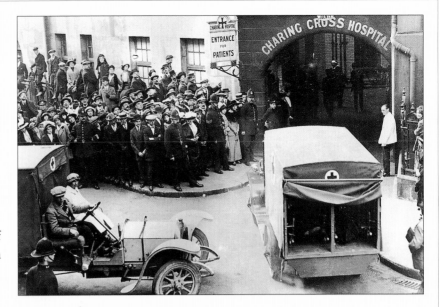

Who's Who? 1897–1998

Contains over 110,000 biographies of people from all walks of life. Includes nine volumes of *Who's Who*.
• Available from Electronic Publishing, Oxford University Press, Great Clarendon Street, Oxford OX2 6DP, UK.
E-mail: ep.info@oup.co.uk

Above: London's History Library contains a large collection of hospital records. The picture shows wounded soldiers arriving at Charing Cross Hospital, London in September 1914.

holdings they have on school records. These records make interesting reading, for as well as an admission book there could be a punishment book and a book of attendance. In village schools you may well discover that a large number of children were absent at harvest time.

In the records for Huntingdon are the school books for the Huntingdon Girls' and Infants' National School, built in 1842–43. The daily routine was strict. In January 1864, Ada Day took over the school and noted: "Found children very trying; very late in dismissing on account of frequent stoppage for talking." Other interesting notes found in the punishment book are "caned Harriett Marshall for being absent from school without leave" (1863) and "Phoebe Barnard flogged for repeated bad behaviour" (1875). School records thus offer not only more details about ancestors, but an important insight into social history.

University records have also been published and copies are held by the Society of Genealogists. Until the nineteenth century, Cambridge and Oxford were the only two universities in England. Other universities were not opened until the mid-1800s. Those records which exist will give such information as the student's name and age, father's name, and other family information.

Above: The Greater London Record Office and History Library are part of the London Metropolitan Archives.

Above: Local newspaper offices may have records which can be of use.

WILLS AND ADMINISTRATIONS

HAVING DISCOVERED our ancestor's dates of birth, baptism, marriage, death, and burial, the next step is to find a will. The term "last will and testament" must come from the English Statute of Wills (1540) which provided that a will should deal with land and property and that a testament would deal with moveable personal property, such as goods, money, crops, and furniture.

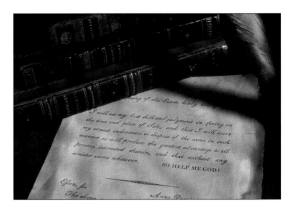

THE VALUE OF WILLS

A will could be made by any male over the age of fourteen years and a female over the age of twelve years, between 1540 and 1837. After 1837 a testator had to be over the age of twenty-one (of full age). A testator is a male or female who makes a will and dies. Very few married women made a will and only with the approval of their husband, though spinsters and widows with property were not subject to any impediment. In England and Wales, a married woman was only allowed to own property following the Married Women's Property Act of 1882; she could then dispose of it in any way she wanted.

For the family historian, a will is a valuable document. They pre-date other documents, such as parish registers, and can go back as far as the fourteenth century. A will could have been made while the person was quite young; whereas at the other extreme, a verbal death-bed request required three witnesses, and the testator had to have been resident in the place of death for more than ten days.

ENGLISH WILLS BEFORE 1858

English wills fall into two time periods: up to and including 1857; and from 1858 onward. In January 1858 the power of granting probate was taken from the jurisdiction of the Church of England and given to the state. Prior to this, wills and administrations had been dealt with by the various ecclesiastical courts up and down the country. If a person of limited means had left a will, and there was no dispute over his estate, the will may not have been put through the formal probate system, so the chances of it having survived are slim. When a person left a will or died intestate during the sixteenth or seventeenth centuries it was common practice for the courts to insist on an inventory. These inventories give a detailed description of a

person's home and the items in each room, even down to the kitchen and dairy. These wills and inventories from the period prior to December 1857 are found in the local county record offices, archive repositories and the Public Record Office at Kew. Almost all of the pre-1858 probates of England are on microfilm at the Family History Library in Salt Lake City.

ENGLISH WILLS AFTER 1858

From January 1858 the state-run department for wills and administrations (admons) has made things more straightforward. They are now proved in the Principal Probate Registry or in the district probate registries. These are indexed into bound, printed alphabetical volumes. From 1858 to 1870 the wills and admons were kept separate but within the same volume, so make sure you search both sections. From 1870 they were combined into one index, thus making the search a little easier. The indexes themselves are quite informative, but to see the full will you have to request a copy. The indexes are free to view, but there is a fee to see a copy of

Above: An antique will from the archives of the Essex Institute, Salem, Massachusetts, USA.

Below: Wills and probate records. A page from an administration act book, illustrating cases dealt with in the Registrar's seat, February 1840.

the will or admon. The information gained from the index will be the name of the deceased, date of death, place of residence, place of death (if different to residence), where the will was proved, total value of the estate, and the identity of the executor(s). Wills can take a while to be proved, so do not expect to discover it in the same year as the individual's death.

These indexes were once kept in Somerset House, but in 1998 they were moved to a new building in High Holborn, London. If you are unable to visit the Probate Department, it is possible to apply by mail. Some local probate registries hold sets of the national printed will and admon indexes, and some have been handed in to the local county record office. If you can conduct a search, you may apply for a photocopy by post from the York Probate Sub-Registry. They will also carry out a three-year search for a nominal fee. You could also use a professional researcher or agent. The degree of information will vary from will to will, but you should gain a lot of valuable family information.

Left: The will of Fearnot Cox, 1784, showing slaves being bequeathed to family members. This document would provide valuable information for both the descendants of Fearnot Cox and those of the named slaves.

WELSH, SCOTTISH, AND IRISH WILLS

In the National Library of Wales is a microfilm index of Welsh wills in the Prerogative Court of Canterbury, covering most of the eighteenth century. The probate records for Scotland are held in the Scottish Record Office, although some could still be in the Sheriffs' court. Irish wills and admon came under the Church until 1858, when a Principal Registry was established. Tragically, the collection of wills dating from 1536 and kept in the Four Courts in Dublin was nearly all destroyed during a fire in 1922, although many indexes did survive (see also pages 86–87).

Left: The will of Able Seaman Joseph Lewis, 1790. Wills and inventories prior to 1857 are found in local county record offices, archive repositories, and the Public Record Office. Almost all of the pre-1858 probates of England are available on microfilm at the Family History Library in Salt Lake City.

Prevost, Provost, Provis—an official name "the provost;" a prefect, the mayor, or the chief magistrate.
Prowse—meaning "a valiant man."
Pugh—"the son of Hugh," of which an early form was Hebrew. The middle-class Welsh seemed to adopt the English style in the seventeenth century.
Pupper—(German) a "doll-maker."
Quail, Quaile, Quayle—a nickname from the bird "a quail." Also a Manx name from the Isle of Man which traveled over into Lancashire; changes could have become Macquail or MacPhail, "son of Paul."
Quick, Quicke—nickname for an active or lively person.
Quickley, Quigley—possibly of Irish origin. A popular name in late nineteenth-century Boston, Massachusetts.

DIRECTORIES

ANOTHER SOURCE for finding out more about our ancestors are the directories. There are many different types of directories, and perhaps the forerunner of the telephone directories are the commercial and trade directories full of information for recent centuries. There are, however, even earlier ones and they were originally aimed at commercial travelers, containing general information about the cities, towns, or villages concerned and their mode of transport. In the UK you will find directories in the reference section of most major county libraries, in the county record offices, the Public Record Office, and all major repositories. The largest collections are in the Library of Congress and state libraries or state archives.

The first London directory was published in 1677, the next was published by Henry Kent in 1734. They were then published annually until 1828. Directories all have a common layout, beginning with a brief history and topography of the area and continuing with a description of the parishes, villages, and towns, then a listing of the clergy, gentry, and traders. They also give details of schools and the modes of transport, and some of the directories also contain detailed maps.

TRADE DIRECTORIES

In the 1830s Pigot & Co published several editions of their county by county *National and Commercial Directory and Topography*, covering all the counties in England and Wales. Facsimile editions of these have been reproduced by Michael Winton and are now on sale from *Family Tree Magazine*. The Essex, Herts, and Middlesex edition, for example, shows us that in the village of Great Baddow in Essex in 1839 "James Larcher is the Post Master, the letters arriving from London every morning at six, and are despatched every evening at eight." The taverns and public houses were "The Bear run by David Daws, The Bell, run by Joseph Sewell, The Blue Lion, run by William Young, there is also the Crown, King's Head and White Horse." Quite a collection for a small village. The "coach to London passes through Baddow every morning and returns every afternoon."

The *June Edition of the Post Office London Directory 1846* is republished as a facsimile edition, and is available from *Family Tree Magazine*. It offers a general index to London,

and includes lists of commercial and professional people, a court directory, official directory, parliamentary directory, and a postal directory.

Local directories were printed too. For example, the *Sittingbourne, Milton and District Directory for 1908–9*, published by W. J. Parrett Ltd (and reprinted in the 1980s), lists heads of households for the two main towns and all the surrounding villages, in address order and alphabetical order, as well as all the churches, schools, and industries. Check your library for these sorts of directories.

Directories with a difference are now available and published every year. There is the *Genealogical Research Directory, National & International* by Keith A. Johnson and Malcolm R. Sainty, published in Australia. It is the largest worldwide surname queries listing published in book form. It contains, on average, 150,000 reference entries submitted by contributors and offers one of the most important and useful genealogical tools ever published. This useful directory acts as a central reference book to which researchers contribute details of the surnames, locations, and dates they are researching. These entries from around the world are collated and published in the directory, enabling you to contact fellow researchers

Above: You will find directories in the reference section of most major county libraries. The picture shows Marsh's Library, Dublin, the oldest of Ireland's public libraries, built in 1707.

Above: Weaver is an occupational surname which could be traced back through trade directories.

> **Pigot's Directory**
>
> Pigot's 1830 Directory of Berkshire, Buckingham, and Oxfordshire.
>
> • Available from S & N Genealogy Supplies:
> http://www.genealogy.demon.co.uk

interested in the same surnames. It is an ideal way to find out if others are also researching your name and saves a lot of time when researchers share information.

Another directory to have on your bookshelf is *The Genealogical Services Directory*, compiled by Robert Blatchford and Geoffrey Heslop. It is an essential source of information for family historians, genealogists, and everyone wishing to trace or have someone trace their family history for them. As well as names and addresses of researchers, it has contact addresses for those businesses which provide a specialist service. It lists associations and organizations from the British Isles, Australia, South Africa, and North America.

Above: Flesher was the English name for a butcher and was once a common surname, although it is now more unusual.

Occupational Names

The origin of our ancestor's surnames plays a large part in the search for our roots. In spite of many names which have become obsolete over the years, the occupational surname is more numerous today than in earlier periods. This makes their classification quite difficult. Some surnames give us a direct link to the ancestor's trade or occupation, while others are rather more obscure: Calvert or Calvard could refer to a calf-herd, while Coltard or Coulthart refers to a colt-herd; the name of Shepherd refers to the occupation of that name, but so too could Looker or Luker.

Over the years names related to early occupations have died out, while others have been replaced with shorter names, losing the actual occupation in the change of surname. In early documents, names would appear in their Latin form—Faber (smith), Pistor (baker) and Sutor (shoe-maker), for example—and these Latin names still survive. It is said that nearly one-third of occupational names are French; remember that following the Norman

Conquest, French was spoken by many well-educated people in Britain while the poorer people still spoke English. The English name for a butcher was "flesh-hewer", giving the once quite common name of Flesher. This was then absorbed with the name of Fletcher, a maker of arrows. (The original name in Nottingham for Fletcher Gate was Flesshewergate: "the street of the butcher.")

When checking the origins of your surname, read several books on the subject and check the various spellings which have been brought about with the change in meanings.

Above: Turner; a person who works with a lathe.
Left: Cooper; a maker or repairer of casks and barrels.

Quin, Quinn—(Celtic) "the son of Quin," found also as McQuinn or as McQueen.
Quincy, Quinsey—a local Normandy name, a person "of de Quency." Also an American name.
Quirk—a surname common to the Isle of Man. A corruption of MacCuire.
Ratcliff, Ratcliffe—a local name, same as Redcliff. Places are found in Devon, Leicestershire, and Nottinghamshire.
Reeves, Reaves—a reeve, a chief magistrate, bailiff, or an overseer. Reeves, a servant or son of "the dweller at the house."
Reagan—of Irish descendants.
Reay—a name of Huguenot origin.

SPECIAL ARCHIVES

UNTIL THE sixteenth century the indigenous population of England was Roman Catholic, nominally owing their allegiance to the Pope in Rome. Under the rule of Henry VIII, a one-time Papal champion, it became a Protestant country with Henry declaring himself the Supreme Head of the Church of England. Many Roman Catholics went into hiding due to the persecution that followed, and many were burned at the stake because of their religious beliefs.

> **Encyclopedia of American Quaker Genealogy**
>
> This CD comprises all six volumes of William Wade Hinshaw's renowned *Encyclopedia of American Quaker Genealogy*, originally published between 1936 and 1950. It contains thousands of Vital Records.
> • Available from the Genealogical Publishing Company: http://www.genealogical.com/cdrom.htm

ROMAN CATHOLIC REGISTERS

It was not until the late 1700s that religious tolerance came about with freedom to worship as one wished, except for Roman Catholics who were still persecuted until the Catholic Relief Acts of the late eighteenth and early nineteenth century came into effect. Despite suffering extra taxes and being forced to take various oaths, with fines for those who refused, many Roman Catholics remained true to their faith, and many young men traveled to Europe, later returning as trained priests. The Roman Catholic faith was strongest in the north of England, and when the Roman Catholic registers were placed in the Public Record Office it was noticeable that the majority came from the north. Many registers and records are still in the custody of local priests. Although Roman Catholics had their own registers, to keep within the law they used the Church of England, so remember to check both registers. A list of surviving registers are in Michael Gandy's *Catholic Missions and Registers 1700–1880*. Details of further books are available from the Catholic Family History Society.

Quaker

JEWISH SYNAGOGUE RECORDS

A small Jewish community settled in London, at the request of the Norman William I, but its members were expelled in 1290 by Edward I. A small group returned in 1541 and by 1734 their numbers had risen to about 6,000, most of whom were traders from Portugal. Other Jews who settled in England in 1734 came from

Below: Most Jewish synagogues preserve their own records. The picture shows a Jewish family photographed celebrating the Feast of the Tabernacle, 1908.

Above: The main altar at the National Shrine of the Immaculate Conception, Washington DC.

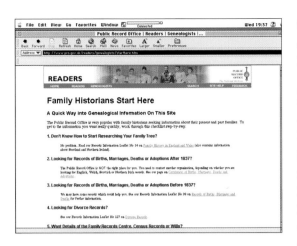

Above: A page from the PRO website which is full of valuable information to help you with your search.

Germany and spoke in Yiddish, a cross between German and Hebrew. The main trade of this group was as skilled engravers and many settled in the East End of London, followed by Leeds and Manchester. (The Leylands area of Leeds, for example, was 80 per cent Jewish by the 1880s.) Many of the synagogue records are deposited in local record offices, but because of the language, there are problems with reading the early records. By 1875 there were about 400,000 Jews in Britain, of whom about 270,000 lived in London. In the 1930s more refugees came to England to escape the Nazi regime in Germany and, later, occupied Europe. Most Jewish synagogues preserve their own records, and while many of the early records have accurate information about marriages and burial, be careful with the births.

THE SOCIETY OF FRIENDS

George Fox, the son of a Leicestershire weaver, was the founder of the Quakers (the Society of Friends). The term "Quaker" appears to have come from two sources, one was after Fox exhorted a judge to "quake" before the Lord, while others say it came from his young followers who were said to "tremble and shake" at early meetings. The Society of Friends started to keep records in 1650, and in due course they became well known for their thorough and conscientious record keeping. In 1840 and 1857, copies were made of their records, called digests, and the originals were handed to the Public Record Office and the digests kept with other records in the library at Friends' House in London. Some records have also been lodged in county record offices. A useful book to refer to is available from the Society of Genealogists called *My Ancestors Were Quakers*, written by E. H. Milligan and M. J. Thomas.

HUGUENOT REGISTERS

After the massacre in 1572 of 100,000 Protestant Huguenots in France, many fled to England followed in the late seventeenth century by a further 45,000 who settled in Britain. The English, however, also tended to use the word Huguenot to describe the Walloon refugees, who came from the Low Countries to avoid Spanish control. On their arrival in England, the Calvinistic Huguenots applied for naturalization or denization. They brought their skills and trades with them, making them an asset to Britain and it was possible to find many of these immigrants working in Spitalfields as silk weavers. Indeed, this weaving legacy remains in some of London's architecture, most notably in London's Fournier Street. The earliest Huguenot register is from their church in Southampton, and the congregations in London soon followed suit. Spellings of names changed and were Anglicized or translated. The registers of births, marriages, and burials have been copied and have been published by the Huguenot Society. The originals are in the Public Record Office. Not all French refugees were Huguenots of course; many French people came to Britain during the 1789–1795 period, fleeing from the French Revolution and The Terror.

Reid—Scots form of Read, one of the most common surnames in Scotland. Also found in Ireland and England, in Northumberland and County Durham. Variants are Read, Reade, Reed. Also a nickname "the red," meaning of one of red complexion or hair.

Reyes—(Spanish) descendants of the king's household or a local of Reyes in Spain.

Rixon, Rix, Rickson—"son of Ricard" or "son of Rick." Also a "dweller among the rushes."

Robinson, Robin, Robbins—"the son of Robert," from the nickname of Rob and the diminutive of Robin. Robin coming from birds, flowers, etc.

Rockefeller—(German) meaning a rye field.

Rodriguez—a descendant of Rodrigo or Roderick.

Rolfe, Rofe, Roffe, Rolf—name meaning "the son of Rudolph;" Rolph or Rolf stand for Rudolph. The form with -e (Rolfe) is found in the UK in Norfolk, Suffolk, and Essex. The husband of Pocahontas was a John Rolfe from Heacham in Norfolk. The name was also common in Normandy, France, where it became Roul or Rou.

Left: The statue of Princess Pocahontas at Gravesend, Kent, England.

DIVORCE AND NAME CHANGES

IN ENGLAND and Wales a *mensa et toro* (from board and bed), the legal separation of husband and wife, could only be granted by ecclesiastical courts (the Church courts' records are in the local records offices). From 1668 to 1857 a *vinculo matrimonii* (from the bands of matrimony or full divorce) could only be granted by a Private Act of Parliament, and this was rather expensive (the House of Lords Record Office holds the files on Divorce Bills from 1669 onward).

There were no changes in the divorce law in England and Wales prior to the Matrimonial Causes Act in 1857 (an Act that was never extended to Ireland). The London Consistory Court did a good deal of matrimonial business, and these records are in the London Metropolitan Archives. Divorce was allowed in Scotland from the mid-sixteenth century on the grounds of adultery or desertion, and the innocent person was allowed to remarry.

For the period 1858–1940 divorce files are in the Public Record Office (reference J 77, with indexes in J 78 going up to 1958). There is, however, a 100-year closure on them, but the public can still inspect the indexes. The files

may contain petitions for divorce and judicial separation, declaration of legitimacy, a copy of the petition, and grounds for divorce. The PRO issue of information leaflet No. 127, "Divorce Records in the Public Record Office," is a useful one to read, and it outlines further divorce legislation from 1873 to 1969. The records for the period from 1941 to date are in the Principal Registry of the Family Division at Somerset House, where for a fee a search will be done for you.

But couples did not always resort to the Church or civil courts; they would separate and bigamously marry another partner, until the law caught up with them, or they would live

Above: Somerset House contains divorce records.

Above: In the United States, divorce details can be traced by area through the court system. The picture shows the US Divorce Court at Reno, Nevada, in 1935.

Premature Death

It is a myth that women married young. They were, however, often pregnant when they did marry, so as to make sure they could provide a family. It was only during the Victorian period that very large families actually came into being—possibly in imitation of the queen herself—and prior to this the average household consisted of two adults and two or three children. There were, of course, large families to be found, but household numbers were kept small by the premature deaths of young children in their first year of life. Many died of infectious diseases, and the evidence can be found in the burial registers of any local parish: about 15 per cent of children died in their first year and about a quarter of all children failed to reach the age of ten.

One of the problems for family historians is that the mother and father would often give a new baby the same name as an earlier, dead child. This could happen two or three times. In checking the baptism registers,

you could find that the parents had three daughters all called Mary, but upon checking the burial registers you will find the first two had died prematurely, only leaving the last Mary surviving into adulthood.

What can also be found in the burial registers is the death of a young mother and her stillborn child. Deaths in childbirth were far from uncommon and, particularly if there were other children in the family, the father would often remarry very soon after the death of his wife. Because he needed to continue to work, he would require someone to look after his children and this was the wife's role. This can cause confusion to the family historian when checking the census records. If you know the name of your ancestor and his birth parents, then you find another wife in the household, different to the birth mother, this might well be the reason and it is because of this that burial registers should be thoroughly checked.

Above: It is thought that Queen Victoria's large family inspired a trend for larger families during her reign.

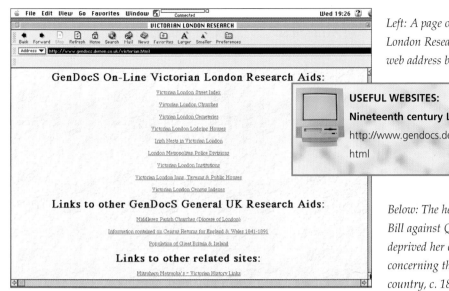

Left: A page of Victorian London Research – see the web address below.

USEFUL WEBSITES:

Nineteenth century London:

http://www.gendocs.demon.co.uk/victorian. html

Above: US President Franklin D. Roosevelt.

Below: The heading of the Divorce Bill against Queen Caroline which deprived her of any future rights concerning the sovereignty of the country, c. 1820.

together without marriage or divorce. The following is an example of what can happen: William Giddings of Kings Cliffe, in Northampton, was convicted and sentenced in 1837 to transportation to Australia. He had to leave his wife Sarah and their three children in England. After serving his time, he was given his ticket of freedom, but had to remain in Australia. He married a young girl and had eighteen more children. On the marriage certificate in Australia he gave his status as a widower. In England, Sarah also remarried, saying she was a widow, but there is no record of a divorce.

As mentioned previously, it is recognized by English common law that a person may change their surname without any formal record, provided that it is not for a fraudulent purpose. There are several methods of surname change, and leaflet No. 38 from the Public Record Office gives details in full.

• By Act of Parliament. This is a costly method, as it requires the promotion of a Private Bill, and has only been used once in the past century (1907), although it was fairly common in previous centuries.
• By royal licence. This method arose in the late seventeenth century. Since 1783 all applications have been referred to the College of Arms for a report.
• By deed poll. By the end of the nineteenth century this had become the normal and most convenient means of name change.
• By statutory declaration. This takes the form of a statutory declaration of the change before a Justice of the Peace or a Commissioner for

A
B I L L

To deprive Her MAJESTY Caroline Amelia Elizabeth of the Title, Prerogatives, Rights, Privileges, and Pretensions of Queen Consort of this Realm, and to dissolve the Marriage between His MAJESTY and the said Queen.

Oaths. It cannot be enrolled in the Supreme Court unless advertised in the press.
• By advertisement in the press. Advertisement to be placed in *The Times* or some other national or local newspaper.

If your ancestor has changed their name in one way or another, it is hoped they did so by one of the above methods, or that there is a family tale to explain it. Without this knowledge, it is an almost impossible task to find him or her.

THE UNITED STATES

Divorce was granted until the mid-1800s through the courts and determined by specific state legislation, but in 1866 the federal government declared this illegal and it then became a civil action determined in local courts. Divorces can thus be traced in the court system records as organized for the particular area; very often, however, they are in a separate book, making it easier for the genealogist to find what they are looking for.

Roosevelt—from the Dutch name of Van Rosevelt meaning "of the rosefield."
Rossenberg—(German) meaning the "rose mountain." Also a local place name in Germany.
Rossiter, Rossitta—a local name from Rochester, a place in Kent, meaning "town on the bridges." The name is more popular in the Somerset and Dorset areas. It is also found in Kent.
Rothechild—a name of Jewish descent.
Rous, Rouse, Rowes, Russ—French nickname for "le rous," from one with a red complexion or hair. Rousso is of Jewish descent.
Rowan—local name "at the rowan," a residence by a rowan tree. A northern English and Scottish surname. Found in great numbers in Philadelphia.
Ryan—a name of Irish descent.

THE PUBLIC RECORD OFFICE

THE PUBLIC Record Office (PRO) has gone through a dramatic change over the last decade with a new purpose-built office having been constructed next to the existing building, which was refurbished. The PRO has one of the best conservation departments in the UK. It is the national archive for England and Wales with all the records of central government and the law courts, spanning 900 years and starting with the Domesday Book of William the Conqueror. The records are preserved on nearly 100 miles of shelving, sufficient to provide storage until the year 2010.

The PRO was set up by an Act of Parliament in 1838, mainly for the convenience of lawyers and a few scholars. The new PRO is for everyone to use. Its aims are to assist and promote the study of the past, through public records, in order to inform the present and the future. What will you find on these miles of shelving? There are documents of incredible historical importance to British history, such as the Domesday Book, illuminated medieval manuscripts, medieval maps, Guy Fawkes's confessions to the gunpowder plot, charts drawn by Captain Cook on his voyages of exploration to the Antipodes, Queen Victoria's personal census return from Buckingham Palace, King Edward's signed abdication, and countless others. There are many others which are less important but just as fascinating: Bligh's account of the mutiny on HMS *Bounty*, the wills of Jane Austen and William Shakespeare, the account of 617 Squadron, "the Dambusters," and so on. A wealth of knowledge at the touch of a button.

INSIDE THE PRO

The PRO is open from Monday to Saturday, but the opening hours vary. It is accessible by car, coach, subway, and bus. To research there you will need a reader's ticket to gain access to the correct secure area and to order records. This ticket is issued on your first visit, but take a formal means of identification with you;

Above: The Public Record Office contains a vast collection of historical documents, including manuscripts, maps, wills, and census returns. The PRO is open for everybody to use but security is tight, so a formal means of personal identification is required when you first visit.

Left: A page from the Domesday Book of William the Conqueror.

Below: A depiction of the conspirators and the letter sent to Lord Monteagle which led to the discovery of the gunpowder plot in 1605.

overseas visitors should take a passport or national ID card. Lockers are provided because you can only take either six loose sheets of paper or a bound notebook into the research area, and pencils only.

There are no charges and no need to book. Most of the documents relate to England and Wales and you can buy photocopies of the majority. A thirty-year ban exists on most things placed there, although some more sensitive records are kept closed for longer still. On the lower floor there is the general inquiries desk, while the research areas are located on the first and second floors. Also on the first floor is a research inquiries room, where the catalogs and indexes are found, together with an instructive video about the PRO and how to use it; the document reading room, where all original records are read, unless they are maps or very large documents; and a microfilm reading room, with the library adjoining it. The second floor is one large room where maps and large documents are held.

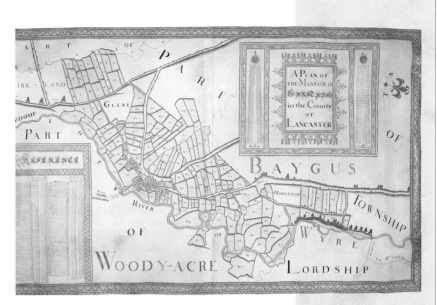

ORDERING DOCUMENTS

The method of ordering documents is fairly simple. To locate your documents you need to find the reference numbers. These are found in the catalogs, called class lists, held in binders in the lobby on the first floor. Before you can order any records you need to get a bleeper (pager) from the long counter in the document reading room. Next, order your documents on the computer terminals, swipe your reader's ticket, key in your seat/bleeper number, and enter the document's reference numbers. You will have

about a thirty-minute wait. When the bleeper goes off, collect your documents. You may order up to three documents at a time, but you are only allowed to read one at a time. As you finish one, take it back and collect the next. If you have any problems or do not understand anything, ask the staff who are available to assist you.

You are allowed to take notes with your pencil, and you may also use word processors or dictaphones. Most records may be photocopied on the spot. The PRO also offers a high-quality color copying service, but it takes a week. The microfilm reading room houses reader-printers for taking copies from film or fiche.

As with all major repositories, you must, of course, go prepared. Check your own research and find out what you are looking for. Are you going to the right place? Should you be at Chancery Lane or the Family Records Centre?

Above: Maps of historical importance are archived at the Public Record Office. The map pictured here is of the Manor of Garstang, Lancashire, England, made in the mid-seventeenth century.

Sale, Sales—meaning "of the hall." "Salle-à-manger," the French word for dining-hall.

Sager, Sagar—an occupational name "sawyer," one whose job it is to saw wood.

Salt, Salter—an occupational name, a person who works with salt, either as an extractor or a seller.

Sass, Sasse—a local name "at the sasse" A "sasse" is a sluice or lock, mainly a river with floodgates, to close or release the water for the passage of boats.

Schneider—(American with a German origin) descendant of a tailor or cutter.

Schol, Scholle, Scholl—(German) a soil farmer, or "clodhopper."

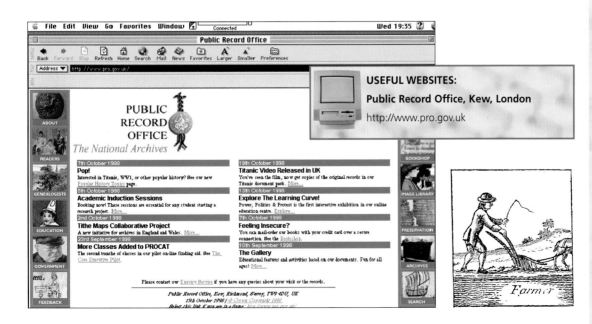

USEFUL WEBSITES:

Public Record Office, Kew, London

http://www.pro.gov.uk

SERVICE RECORDS—

ARMY, NAVY, AND AIR FORCE

BRITAIN, AND before that England, Scotland, and Wales, has long been involved in the power struggles and wars of the European nations. Since the English Civil War in the seventeenth century, a standing army has been maintained, but it was at sea where strength was deployed most effectively for so long. The size and power of the merchant fleet and the Royal Navy enabled Britain to build the largest empire ever seen in the world, carved out and defended by military forces of historic regiments in which tens of thousands of men have served, fought, and died in countless conflicts and two world wars. One of many wars was the struggle for control of North America, and during the Revolutionary War militias obtained independence for a new country, the United States, and a new continental-sized nation was born that today, just over 200 years later, possesses the greatest military power ever known to humankind.

Above and left: The Regular Army Certificate (above) of Leslie John Turnbull, issued at Canterbury, Kent, England, on December 29, 1925, and the Royal Artillery certified copy of Attestation (left) issued on the same day.

Below: The British Army records of soldiers are arranged by regiment.

THE ARMY

Before 1642 and the outbreak of civil war there was no regular standing army in England. Armies were formed to meet special requirements, usually named after the colonel who raised them. No records relating to them have survived. For the English Civil War and Commonwealth period, officers of both armies are listed by regiment in Edward Peacock's *The Army List of Roundheads and Cavaliers* (1863); the second edition (1874) of which contains an index.

After 1660 records became more abundant and information is easier to trace. Family details and birthplaces of officers are seldom recorded until the end of the eighteenth century, although they are sometimes found in widow's pension applications. (Information about retired officers and their widows are found in the records of the Paymaster General's Office, in classes PMG 3 to PMG 4, and these give a date of death.)

The records of other ranks are arranged by regiment. If a man was discharged before 1873 it is essential to know which regiment he served with. If it is known where the individual you are interested in was at a particular time, it may be possible to identify his regiment from the published Monthly Army Lists or from the Monthly Returns (WO17 and WO 73) which show where the regiments were stationed. The most detailed records of a soldier's service are his discharge documents in WO 97. These documents give a record of his service and the later ones give birth, age on enlistment, and a physical description; from 1883 onward they offer details of the next-of-kin, his wife, and any children. Records of soldiers who died while serving, and would not receive a discharge certificate, were destroyed, but providing his regiment is known it may well be possible to find him in pay lists and muster rolls.

Soldiers Who Died in the Great War 1914–1919

This CD-ROM contains the complete set of all eighty-one volumes with software that allows a search of every element in each record. Searches can be executed for regiments, battalions, surnames, forenames, initials, born (town and county), enlisted (town and county), and regimental number etc.

• Available from: The Naval & Military Press.

Website: http://www.great-war-casualties.com

Left: The Family Records Centre, London.

Schultz—a descendant of the magistrate, sheriff or steward.

Seymour—a local name "of Saint Maur" a place in France; could have come to England with the Huguenots.

Shrubsall, Shrubsole, Shrubshall—said to be a local of Shrubsole, but no locality found. The suffix of sale, sall, or sole means "a hall." This name was found only in Kent and London in the early 1800s, but is now found in Australia, Canada, and the USA.

Silkman—a dealer or weaver in silk, possibly of Jewish descent.

Silva—(American) a dweller in or near a wood.

Simonds, Simon, Simmonds—"the son of Simon." The spelling with the "d" possibly comes from the Huguenots.

Smith (English), **Kowalsky** (Ukrainian), **Kuznetsov** (Russian), **Schmidt** (German), **Lefevre** (French)—occupation "the smith," a blacksmith, a farrier. Easily the most common name in the English-speaking world.

Spencer—a house steward, one who has charge of the buttery or "the spence."

Left: The names of US servicemen who died serving their country are listed at the US National War Memorial, Washington DC.

Surviving records of soldiers discharged after 1913 are currently being released by the Ministry of Defence at Hayes. However, two-thirds of those covering the period 1914–1920 were destroyed or badly damaged by bombing during World War II. These are now known as the "burnt" documents and the "unburnt" documents.

The "burnt" documents are at present stored in 33,000 boxes on two miles of shelving, with each box containing between 840 and 1,200 items. The Public Record Office has received a grant from the National Heritage Lottery Fund to start a project of microfilming the documents. Providing funds are available the project could be completed by the end of 2001. By June 1998 the alphabetical letters of N, O, Q, U, V, and Z had been filmed, but you should check with the PRO to find out the latest situation. These records are under reference WO 363. The "unburnt" records (WO 364) are a collection of records which were an attempt to put together a second collection from duplicated forms held by the Ministry of Pensions.

World War I medals are found in the medal rolls WO 329. More can be learned from the PRO publication called *Army Service Records of the First World War* by Simon Fowler, William Spencer, and Stuart Tamblin.

THE ROYAL NAVY

Tracing a sailor before 1853 may be difficult unless you have the name of the ship on which he served. If he was serving in 1861, start by looking in the index of seamen in the 1861 census returns which are at the Family Records Centre. The list contains the names of seamen on ships abroad and in home waters on census night. The records are more informative after 1852 when the introduction of continuous service engagement began. You will be able to find where he sailed, his promotions and punishments, and the ships he sailed in. The Royal Navy is divided into ratings, warrant officers, and officers. The records available are ship's books and muster rolls for 1688–1798; there is no name index and you will need to know his ship. Muster books list the crew and sometimes their age and date of birth (ADM 36–ADM 39). Pensioned seamen (ADM 29) files give a brief service record for seamen in 1802–1919 who received a pension only. Continuous service engagement books cover all seamen for 1853–1872, as do seaman's service books for 1837–1891. Don't forget to look at naval wills. Service records of ratings who enlisted between 1891 and 1939 are not yet released. Write to the Ministry of Defence at Bourne Avenue, Hayes, Middlesex, and for the period after 1939 write to HMS *Centurion*.

THE ROYAL AIR FORCE

Founded in 1911 as the Royal Flying Corps, its records are among the World War I service records and they relate only to men who left the service before the Royal Air Force was formed on April 1, 1918. The Royal Air Force's records from 1918 onward are still with the Ministry of Defence and you will need to write to RAF Innsworth. Records of RAF medals are in class AIR 2.

SHIPPING RECORDS AND
MERCHANT SEAMEN'S RECORDS

IN GREAT Britain there is a long and detailed history of maritime conquest, trade, and exploration, and for many years the country had the strongest navy in the world. But things maritime are not just about the sailors who went to sea, there are people who worked in the dockyards around the world, the local fishermen, the whalers and, of course, the shipbuilders.

USEFUL WEBSITES:

National Maritime Museum:
http://www.nmm.ac.uk

Passenger List for Ships from British Ports:
http://shipping.cohsoft.com.au/db/britship.html

Merchant shipping was the responsibility of the Register Office of Merchant Seamen from 1835, and later the Registrar General of Shipping and Seamen who would report to the Board of Trade. These records are found in the PRO under class BT. From 1747 onward it was required that merchant ships' masters or owners keep muster rolls listing the crew on each voyage. The musters were filed at the port of arrival or departure and they contain various information on the seaman including, name, home address, dates of engagement and discharge, and the name of his previous ship. The surviving records are at the PRO in class BT 98, filed by port numbers.

Registers of seamen from 1835 to 1836 are under class BT 120 at the PRO. These are alphabetical lists of the seamen, detailing age, place of birth, his position in the crew, and the name of his ship. Having found this you then check the ship's crew list. The registers for 1835–1844 are in class BT 112, separated into foreign voyages and home trade. There is an overall index in BT 119, but it does not state whether it is foreign or home trade.

Masters and mates having the necessary examinations and qualifications could apply for their certificate. These documents would give the year and place of birth, date and place of certification as master, mate or engineer. Having found the number of the certificate, the National Maritime Museum holds many of the application forms for them.

SENT TO SEA

The overseer from the parish could bind a young pauper boy as an apprentice to a ship's master for seven to nine years. Indentures may

survive in the parish records (now held in the county record office); also check in PRO class BT 167. The death of a seaman could leave his widow and children in poverty, with the possibility of being put in the Poor Law Union workhouse. From 1514 to 1854, charity funds were distributed by the Corporation of Trinity House, and petitions were sent describing the circumstances, usually with supporting documents. The surviving petitions are in the Guildhall Library in 113 volumes, and an indexed calendar by A. J. Camp is in the library of the Society of Genealogists.

Above: Maritime museums and attractions such as Chatham Dockyard, Kent, England, may be a good place to begin the search for your seafaring ancestors.

Above: USS Constitution, *preserved in Boston, Massachussetts.*

Left: The record of service for Petty Officer 1st Class Charles Callaghan, from 1879, documenting his career, his wages, and the ships on which he served.

cards, official papers, and discharge papers. They were in the custody of the Glamorgan County Record Office, with no public access. Also due to be transferred to the PRO are the indexes of mercantile marine medals for World War I and the indexes of certificates of competency (all deck officers) for 1910–1930.

The PRO has an information leaflet called "Dockyard Employees" that lists the surviving records from 1660 of British naval dockyards all over the world. These lists will include yard musters, giving details of the different tradesmen, their entry, pay, pension, and discharge. References are found in ADM 32, ADM 36, ADM 42, and ADM 106.

Left: An extract from the register of merchant ships in England, 1572, with the names of their masters compiled by Thomas Colshill, the surveyor of the Port of London.

Below: Old photographs showing relatives in uniform may have maritime service details written on the back.

Spittey, Spitty—from the Welsh word for hospital: "Yspytty." Spittel, Spittle meaning "attendant at the hospital."

Steiger—a "climber," or "dweller by the footpath."

Sturgeon—a nickname from the fish of the same name, but also a known Huguenot name.

Taylor, Tayler, Tailor, Tailer—an occupational name, "the taylor," a cutter of cloth, a maker of clothes.

Telfair, Telfer, Telford—one who could pierce his enemy's armor, using a cleave or cut iron. The name started in Scotland and traveled over the border to Northumberland.

REGISTERS OF SHIPS

There are also registers of ships, which name their masters and owners. Some registration of ships took place in the home port from the seventeenth century, and if they have survived these records are available in the relevant county record office. A national system was started in 1786, when ships over 15 tonnes were registered by the customs' office in the home port. This register gives details of the ship's name, its home port, its owner's name, the master's name, and the date and place of the ship's construction. Check the PRO class BT 107 and BT 111. Some registers are in county record offices or customs' houses in the provincial ports. A new registration system was begun in 1854 and these records (up to 1889) are at the PRO in class BT 108.

THE EAST INDIA COMPANY

The East India Company also owned and chartered merchant ships for its trading. Nearly 10,000 journals and logs of the East India Company have survived, held in the India Office Library, covering the period 1605–1863.

The records of 250,000 seamen born after 1910 are currently being filmed and will soon be available in the PRO. These are known as "seamen's pouches," and they contain identity

TRADES, PROFESSIONS, GUILDS,

AND LIVERY COMPANIES

THE TRADE and commercial directories as a means of discovering our ancestors' trades have already been discussed, but there are other records where their trades will also show: civil registration, parish registers, probate, and the census. Businesses were advertised in newspapers in years gone by, just as they are today. County record offices also have collections of local photographs, and it might well be possible to find a picture of a shop or premises, especially if it was a long-established family business. It is worth knowing that there is an index to the *London Gazette* which lists notices of partnership dissolutions from 1785 to 1811.

British business records can be located through the National Register of Archives, a computer database which has a catalog of many items held by the county record offices, libraries, museums, businesses, and private collections. Searches are conducted through three indexes—personal names, businesses, and subjects—held at the Historical Manuscripts Commission in Chancery Lane, London, and soon to be available on the Internet.

A Judge

THE PROFESSIONS

Under the title of the "professions," are barristers, solicitors, proctors and advocates (all various types of lawyer), judges and justices of the peace, doctors, nurses, architects, clergy, and teachers. It is advisable to read and learn all you can about these professions before trying to find the records to trace your ancestors. If your ancestors were from an agricultural or laboring background, they would be very unlikely to have entered one of these professions, for it required a very good education, which was not always available in the small parishes.

Barristers would have practiced through one of London's four Inns of Court—Lincoln's Inn, Middle Temple, Inner Temple, and Gray's Inn.

Most barristers can be found through the law lists and university records. The admission registers for the four inns have been published and are held in the Society of Genealogists' library (covering the period 1501–1975). Proctors and advocates were also doctors of law and therefore would have attended university; most of the surviving records are at Lambeth Palace Library, and there are a few in the Public Record Office. An article called "The Proctor", by John Titford, in *Family Tree Magazine* of January 1991, provides a lot of useful information. Lawyers have been included in published lists since the late eighteenth century: Brown's *General Law List* and then *The Law Lists*. These published

Above: Many thousands of application forms were handwritten by the first female nurses to be recruited for service in the Crimean War in 1855. The forms which survived are held by the PRO.

Below: Shopkeepers. Guilds and livery companies were formed to regulate a wide range of trades and traders.

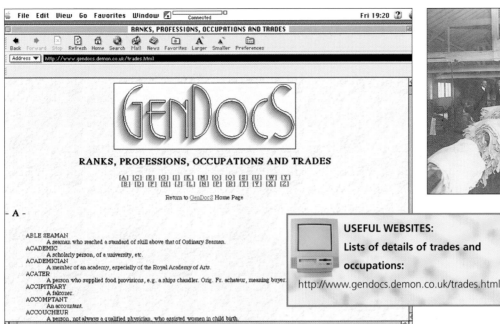

GenDocs

RANKS, PROFESSIONS, OCCUPATIONS AND TRADES

[A] [C] [E] [G] [I] [K] [M] [O] [Q] [S] [U] [W] [Y]
[B] [D] [F] [H] [J] [L] [N] [P] [R] [T] [V] [X] [Z]

Return to GenDocs Home Page

- A -

ABLE SEAMAN
A seaman who reached a standard of skill above that of Ordinary Seaman.
ACADEMIC
A scholarly person, of a university, etc.
ACADEMICIAN
A member of an academy, especially of the Royal Academy of Arts.
ACATER
A person who supplied food provisions, e.g. a ships chandler. Orig. Fr. achateur, meaning buyer.
ACCIPITRARY
A falconer.
ACCOMPTANT
An accountant.
ACCOUCHEUR
A person, not always a qualified physician, who assisted women in child birth.

USEFUL WEBSITES:

Lists of details of trades and occupations:

http://www.gendocs.demon.co.uk/trades.html

Above: Prepared hides in a tannery. There is a lot of information about trades and industry available from books and various other documents.

volumes are in the British Library and the Guildhall Library. As most professionals were well educated, it is safe to assume that they attended one of the universities or colleges, and records will be found there. Other places for records would be in the *Medical Directory*, the *Medical Register* and *Crockford's Clerical Directory*.

GUILDS AND LIVERY COMPANIES

The livery Ccompanies, or the guilds of the City of London, have existed since the twelfth century. They were later incorporated by royal charter during the reign of Edward III, and were known as livery companies from their distinctive dress or livery. It was required that all Freemen of the City should be a member of one of the guilds. Their function was to regulate trade and traders in their particular occupation. Freedom of a company could be obtained in three ways:

• After apprenticeship to a freeman of the company.
• By the son of a freeman of the company.
• By buying the freedom of the company.

On gaining their freedom, a company could then apply for the freedom of the City of London. The charitable work of the City companies can be seen in the schools which they founded. The following is a very small percentage of the present livery companies: Apothecaries, Bakers, Barbers, Blacksmiths, Brewers, Carpenters, Clockmakers, Cooks, Cordwainers, Dyers, Farriers, Fletchers, Girdlers, Glovers, Joiners, Masons, Playingcard Makers, Shipwrights, Turners, and lots more. The records for these are in the Guildhall Library.

TRADE UNIONS

Trade unionism was well established by the eighteenth century among groups of industrial workers and there is a lot of information available about them, both books and documents. Read the local newspapers which will detail meetings and social events, and will give names and details. The main collection of trade union records is housed at Warwick University and the Nuffield College in Oxford. The Scottish trade union records are kept at the Department of Manuscripts in the National Library of Scotland. Some branch records are in the local county record offices, but more still have been lost.

Above: Trade union records date back to the eighteenth century. There are various sources of information which list names, detail meetings, and record social events.

Thatcher—an occupational name: "the thacker or thatcher." A medieval name also linked with the Roman toga, a means to cover.

Thomas—"the son of Thomas;" from the nickname of Thome or Tom. In 1939 this was the eleventh most common name in the United States.

Thompson—a diminutive of Thomas. Fifteenth most common name in England and Wales in 1853, forty-second in Ireland in 1890, and fifteenth in America in 1939.

Thormann—(German) A "gatekeeper."

Tobin—a diminutive of Tobias, a Jewish name.

Todd—nickname "the tod" or "fox;" the todhunter or foxhunter. A surname from the north of England.

Toller, Tolman—a toll-collector or a tax-gatherer. Also a local name "stream in a hollow;" a place name in Devon.

TAXATION AND INSURANCE RECORDS

TAXATION RECORDS in the UK are very varied and date back several hundred years, as do those in a number of US states where many have been microfilmed and placed in the state archives. They are usually found in the Public Record Office and the county record offices. There are many types of tax, but it all comes back to one thing: tax is a means by which the state transfers from the citizen a part of his or her wealth for the support and maintenance of the country. Taxpayers over the years have disliked paying taxes and would always find a way around it, and because of this the efficiency of individual taxation systems have tended to decay and another taxation system would be developed. Thankfully for the family historian, proper tax records with names and details are good news. Taxes were, as today, levied either on behalf of the nation state or by local government.

Right: A sheriff's pouch and papers relating to an inquest into Alien Subsidy Tax, 1469.

Lay subsidies were a series of taxes which were levied on the moveable assets of the lay population. The sum that was required varied, according to the need of the country (the very poor were exempt from it). In 1542–1545 the Great Subsidy listed all people over sixteen years of age. Original lay subsidy records are in the Public Record Office (Exchequer series E179), dating from the fourteenth to the end of the seventeenth century. Subsidies were also raised on land and buildings.

HEARTH TAX RETURNS

Hearth tax returns were levied from 1662 to 1689 in England and Wales and offer one of the most valuable lists of name documents compiled in the seventeenth century. The tax was for two shillings each year on each hearth, fireplace, or stove in a household. The parish constable in each county made a return with names, showing the number of taxable hearths for each person. A separate list would be made for those who were too poor to pay. The taxes were paid twice a year on Lady Day, March 25, and on Michaelmas, September 29. It was sometimes difficult to collect the taxes and the court would send in a receiver to do so. Hearth Tax records for 1662–1666 and 1668–1674 are lodged in the Public Record Office; some are found in the appropriate county record office.

Right: Most of the existing hearth tax records in the UK are lodged at the Public Record Office.

122

THE MARRIAGE DUTY ACT

The Marriage Duty Act of 1695 levied a tax on births, marriages, and burials, payable on a sliding scale. The Stamp Duty Act of 1783 meant an annual tax was payable by bachelors over twenty-five years of age and childless widows were also taxed. Only the paupers who received poor relief were exempt.

POLL TAXES

Poll taxes were first paid in the fourteenth century and then between 1660 and 1697, but very few records have survived (some can be found in city archives and a few in the Public Record Office).

WINDOW TAX

Window Tax was first levied from 1696, an unpopular tax (a replacement to the equally unloved Hearth Tax) which continued until 1851. This tax applied to the occupiers not the owners. Many householders would brick up their windows, the evidence of which can still been seen today. The returns would show the name and address of the taxpayer, the number of windows, and the amount of tax paid. Records are found in the county record offices, with a few in the Public Record Office under E181.

LAND TAX

Land Tax was started in 1693, levied on land with a value of more than twenty shillings. The majority of surviving records are from 1780 to 1832. During the 1692–1831 period Roman Catholics paid double. Collections and documents are arranged in county, hundred, and then parish. The records show the landowner's name, and from 1772 all the occupiers were listed. From 1780 a duplicate copy was made of the return which was lodged with the Clerks of the Peace. A Land Tax return would give the names of the occupier and owners, acreage, type of land, and the amount of tax paid. These deposited returns are found in the county record office, while the 1798 land tax for the whole of England and Wales, except Flintshire, is in the Public Record Office.

Left: Part of a lay tax assessment dated 1587. The document shows the apportionment of tax between various tenements of land.

INSURANCE POLICIES

In your family records you may have copies of life insurance policies, the policies may have been kept, as well as the death certificate or will which were used to support these claims. Another type of insurance is fire insurance. Companies started from the seventeenth century to insure buildings against fire; most of their records have been lost, but the surviving records will be in the county record office or the Guildhall Library. If a building was insured against fire, it would have a plaque embedded in its wall to let the fire brigade know there was insurance cover. There are various microfiche indexes to registers of the Sun Fire Office and the Royal Exchange. Do look for these records, because the small companies also had their own records. Hedley Peters & Son of Sittingbourne hold insurance records for property, fire and life, which are on microfiche and can be bought through the Kent Family History Society. The property certificates give the name of the owner, the occupier, the full address, and the value of the property.

Torres—a local name meaning "dweller at or near the tower or spire." An early English name, also popular in America.
Trewen—(Celtic) meaning "a dweller in the white homestead."
Tucker—(Old English) "one who teased and burled the cloth." Mainly from the Devon area, where they had a great medieval cloth industry.
Tulloch—a local name "at the tulloch;" a Scots name from the Gaelic, "tulach" meaning "a hillock." Therefore a residence by the hillock.
Turnbull—a nickname; whether the bearer could "turn a bull" in the course of his duties or as an act of daring and strength is not clear. A common Scottish border family name, now found in Northumberland and Durham, also worldwide.
Turner—"one who works with a lathe," making objects of wood, metal, bone, etc. This was the twenty-third most common surname in England and Wales in 1853, and thirtieth in the USA in 1939. Also a family name of the barons Netherthorpe.

COURT RECORDS

HAVE YOUR ancestors appeared before a court, whether it be civil, ecclesiastical, or criminal? Most of us have tales about "black sheep" in our families and one of the fascinations of genealogy is that it provides you with a window into history. In times gone by there were many more ways of finding oneself on the wrong side of the law. What we would regard today as relatively minor matters may well have resulted in the transportation of our ancestors to colonies in Australia and North America (see page 81). Tens of thousands of people were dealt with in this way and, therefore, many people today are descended from those who suffered this punishment. Some of the very best kept papers of all are court records which are likely to contain a wealth of interesting details, including the names of convicted criminals, the nature of their offences, and the penalties awarded.

Above: Did your ancestors have criminal records?

In England and Wales, civil disputes went through the Court of Chancery, the procedure of which was very complex, slow, and expensive. The records for it date back to the beginning of the accession of King John I in 1199, and the Chancery became a court of law during the reign of Edward III in 1348. The court acted as a court of equity to deal with cases which had no provision under English common law. They dealt with an enormous amount of business: disputes over inheritance, lands, debts, and marriage settlements. It functioned until 1873, when all equity jurisdiction passed to the Chancery Division of the Supreme Court of Judicature.

CHANCERY RECORDS

The extensive Chancery records are found in the Public Record Office (see leaflet No. 30); from about 1873, they fall into a number of different categories and each is filed separately. The classes, each with a reference, are listed numerically in the typescript "Summary of Records" available on the search room shelves.

ECCLESIASTICAL COURTS

Ecclesiastical or Church courts are full of records of your ancestors. Wills and marriage licences are just two of the documents which passed through the hands of these courts. Under the Norman kings, separate courts were created for the hearing of cases; they were on two levels: the Bishops' Courts and the Archdeacons' Courts. Records since the fifteenth century have survived and they deal with

heresy, attendance and behavior in church and the churchyard, the conduct of the parson and church officials, the state of the church building and its furniture, the payment of parish dues,

Below: Mariposa County Courthouse, California's oldest seat of justice still in use, built in 1854.

Above: Judges and barristers leaving Westminster Abbey in 1938 after a service to mark the reopening of the law courts following the long annual vacation.

Left: The Royal Courts of Justice, London.

betrothal, marriage, immorality, slander, wills, and parish boundaries. Many cases were concerned with adultery and fornication, and because of this the court was known as "The Bawdy Court" in some places. The following was written in the baptismal parish register of Milton Regis in Kent during September 1783:

"Joseph George, son of George & Elizabeth Bass, age 6 years. And what is further to be recorded, as a striking instance of the immorality of the times, the sponsors of the said Joseph George Bass, viz. Henry South and Joseph Hodge, behaved themselves at the Font in a most shameful manner, by drinking of liqueur and handing about the same in the face of a large congregation for which offence they were presented."

Are they your ancestors? Were they presented before the Ecclesiastical courts? The original records of the archbishops of Canterbury are in Lambeth Palace Library, the probate records are in the Public Record Office. The records for the Archbishop of York and the Diocese of York are in the Borthwick Institute of Historical Research. Some records are also in diocesan registries and could possibly be in the county record office.

ASSIZE COURTS

From the thirteenth century onward, justices were sent from the central courts in Westminster on circuits, usually in pairs, to cover all the counties of England, except London and Middlesex. By the fifteenth century this criminal jurisdiction had come to dominate the business of sessions of the Assize Courts, which continued until they were abolished by the Courts Act of 1971 and replaced by the crown court. The justices would hear cases about murder, rape, robbery, burglary, larceny, and arson, and any other crimes which were too serious to be heard by the Quarter Sessions.

The records of the Assize Courts are held in the Public Record Office, for although the case was heard in the county, the records are termed as national records. For convicts sentenced to transportation you will need to find out where the convict was tried. At the Assize Courts, Quarter Sessions or the Old Bailey. Begin with the convict transportation records class HO11 1787–1871. Lists of prisoners tried at Newgate 1782–1853 are in class HO 77 and calendars of prisoners held for trial at Quarter Sessions and Assizes 1774–1882 are in class PCOM 2.

Ulbrich—(German) meaning "inheritance" or "bright."
Underdown, Underhill—local name "at the foot of the hill." Underhill is a very popular name in Devon.
Unfried—(German) a disturber of the peace.

Hound

Unsworth—a local name meaning "enclosure of hound or dog." Also a place in Lancashire.
Unterberg—(German) meaning "living below the mountain."
Unwin—"a foe" or "unfriendly," found in Derbyshire and Essex.
Upton—an upper place or farm, common in most of England. Also local "of Upton," with place names in several English counties.
Usher—a name for a doorkeeper, chamberlain or usher; one who introduces strangers.

EMIGRATION

EMIGRATION means leaving one country for permanent settlement in another, often involving the upheaval of whole families. It is a phenomenon as old as humankind itself. As a more systematic and concerted economic facet of life it really became significant in the sixteenth century—although there was migration and emigration in medieval Europe—with the discovery of the New World and has become increasingly important ever since; today, more than ever.

There are so many reasons for emigration: a need to escape poverty and better one's life and one's family's future; to escape religious or political persecution; or transportation due to criminal acts, indentures, and apprenticeships. The most popular destinations for groups of emigrants were North America, the West Indies, Australia, South Africa, and New Zealand. Practically the whole modern populations of these countries have ancestors from elsewhere. In the United States and Canada, for example, the modern indigenous Native American population is tiny in percentage terms.

It is a well-covered subject and numerous books are available which give ships' passenger lists and related records. Check libraries first, if the information is published it should be easy to find your ancestors in the original records.

Early in the seventeenth century, emigration from Britain began in significant numbers—to Ireland. For religious and political reasons the British government encouraged people to settle in Ireland by providing land. From the government's perspective this policy was successful, displacing indigenous Catholics and replacing them with Scottish and English settlers who, by 1659, accounted for 37 per cent of the 70,800 householders in Ulster, the territory nearest to Britain. Generations later, many of these may have been among the people that went to the US, or back to Britain, to escape the potato famine.

NORTH AMERICA

During the 1630s the really popular place to go was North America and the West Indies. Today about 20 per cent of Americans can trace their ancestry to England and 16 per cent back to Ireland. It is suggested that approximately

Above: Steerage passengers emigrating to America, sail from London to New York, in 1896.

Left: Irish emigrants preparing to sail to America from Clifden, County Galway, in 1883.

540,000 people left England to settle in America between 1630 and 1700, of whom 21,000 went to New England. By the end of the 1700s they were settling in the southern states and the Caribbean. Cheaper labor was in great demand, and young men and women left the central and southern parts of England emigrate as indentured servants—a position only one step up from slavery. Younger sons from gentry families traveled out with servants and laborers, seeking to buy land, settle, and make their fortune in places such as Virginia. They sought an adventurous life in a new land, because the English system of inheritance meant the eldest son would always acquire the family title, property, and fortune.

IN PURSUIT OF LIBERTY

During the nineteenth century it is thought that about ten million people left the British Isles for America, and in Ireland by 1900 the population was half what it had been fifty years earlier. But in the US the population rose dramatically: in 1790 there were about four million and by 1850 this had risen to 23 million. Emigrants flocked to the US from every European country, taking people from all trades, occupations, and social classes. The journey across the Atlantic was long

Above: Gold prospectors developed towns across America which often became ghost towns when the gold ran out or mining failed.

and hard, and many did not survive. The dominant culture, however, in the US remained Anglocentric and upon arrival many Europeans Anglicized their names in order to fit in better—many others had their names changed by immigration officials who found it troublesome to spell the originals proffered. Every upheaval in Europe—of which there were many during the nineteenth century—created new waves of people heading to this haven which promised greater liberty and a better future.

The records on both side of the Atlantic are many and varied. If your ancestor left the UK between 1890 and 1960 and you also know the port of leaving, then check in the Public Record Office in class BT 27. This gives name, age, occupation, and an address. The registers of ships' passenger lists, class BT 32, includes ships leaving each port and might help you to find the right VT 26 register. Prior to 1890 tracing emigrants to North America is more difficult as there is no regular documentation in the Public Record Office. Various research has been done which has resulted in published books and

Cornish Roots CD

This CD-Rom is produced by Cornish American Connection in Redruth and Cornwall Business Systems, the producers of *Cornish Multimedia*. Includes a full transcript of substantial parts of the 1851 census and the Cornish American Connection database (with over 24,000 Cornish emigrants to the USA), a collection of old pictures of churches and chapels, a gazetteer of 15,000 Cornish place names, historical information for each parish, Cornish names and their meanings, and famous men and women.

• Available from Cornwall Business Systems and the Cornish American Connection.

http://www.cornwall-net.co.uk/multimed/roots.htm

indexes. Mr F. Leeson has a name index to about 100 published and unpublished sources for the period 1660–1850, and Mr N. Currer-Briggs has an index of about 50,000 names for 1560–1690. Many of the books available are published by the Genealogical Publishing Company and there are many available in public libraries in the United States.

Valentine—nickname for "a sweetheart." Also "a son of Valentine," originating from St Valentine's day, February 14. Also a pagan festival when lots were drawn for lovers.
Vann, Van—a local name meaning "at the van;" the threshing floor or a residence near by.
Varney—a local name, a variant of Verney.
Vaughan, Vaughn—a nickname meaning "the little" in Welsh.
Venables, Venable, Vennable—a local name "from Venables," a parish of Louviers in Normandy, France.

Huntsman

Venner, Fenner—an occupation of "le veneur," a huntsman.
Vincent, Vincett—"the son of Vincent." Vincett is a corruption of the name, not a diminutive.
Voller—a fuller or a bleacher of cloth.
Wagner—a descendant of a wagon-driver or of a wagon-maker.
Wainwright—a wagon-maker and repairer.

Taking Names to the World

Many foreign surnames brought into England have been Anglicized immediately or over the course of time. For example, the French names of Hervé and Charpentier can be found in the English form of Harvey and Carpenter. The Dutch name of Van Rosevelt traveled across to the United States; the identifiably "foreign" Van was dropped and the surname became Roosevelt.

As well as surname changes there have been effects on first or Christian names too. During the twelfth and thirteenth century, Christian names which were popular in Anglo-Saxon and Anglo-Scandinavian England became nearly extinct. Edward survived, but new names such as William, Robert, Richard, Ralph, and Hugh were made popular by the barons and kings of Norman France. During this period names from the Bible were also to be found, mainly those of the apostles. Girls received the names of Catherine, Mary, Elizabeth, and Anne, names which continue to be popular even today.

Right: Headstones in the Sonora Pioneer Cemetery, California, show that Edmund Parnell was born in Cornwall, England in 1802, and Mrs McCormick was born in Cliffony, County Sligo, Ireland in 1824.

In the United States the Christian names which appeared in the New England area were from the Puritans, who also favored Biblical names, hence Benjamin, Hannah, Jacob, Joseph, Samuel, and Sarah. During the nineteenth century new names appeared: Amos, Caleb, Ebenezer, Noah, and Zachary, as well as Faith, Hope, Charity, and Patience—the Puritans had a greater effect on names in America than in their native England.

The movement of emigrants from country to country has meant a wide dispersal and variety of surnames and forenames, with each nationality taking its own culture with them.

IMMIGRATION

AS PEOPLE emigrated to a new life overseas so we must consider the impact of immigration on the country receiving an influx of settlers. We all think of the United States as a country built on mass immigration, but few people consider that people have arrived on British shores from the continent of Europe for centuries: Celts, Romans, Angles, Saxons, Danes, Vikings, and Normans, creating the mix which became the British. We have looked at the Huguenots, the Jews, and the French fleeing from persecution, but more recent additions to the British make-up from further afield are those immigrants who have come from the West Indies and the Indian subcontinent.

Above: An American slave market, 1852. Many slaves were not given a surname and may not be very well recorded.

THE UNITED KINGDOM

It should be realized that the West Indians who went to the UK in the aftermath of World War II were not the first black people to settle there. Many first arrived as slaves, as early as 1555, and it has been suggested that there were between 10,000 and 20,000 living in the black community in London by the end of the eighteenth century (by which time the trade in slaves had been illegal in Britain for almost a century). These people were, however, not very well recorded; many had no surname, until civil registration in 1837, but they may appear in Anglican burial registers.

A few immigration records are in the Public Record Office (class BT 26), but they refer only to the late nineteenth century and the first half of the twentieth. They give name, age, occupation, date of entry, and possible place of residence. They are arranged by port, then year, and then ship. You would need to know the port of entry and a possible date, as these records are not indexed. If immigrants decided to become naturalized, the relevant papers would be found in the Public Record Office. In RG 4, Nonconformist registers on microfilm in the Family Records Centre, are registers of birth, baptism, marriages, and burials for the French, Dutch, German, and Swiss churches. They cover various periods between 1567 and 1857.

The King's Bench Swearing, or Oath, Rolls include Oath Rolls of Naturalization from 1708 to 1712. They are the oaths of foreign Protestants who were deemed natural-born British subjects (class KB 24). The Public Record Office leaflet No. 70 gives a full list of the records available.

THE UNITED STATES

The immigration records available in the United States are, as one might expect, entirely different. The sheer scale and process of immigration was of a wholly different order. Did one of your ancestors arrive in the United States between the years 1892 and 1954? If they did, they must have certainly passed though the immigration depot of Ellis Island, New York. More than twelve million people from all over the world landed here and 40 per cent of the population of America can trace their ancestry to a steamship passenger in the registers at Ellis Island.

ELLIS ISLAND

Ellis Island is a small island in Upper New York Bay. Although in New Jersey waters, it is under the political jurisdiction of New York. Since 1965 it has been part of the Statue of Liberty National Monument. It was once a picnic ground used by the early Dutch settlers, and the island was

Below: Newly arrived immigrants await inspection in the Great Assembly Hall at Ellis Island, New York, in 1911.

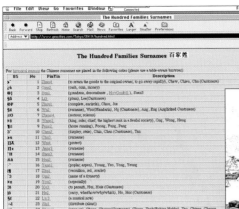

USEFUL WEBSITES:

Chinese surnames; one of the few non-Western genealogy sites:

http://www.geocites.com/Tokyo/3919/

Kindredkonnections:

http://www.209.40.72.162/indexeng.html

Left: A page from The Hundred Families Surnames website.

Left: Jewish refugees from Russia see the Statue of Liberty as they arrive at Ellis Island in 1892.

Below: Emigrants sail to America aboard the S.S. Westernland, c. 1890.

named after Samuel Ellis, who owned it in the 1770s. It was purchased by the federal government from New York State in 1808 for use as a government arsenal and fort. By 1847 it was clear that some form of immigration department was required in the United States.

The potato famine in Ireland during the mid-1840s had sent thousands of emigrants to New York and New England. A request to use the old fort on Ellis Island was turned down and Castle Clinton was used instead. It was not until January 1, 1892, that the first immigrant landed on Ellis Island, she was fifteen-year-old Annie Moore from County Cork in Ireland. John Webster, the New York State Immigration Commissioner, gave her a ten-dollar gold piece.

Five years later the depot was burned to the ground, but only after 1,500,000 people had passed through. Cost and delays meant that a new building, complete with hospital complex, on a nearby island was not opened until December 1900. Once again the immigrants passed though Ellis Island, although the journey across the Atlantic Ocean now took only two weeks instead of the previous three months. On-board conditions were terrible; the steerage class slept in rooms with triple-level bunks, and the lack of privacy and limited toilet facilities made the journey very unpleasant. On arrival in the US they waited on the ships for several days, because as many as 20,000 people were waiting to be ferried to Ellis Island. On landing, they underwent a medical check from the Public Health officials, but even these doctors only had seconds to check for sixty different symptoms which would indicate any disease and disability. Children over two years of age were made to walk, asked for their name, and checked to see if they had any speech or hearing difficulties.

People were watched to see if they could climb stairs without difficulty. Any who were sick were marked with blue chalk and taken to the hospital to recover; those with incurable illnesses or disabling complaints were returned to their port of departure, usually at the expense of the steamship on which they arrived.

Once through the medical examination, the immigrants passed on to the main registry room where they had to convince the inspectors that they were strong and able to work. In 1917 the government imposed a literacy test, thus restricting immigration further. In 1954 Ellis Island finally closed its doors. In 1990 the doors opened again but this time as a museum and research center for visitors. The records and registers for these immigrants are now indexed and available. Did your ancestors land there?

Walch, Walcher—(German) a foreigner, a non-German.

Walker—a cloth worker who trod cloth to clean or bleach it.

Washington—a local name of a place or farm; also a parish in Durham. A popular name in the Boston area of the United States.

Waterman—a waterman or carrier; also "son of Walter."

Weber—descendant of a cloth weaver; also a county name in Utah.

Weiss—descendants of a man with a white complexion or hair.

Whitwell—a local of "white springs or stream." Also a local of Whitwell, with many parishes in England.

Wicken, Wickin—local "of the dairy farm." Also "the son of William."

Williams—"son of William;" a name dating back to the 1300s.

Wilson—"the son of William," from the nickname of Will. This name is found all over England and is common in the USA.

CORONER'S RECORDS

THE CORONER'S office in England dates back to 1194, when their job even then was to hold inquests into sudden or suspicious deaths. Also, if valuables were found, they were to decide if they were treasure trove. An inquest jury was made up of twelve to twenty-three people, and was not altered until 1926 (when it was reduced to between seven and eleven). A coroner was elected by the freeholders and had jurisdiction over his county until the nineteenth century, when, from the late 1880s, counties were sub-divided into districts, each with its own coroner elected by the local authorities.

Very few records have survived prior to 1875 because a coroner was allowed to destroy any records which were more than fifteen years old. These existing records are closed to the public for seventy-five years, although at the coroner's discretion you may be allowed access.

If you know that a coroner's report was issued on the death of an ancestor, and the report is missing, check the local newspaper. From the eighteenth century onward, inquests were reported in local, and sometimes national, papers. These accounts are an almost verbatim report of the inquest. The following is a very small part of a report into the inquest of two young children who died in a house fire in Sittingbourne, Kent, on August 13, 1882; the children, George, aged three and a half years, and Agnes, aged nearly two, were suffocated by the smoke, while alone in the house:

"The following evidence was taken: Pricilla Shrubsall, mother of the deceased children, deposed:

I am the wife of Alfred Shrubsall and reside at No. 25 Cheapside, Sittingbourne. I left my home at about a quarter to six last evening. My little girl, Elizabeth, aged eleven, had put the two deceased children to bed, as she was in the habit of doing. . . "

The report goes on for two columns in the newspaper; statements were given by Elizabeth, the two neighbors who tried to save them, the fire superintendent, and the local doctor. Even from tragedy, so much information is available. An inquest can be held very quickly, therefore the report should be in the next issue of the local paper. Check the following week's papers for more details; in the case of this fire, letters were sent in condemning the poor woman for leaving her children alone, and this could be the reason the family soon moved to Margate.

Coroners would hand their records to the Assize justices, and therefore some reports will be in the Assize records in the Public Record Office, while others may be found in the county record offices.

If an inquest returned a verdict of murder, a criminal trial would have taken place. From the sixteenth to the eighteenth century, coroner's reports were forwarded to the Court of King's Bench (see class KB 9 to 12). Any surviving reports from the coroner may include notes from the inquest: details of the deceased, the death, names, and verdict of the jury, and, from 1837, a certificate sent to the registrar to notify details of death. A death certificate and a burial register may show that the burial is allowed by the coroner. If no inquest record is found, check any information on the coroner's bills; any surviving bills will be found in the Quarter Sessions records.

Above: National and local newspapers are an important source of information, recording events which document the social history of a country or area at any given time.

Newspaper Libraries

Newspapers can be regarded as a very important document for local and family history. As well as recording events in which our ancestors are mentioned, they also give a good social history of the local area, providing an indication of how our ancestors lived.

Most local newspapers are found on microfilm in the local county library, but for a truly wide range of local and national newspapers you will need to find the national holdings. For England and Wales, these are housed with periodicals at the Newspaper Library at Colindale in North London, a part of the British Library. It is the home of one of largest the single collections of newspapers in the world.

In Germany many newspapers published notices of residents who had emigrated. During the period 1820–1914, the *Deutscher Reichsanzeiger* mentions 277,000 names, and all these are in a book called *The Germanic Emigrations Register,* published in 1992.

In the United States, old newspapers are often more difficult to locate. There are several aids which are available to help you: *History and Bibliography of American Newspapers, 1690–1820,* in two volumes, by Clarence Saunders Brigham; *American Newspapers 1821–1936: A Union List of Files Available in the United States and Canada,* by Winifred Gregory; and *Newspaper Indexes: A Location and*

Subject Guide for Researchers, by Anita Milner. These will help with the location of the library, historical society or newspaper office in which you will find your relevant newspaper.

THE STEAMBOAT COLLISION ON THE MERSEY.

INQUEST ON THE BODIES.

LIVERPOOL, JULY 9.

The inquest on the bodies of the eight unfortunate Irish-men who died from injuries sustained in the collision of the iron steamboats Mail and Excelsior, on the Mersey, on Sunday morning, was continued to-day before Mr. F. P. Curry and a respectable jury, in the Crown Court, St. George's-hall.

Mr. Blair, barrister, instructed by Messrs. Duncan, Squarey, and Duncan, watched the case on behalf of the owners of the Mail; Mr. Aspinall, instructed by Messrs. Lowndes, Bateson, and Robinson, for the owners of the Excelsior; Mr. T. S. Raffles, instructed by Mr. John Yates, jun., for the representatives of the deceased; and Mr. Bremner, attorney, for Brewer, the pilot who was in charge of the Excelsior at the time of the collision.

Captain Cooke, superintendent of the pilots of Liverpool, and Mr. Hodgson, Harbour-master, sat on the bench, assist-ing the coroner and the jury with models and charts show-ing the positions of the vessels as the evidence proceeded.

The court was crowded, and the greatest interest was manifested throughout the hearing.

The jury having been to inspect both vessels, for the purpose of making themselves acquainted with the position of the lights,

Joseph Bailey, the captain of the Mail, was sworn. He said,—I am master of the iron screw steamer Mail, 194 tons register, plying between Dublin and Liverpool. The crew, including officers, consists of 16 men. There are two en-gines of 30-horse power each. We sailed from Dublin on Saturday, at 1 55 p.m., with 76 deck-passengers, eight cattle-dealers, and four cabin-passengers. We had a fair wind, but took the sails in. The chief-officer (White) was on the first nightwatch, which consisted of chief-officer, carpenter, and two sailors on the look-out on the forecastle. One of the sailors was at the helm. When the night set in we had our usual lights all right. We approached the Mersey by the Rock channel, all going well till we got there. We rounded the Rock light at 1 30, half an hour after entering the channel. At that time the boatswain, Thomas Gurney, was in charge of the helm, and all hands were then on deck, in accordance with custom on coming into port. We kept as close to the Cheshire shore as we could get. Immediately after rounding the Rock light the chief officer reported a steamer coming down the river, about half a point on our port bow. We were going at full speed at that time. I then distinctly observed the three lights of the steamer. The head of the Mail was a .... littll......

Above: This coroner's inquest concerning the death of eight Irishmen in a steamboat accident appeared in The Times *newspaper, London.*

Left: The British Library in London is a large new building, but the archived material is so vast that some departments have to be housed separately in other buildings.

USING A PROFESSIONAL GENEALOGIST

AT SOME point you may have to use the services of a professional genealogist, whether in your own country or abroad. How you find them can vary. The best approach is through the recommendation of someone else. Ask at your local family history society or genealogical society, consult the journals of your group and also look in family history magazines. Sometimes it is not practical to carry out a certain piece of research yourself, either because you want more professional help and/or the research is some distance away—perhaps even in a different continent.

Try to choose a researcher who is specifically working in the area you want your research done. If the research is to be done in an English record office, write them and find out if they will do a mail search and, most importantly, find out their charges. If you are using a professional researcher, do try to find two or three whom you might consider. There are organizations which a researcher can join; they have certain codes of practice, so if you have any complaints let them know. Professional researchers can fall into several categories: someone who researches for a living, or another who is a keen family historian supplementing their income. Whoever you choose, you should expect a professional job without hidden additional charges.

Having obtained several names, write to them, giving a clear idea of who and exactly what you want researched. Do not send a long rambling letter about your complete family history for the last two centuries; keep it short and to the point. Don't keep any information back to see if the researcher finds it out for themselves, they will charge you for it and it would be a waste of money. If you telephone the researcher, always confirm in writing so as to avoid mistakes. Send a stamped self-addressed envelope or International Reply Coupons; do not send any money with your inquiry.

When the researcher has had the opportunity to decide whether they can help you and, of course, has the capability and knowledge to do so, you would expect a reply to advise whether your request is reasonable in research terms, and also whether you have provided enough information. You should receive details of their terms of business, either in their letter or a separate enclosure. You would expect to be told their rates, any possible extra costs and whether a deposit is required. You should have the opportunity to accept or question the terms before the work is carried out. Their rates could be quoted as an hourly

Above: Your researcher requires as much information as possible. Letters of sentimental value often give many clues, including names, addresses, dates, and details of events.

Below: Do not send original documents through the mail—send a photocopy in case it gets lost.

Above: Your relatives may have documents which suggest your search may take you abroad, such as this French wine merchant's invoice, dated 1874.

out how long the research will take and an idea of when the report will be sent back to you. When choosing a researcher, look at how he presented his initial details: is it a well-presented letter, a leaflet or a scribbled note on an equally scrappy piece of paper? This could be an important indication of how his final report will be presented.

Now prepare your reply. If are you sending any details of documents or certificates, send a photocopy, not the original. If you haven't any means of copying a document yourself, the local library or a print shop will be able to offer a photocopying service. Having posted your information, wait for the researcher's reply; the average time is usually five to six weeks. If they gave you an approximate date, give two weeks grace before you send a polite chasing letter.

When your report arrives, it should list all the sources consulted and the results. Each researcher has their own way of setting out their research. One thing to remember is however good or bad your researcher is or how much you pay, if your ancestor was not in a particular place at a certain time, however much you look, they will not be found.

rate plus expenses, but be careful, these extras could be charges for travel and time, as well as a charge for writing up the report. Ask for an estimate of expenses and a full itemization. Find

Wright—a workman, skilled in many things; a carpenter, a joiner.

Above: The village church at Yalding, Kent, England.

Yalden—a local "of Yalding," a parish near Maidstone in Kent.
Yale—a local of fertile land.
Yelland—"a local of Yealand;" parishes are found in Lancashire.
Yardley—a local wood-clearing for gathering sticks, spars, and poles.
Yeoman, Yeman, Yeaman—an occupation, a yeoman or a small freeholder; earlier use was a servant or attendant in a noble household.
York, Yorke—"a man of York;" or from the city of York.
Young—a nickname for "the young;" could have been used instead of "junior."
Zachary—"the son of Zachary."
Zimmerman—descendant of a carpenter.

Left: Bibles handed down through the generations are good places to start to discover details about your family tree.

USEFUL ADDRESSES AND ORGANIZATIONS

UNITED KINGDOM

IMPORTANT ARCHIVES
• Church of Jesus Christ of Latter-day Saints, Family History Centre, 64–68 Exhibition Road, South Kensington, London SW7 2PA
(Write for a full list of Family History Centres in the UK, to: Genealogical Society of Utah (UK), 185 Penns Lane, Sutton Coldfield, West Midlands B76 1JU)
• Corporation of London Record Office, PO Box 270, Guildhall, London EC2P 2EJ
• General Register Office, 1 Myddelton Street, Islington, London EC1R 1UW
Tel: 0181 392 5300
Website: http://www.open.gov.uk/prohome.htm
• General Register Office (Northern Ireland), 49–55 Chichester Street, Belfast, Northern Ireland BT1 4HL
Tel: 01232 252021/2/3/4
Website: http://www.nics.gov.uk/nisra/gro
• General Register Office (Scotland), New Register House, Edinburgh EH1 3YT
Tel: 0131 334 0380
E-mail: nrh.gros@govnet.gov.uk
Website: http://www.open.gov.uk/gros/groshome.htm
• Imperial War Museum, Department of Documents, Lambeth Road, London SE1 6HZ
• London Metropolitan Archives, 40 Northampton Road, London EC1R 0HB
Tel: 0171 332 3820
• National Army Museum, Royal Hospital Road, London SW3 4HT
Tel: 0171 730 0717
E-mail: nam@enterprise.net
Website: http://www.failye.com/nam/
• National Maritime Museum, Romney Road, Greenwich, London SE10 9NF
Tel: 0181 312 6691
Website: http://www.nmm.ac.uk
• National Monuments Record Centre, Kemble Drive, Swindon
Tel: 01793 414600
• Post Office Archives and Record Services, Freeling House, Mount Pleasant Complex, Phoenix Place entrance, London EC1A 1BB
Tel: 0171 239 2570
E-mail: catherine.orton@postoffice.co.uk
• Principal Probate Registry, First Avenue House, 42–49 High Street, London WC1V 6NP
• Public Record Office, Ruskin Avenue, Kew, Richmond, TW9 4DU
Tel: 0181 878 8905
E-mail: enquiry.pro.rsd.kew@gtnet.gov.uk
Website: http://www.open.gov.uk/pro/prohome.htm
• Public Record Office, Census Reading Rooms, 1 Myddelton Street, Islington, London EC1R 1UW
• Public Record Office of Northern Ireland, 66 Balmoral Avenue, Belfast, Northern Ireland BT9 6NY
Tel: 01232 251318
E-mail: proni@nics.gov.uk
Website: www.proni.nics.gov.uk/index.htm
• Scottish Record Office, HM General Register House, Princes Street, Edinbugh EH1 3YY
Tel: 0131 535 1314

LIBRARIES
• British Library, Department of Manuscripts, 96 Euston Road, London NW1 2DB
Tel: 0171 412 7513
Website: http://www.bl.uk
• British Library Newspaper Library, Colindale Avenue, London NW9 5HE
Tel: 0171 412 7353
Website: http://www.bl.uk/collections/
• British Library, Oriental and India Office Collections, 197 Blackfriars Road, London SE1 8NG
Tel: 0171 412 7873
Website: http://www.bl.uk.collections/oriental
• Edinburgh Central Library, George IV Bridge, Edinburgh EH1 1EG
Tel: 0131 225 5584
• Guildhall Library, Aldermanbury, London EC2P 2EJ
Tel: 0171 332 1863
Website: http://lhr.sas.ac.uk/ihr/ghmnu.html
• Lambeth Palace Library, London SE1 7JU
Tel: 0171 928 6222
• Library of the Religious Society of Friends (Quakers), Friends' House, Euston Road, London NW1 2BJ
Tel: 0171 663 1000/1135
• Linenhall Library, 17 Donegall Square North, Belfast, Co Antrim, Northern Ireland BT1 5GD
Tel: 01232 321707
• National Library of Scotland, Department of Manuscripts, George IV Bridge, Edinburgh EH1 1EW
Tel: 0131 226 4531
Website: www.nls.uk
• National Library of Wales, Aberystwyth, Dyfed SY23 3BU
Tel: 01970 623816
E-mail: holi@llgc.org.uk
Website: http://www.llgc.org.uk
• Polish Library, 338–346 King Street, London W6 0RF

SOCIETIES AND SPECIAL INTEREST GROUPS
• Anglo-French FHS, 31 Collingwood Walk, Andover, Hants SP10 1PU
• Anglo-German FHS, Mrs J. Towey, 14 River Reach, Teddington, Middlesex TW11 9QL
• Anglo-Jewish Association, Woburn House, Upper Woburn Place, London WC1H 0EZ
• Borthwick Institute of Historical Research (University of York), St Anthony's Hall, Peasholme Green, York YO1 2PW
• British Association of Local History (BALH), PO Box 1576, Salisbury, Wiltshire SP1 8SY
• British Telecommunications (BT) Archives, 3rd Floor, Holborn Telephone Exchange, London WC1V 7EE
• Business Archives Council, The Clove Building, 4 Maguire Street, London SE1 2NQ
• Catholic FHS, Mrs B. Murray, 2 Winscombe Crescent, Ealing, London W5 1AZ
• Centre for Kentish Studies, County Hall, Maidstone, Kent ME4 1XG
Tel: 01622 694363

• College of Arms, Queen Victoria Street, London EC4 4BT
• Commonwealth War Graves Commission, 2 Marlow Road, Maidenhead, Berkshire SL6 7DX
Website: http://www.cwgc.org
• Dr Williams Library, 14 Gordon Square, London WC1H 0AG
Tel: 0171 387 3727
• Federation of Family History Societies, Administrator, The Benson Room, Birmingham and Midland Institute, Margaret Street, Birmingham B3 3BS (Write for a full list of family history societies in England and Wales)
• Gordon Highlanders Museum, St Luke's, Viewfield Road, Aberdeen AB15 7XH
Tel: 01224 311200/31874
• Guild of One-Names Studies, Box G, 14 Charterhouse Buildings, Goswell Road, London EC1M 7BA
Website: www.one-study.org
• Huguenot and Walloon Research Association, Mrs J. Tsushima, "Malmaison," Great Bedwyn, Wiltshire SN8 3PE
• Huguenot Society, Huguenot Library, University College, Gower Street, London WC1E 6BT
• Institute of Heraldic and Genealogical Studies, 10 Northgate, Canterbury, Kent CT1 1BA
Tel: 01227 768664
E-mail: ihgs@dial.pipex.com
• Jewish Historical Society, 33 Seymour Place, London W1HM 5AP
• Jewish Genealogical Society of Great Britain, 32 Tavistock Street, Covent Garden, London WC2E 7PD
• The Jewish Museum, London's Museum of Jewish Life, 80 East End Road, Finchley, London N3 2SY
Tel: 0181 349 1143
Website: http://www.ort.org/jewmusm/
• North Devon Maritime Museum, Odun House, Odun Road, Appledore, Devon
Tel: 01237 474852
• Presbyterian Historical Society of Ireland, Church House, Fisherwick Place, Belfast, Northern Ireland BT1 6DW
Tel: 01232 322284
• Quaker FHS, Mr C. Pitt Lewis, 5 Rad Valley Gardens, Shrewsbury, Salop SY3 8AW
• Roman Catholic Archdiocesan Archives, Cathedral House, St Chad's Queensway, Birmingham B4 6EX
Tel: 0121 236 2251
• Roman Catholic Record Office, The Bishopric of the Forces, AGPDO, Middle Hill, Aldershot, Hants GU11 1PP
Tel: 01252 349007
• Scots Ancestry Research Society, 3 Albany Street, Edinburgh EH1 3PY
• Scottish Association of Family History Societies, 51/3 Mortonhall Road, Edinburgh EH9 2HN
• Scottish Genealogy Society, Library and Family History Centre, 15 Victoria Terrace, Edinburgh EH1 2JL
Tel: 0131 220 3677
E-mail: scotgensoc@sol.co.uk
Website: http://www.scotland.net/scotgensoc
• Society of Genealogists, 14

Charterhouse Buildings, Goswell Road, London EC1M 7BA
Tel: 0171 250 0291/251 8799
Website: http://www.cs.ncl.ac.uk/genuki/SoG

REGIONAL RECORD OFFICES AND ARCHIVES
England
• Barnsley Archives & Local Studies Dept, Barnsley Central Library, Shambles Street, Barnsley, West Yorkshire S70 2JF
Tel: 01226 773950
E-mail: archives@barnsley.ac.uk
Website: http://www.barnsley.ac.uk
• Bedfordshire & Luton Archives & Record Service, Record Office, County Hall, Bedford, Beds MK42 9AP
Tel: 01234 228833/228777
• Berkshire Record Office, Shinfield Park, Reading, Berks RG2 9XD
Tel: 0118 901 5132
• Berwick-upon-Tweed Record Office, Council Offices, Wallace Green, Berwick-upon-Tweed, Northumberland TD15 1ED
Tel: 01289 330044 Ext. 230
E-mail: archives@berwickc.demon.co.uk
Website: http://www.swinhope.demon.co.uk/genuki/NBL/NorthumberlandRO/Berwick.html
• Birmingham City Archives, Central Library, Chamberlain Square, Birmingham B3 3HQ
Tel: 0121 235 4217
Website: http://birmingham.gov.uk/libraries/archives
• Bristol Record Office, "B" Bond Warehouse, Smeaton Road, Bristol, BS1 6XN
Tel: 0117 922 5692
• Buckinghamshire Record Office, County Hall, Walton Street, Aylesbury, Bucks HP20 1UU
Tel: 01296 382587
• Cambridgeshire Record Office, Shire Hall, Castle Hill, Cambridge, Cambs CB3 0AP
Tel: 01223 717281
E-mail: county.records.cambridge@camcnty.gov.uk
• Canterbury Cathedral Archives, The Precincts, Canterbury, Kent CT1 2EH
Tel: 01227 463510
Website: http://crane.uhc.ac.uk/english/cmed.htm
• Cheshire Record Office, Duke Street, Chester, Cheshire CH1 1RL
Tel: 01244 602574
E-mail: recordoffice@cheshire-cc.btx400.co.uk
• Cornwall Record Office, County Hall, Truro, Cornwall TR1 3AY
Tel: 01872 323127/273698
• Cumbria Record Office, Barrow, 140 Duke Street, Barrow-in-Furness, Cumbria LA14 1XW
Tel: 01229 894363
• Devon Record Office, Castle Street, Exeter, Devon EX4 3PU
Tel: 01392 384253
Website: http://www.devon-cc.gov.uk/dcc/services/dro/homepage.html
• Dorset Record Office, 9 Bridport Road, Dorchester, Dorset DT1 1RP
Tel: 01305 257184
E-mail: dcc_archives@dorset-cc.gov.uk

Website: http://www.dorset-cc.gov.uk/records.htm
• Durham County Record Office, County Hall, Durham DH1 5UL
Tel: 0191 383 3253/3474
• East Riding of Yorkshire Archive Office, County Hall, Beverley, East Yorkshire HU17 9BA
Tel: 01482 885007
• East Sussex Record Office, The Maltings, Castle Precincts, Lewes, Sussex BN7 1YT
Tel: 01273 482349
• Essex Record Office, County Hall, Chelmsford, Essex CM1 1LX
Tel: 01245 430067
E-mail: ero.enquiry@essexcc.gov.uk
Website: www.essexxx.gov.uk
• Gloucestershire Record Office, Clarence Row, Alwin Street, Gloucester, Glos GL1 3DW
Tel: 01452 425295
E-mail: records@gloscc.gov.uk
Website: http://www.gloscc.gov.uk/corpserv/archives/Index.htm
• Greater Manchester County Record Office, 56 Marshall Street, New Cross, Manchester M4 5FU
Tel: 0161 832 5284
E-mail: archives@grmcro.u-net.com
Website: http://www-u-net.com/~gmcro/
• Hampshire Record Office, Sussex Street, Winchester, Hants SO23 8TH
Tel: 01962 846154
• Hereford & Worcester Record Office, Old Barracks, Harold Street, Hereford HR1 2QX
Tel: 01432 265441
• Hertfordshire Archives & Local Studies, County Hall, Pegs Lane, Hertford, Herts SG13 8EJ
Tel: 01992 555105
E-mail: iris.white@hertscc.gov.uk
Website: http://hertslib.hertscc.gov.uk
• Huntingdon Record Office, Grammar School Walk, Huntingdon, Cambs PE18 6LF
Tel: 01840 375821
E-mail: county.records.hunts@camcnty.gov.uk/
• Lancashire Record Office, Bow Lane, Preston, Lancs PR1 2RE
Tel: 01772 263026
E-mail: lancsrecords@treas.lancscc.gov.uk
Website: http://www.lancashire.com/lcc/ri/index.htm
• Leicestershire Record Office, Long Street, Wigston Magna, Leicester LE18 2AH
Tel: 0116 257 1080
• Lincolnshire Archives, St Rumbold Street, Lincoln LN2 5AB
Tel: 01522 526204
E-mail: archives@lincsdoc.demon.co.uk
Website: http://www.lincs-archives.co
• Liverpool Record Office, Central Library, William Brown Street, Liverpool, Merseyside L3 8EW
Tel: 0151 225 5417
E-mail: ro@lvpublib.demon.co.uk
Website: http://www.liverpool.gov.uk/public/council_info/direct-info/leisure/libraries/ro.htm
• Norfolk Record Office, Gildengate House, Anglia Square, Upper Green Lane, Norwich, Norfolk MR3 1AX
Tel: 01603 761885
E-mail: norfrec.nro@norfolk.gov.uk
Website: http://www.ecn.co.uk/norfolkcc/htm/council/departments/no/nr oindex.html
• Northampton Record Office, Wootton Hall Park, Northampton NN4 8BQ

Tel: 01604 762129
E-mail: archivist@nro.northamptonshire.gov.uk
Website: http://www.nro.northampton shire.gov.uk
• Northumberland Record Office, Melton Park, North Gosforth, Newcastle NE3 5QX
Tel: 0191 236 2680
Website: http://www.swinhope.demon.co.uk/genuki/NBL/NorthumberlandRO/
• North Devon Record Office, Library & Record Office, Barnstable, Devon EX31 1EL
Tel: 01271 388608
• Nottingham Archives, County House, Castle Meadow, Nottingham NG2 1AG
Tel: 0115 958 1634/950 4524
• Oxford Archives, County Hall, New Road, Oxford, Oxon OX1 1ND
Tel: 01865 815203/810801
• Shropshire Records & Research Centre, Castle Gates, Shrewsbury, Salop SY1 2AQ
Tel: 01743 255350
• Somerset Record Office, Obridge Road, Taunton, Somerset TA2 7PU
Tel: 01823 337600
• Suffolk Record Office, 77 Raingate Street, Bury St Edmunds, Suffolk IP33 2AR
Tel: 01284 352352
E-mail: gwyn.thomas@libber.suffolkcc.gov.uk
Website: http://www.suffolkcc.gov.uk/libraries_and_heritage
• Teeside Archives, Exchange House, 6 Martin Road, Middlesborough, Teeside TS1 1DB
Tel: 01642 248321
• Warwickshire County Record Office, Priory Park, Cape Road, Warwick CV34 4JS
Tel: 01926 412735
• West Sussex Record Office, Sherburne House, Orchard Street, Chichester, Sussex
Tel: 01243 533911
E-mail: recordsoffic@westsussex.gov.uk
Website: http://www.westsussex.gov.uk/ro/rohome/htm
• West Yorkshire Archives Service (Bradford) 15 Canal Road, Bradford, West Yorkshire BD1 4AT
Tel: 01274 731931
• Wiltshire & Swindon Record Office, County Hall, Bythesea Road, Trowbridge, Wilts BA14 8JG
Tel: 01225 713139

Scotland
• Edinburgh City Archives, Department of Corporate Services, City of Edinburgh Council, City Chambers, High Street, Edinburgh EH1 1YT
Tel: 0131 529 4616
• Strathclyde Regional Archives, Mitchell Library, North Street, Glasgow G3 7DN
Tel: 0141 287 2910/2913

Wales
• Anglesey County Record Office, Shirehall, Glanhwfard, Llangefni, Isle of Anglesey LL77 7TW
Tel: 01248 752080
• Archifdy Ceredigion Archives, County Offices, Marine Terrace, Aberystwyth, Ceredigan SY23 2DE
Tel: 01970 633697
• Archifdy Meirion Archives, Cae Penariag, Dolgellau, Gwynedd LL40 2YB
Tel: 01341 424444/424442

• Carmarthenshire Archives Service, County Hall, Carmarthen, SA31 1JD
Tel: 01267 224180
E-mail: archives@carmarthenshire.gov.uk
Website: http://www.carmarthenshire.gov.uk/
• Denbighshire Record Office, 46 Clwyd Street, Ruthin, N. Wales LL15 1HP
Tel: 01824 703077
Website: http://www.llge.org.uk/cac/cac0011.html
• Flintshire Record Office, The Old Rectory, Hawarden, Deeside CH5 3NR
Tel: 01244 532364
Website: http://www.Ugc.org.uk/cac 0011.html
• Glamorgan Record Office, Glamorgan Building, King Edward VII Avenue, Cathays Park, Cardiff CF1 3NE
Tel: 01222 780282
Website: http://www.llgc.org.uk/cac (for information on all Welsh County Record Offices)
• Gwent Record Office, County Hall, Cwmbran, Gwent NP44 2XH
Tel: 01633 644888/644886
E-mail: 113057.2173@ compuserve.com
• Pembrokeshire Record Office, The Castle, Haverfordwest, Pembrokeshire SA61 2EF
Tel: 01437 763707
• Powys County Archives Office, County Hall, Llandrindod Wells, Powys LD1 5LG
Tel: 01597 826088
E-mail: archives@powys.gov.uk
Website: http://www.powys.gov.uk

SPECIALIST PUBLISHERS
• *Family History Monthly*, 45 St Mary's Road, Ealing, London W5 5RQ
• *Family Tree Magazine* and *Practical Family History*, 61 Great Whyte, Ramsey, Huntingdon, Cambridgeshire PE17 1HL
• *Genealogical Research Directory*, Mrs Elizabeth Simpson, 2 Stella Grove, Tollerton, Nottingham NG12 4EY
• *Genealogical Services Directory*, 33 Nursery Road, Nether Poppleton, York YO2 6NN
• Oxford University Press, Great Clarendon Street, Oxford OX2 6DP
• Phillimore & Co Ltd, Shopwyke Hall, Chichester, Sussex
• Public Record Office Publications, Ruskin Avenue, Kew, Surrey TW9 4DU
• Society of Genealogists, 14 Charterhouse Buildings, Goswell Road, London EC1M 7BA

AUSTRALIA

LIBRARIES
• National Library of Australia, Parkes Place, Canberra, ACT 2600
• State Library of New South Wales, Macquarrie Street, Sydney 2000, New South Wales

MAIN ARCHIVES
• Archives Office of New South Wales, 2 Globe Street, Sydney 2000, New South Wales

SOCIETIES
• Society of Australian Genealogists, Richmond Villa, 120 Kent Street, Observatory Hill, Sydney 2000, New South Wales

SPECIAL INTEREST GROUPS
• Australian Institute of Genealogical Studies, PO Box 339, Blackburn, Victoria 3130

SPECIALIST PUBLISHERS
• *Genealogical Research Directory*, Keith Johnson, 17 Mitchell Street, Sydney 2000, New South Wales

CANADA

MAIN ARCHIVES
• National Archives of Canada, 395 Wellington Street, Ottawa, ONT, K1A 0N3
Tel: (613) 995-5138
• Archives Nationales du Quebec, PO Box 10450, Sainte-Foy, Quebec

SOCIETIES
• Canadian Federation of Genealogical and Family History Societies, 227 Parkville Bay, Winnipeg, MB, R2M 2J6

SPECIALIST PUBLISHERS
• *Family Chronicle*, 10 Gateway Blvd, Suite 490, North York, ONT M3C3T4
• *Genealogical Research Directory*, Mrs Jeanette Tyson, 94 Binswood Avenue, Toronto, ONT, M4C 3N9

REPUBLIC OF IRELAND

MAIN ARCHIVES
• Genealogical Office, Office of the Chief Herald, 2 Kildare Street, Dublin 2, Republic of Ireland
Tel: 01 603 0302/303 0311
• General Register Office, 8–11 Lombard Street East, Dublin 2, Republic of Ireland
• Dublin City Archives, City Assembly House, 58 South William Street, Dublin 2, Republic of Ireland
Tel: 01 677 5877
• National Archives, Bishop Street, Dublin 8, Republic of Ireland
Tel: 01 409 2300
Website: http://www.kst.dit.ie/nat_arch/

LIBRARIES
• National Library of Ireland, Kildare Street, Dublin 2, Republic of Ireland

SOCIETIES
• Irish FHS, The Secretary, PO Box 36, Naas, Co Kildare, Republic of Ireland
• Irish Genealogical Society, 82 Eaton Square, London SW1W 9AJ

SPECIAL INTEREST GROUPS
• Irish Genealogical Society International, PO Box 16585, St Paul, MN, 55116-0585, USA
• Presbyterian Historical Society of Ireland, Church House, Fisherwick Place, Belfast, Northern Ireland BT1 6DW
Tel: 01232 322284

SPECIALIST PUBLISHERS
• Gill & Macmillan Ltd, Goldenbridge, Dublin 8, Republic of Ireland

NEW ZEALAND

MAIN ARCHIVES
• National Archives of New Zealand, PO Box 6162, Te Aro, Wellington

SOCIETIES

• Genealogical Research Institute of New Zealand, PO Box 36-107, Moera, Lower Hutt
• New Zealand FHS Inc., Mrs J. Lord, PO Box 13301, Armagh, Christchurch
• New Zealand Society of Genealogists, PO Box 8795, Symonds Street, Auckland 1035

SOUTH AFRICA

MAIN ARCHIVES

• South African Government Archives Service, Union Building, Private Bag X236, Pretoria

SOCIETIES

• Genealogical Society of South Africa, PO Box 2119, Houghton 2041

UNITED STATES

MAIN ARCHIVES

• Bureau of Indian Affairs, Department of the Interior, 1849 C Street NW, Washington DC 20240
Tel: (202) 343-1334
• Bureau of Land Management, Department of the Interior, 1849 C Street NW, Washington DC 20240
Tel: (202) 343-9435
• Bureau of the Census, PO Box 1545, Jeffersonville, IN 47131
Tel: (812) 285-5314
• Immigration and Naturalization Service (INS), US Department of Justice, INS Historical Reference Library and Reading Room Section, Chester Arthur Building, 425 I Street NW, Room 1100A, Washington, DC 20536
Tel: (202) 514-2837
• National Archives, 700 Pennsylvania Avenue at Eighth Street NW, Washington DC 20408
Tel: (202) 501-5525, 501-5400
Also at: 8601 Adelphi Road, College Park, MD 20740-6001
Tel: (301) 713-6800, 713-7250
Website: http://www.nara.gov
• National Archives Microfilm Rental Program, PO Box 30, Annapolis, Junction, MD 20701-0030
• National Archives—New England Region, 380 Trapelo Road, Waltham, MA 02154
Tel: (617) 647-8100
• National Archives—Northeast Region, 201 Varick Street, New York, NY 10014-4811
Tel: (212) 337-1300
• National Archives—Mid-Atlantic Region, Ninth and Market Street, Room 1350, Philadelphia, PA 19107
Tel: (215) 597-3000
• National Archives—Great Lakes Region, 7358 South Pulaski Road, Chicago, IL 60629
Tel: (312) 353-0162
• National Archives—Southeast Region, 1557 Saint Joseph Avenue, East Point, GA 30344
Tel: (404) 763-7477
• National Archives—Central Plains Region, 2312 East Bannister Road, Kansas City, MO 64131
Tel: (816) 926-6272
• National Archives—Southwest Region, 501 West Felix Street, PO Box 6216, Fort Worth, TX 76115
Tel: (817) 334-5525

• National Archives—Rocky Mountain Region, Denver Federal Center, Building 48, PO Box 25307, Denver CO 80225-0307
Tel: (303) 236-0817
• National Archives—Pacific Sierra Region, 1000 Commodore Drive, San Bruno, CA 94066
Tel: (415) 876-9009
• National Archives—Pacific Southwest Region, 24000 Avila Road, First Floor, Laguna Niguel, CA 92656-6719
Tel: (714) 643-4241
• National Archives—Pacific Northwest Region, 6125 Sand Point Way NE, Seattle, WA 98115
Tel: (206) 526-6507
• National Archives—Alaska Region, Federal Office Building, 654 West Third Avenue, Room 012, Anchorage, AK 99501
Tel: (907) 271-2441
• National Park Service, Office of Library, Archives and Graphics Research, Harpers Ferry Center, Harpers Ferry, WV 25425-0050
Tel: (304) 535-6261
• Rhode Island State Archives, 337 Westminster Street, Providence, RI 02903

LIBRARIES

• Allen County Public Library, Reynolds Historical Genealogy Department, 900 Webster Street, PO Box 2270, Fort Wayne, IN 46802
Tel: (219) 424-7241
• American Genealogical Lending Library PO Box 244, Bountiful, UT 84011
• The Burdick International Ancestry Library, 2317 Riverbluff Parkway #249, Sarasota, FL 34231-5032
Tel: (813) 922-7931
• Dallas Public Library, Genealogy Section, 1515 Young Street, Dallas, TX 75201
Tel: (214) 670-1433
• Denver Public Library, Genealogy Division, Western History Collection, 1357 Broadway, Denver, CO 80203-2165
Tel: (303) 571-2190
• Duke University, Perkins Library, Durham, NC 27706-2597
• Family History Department (LDS), Family History Library, 35 North West Temple, Salt Lake City, UT 84150
Tel: (801) 240-2331
• Historic Trails Library, Rt. 1, Box 373, Philadelphia, MS 39350-9762
Tel: (601) 656-3506
• Library of Congress, Local History and Genealogy Reading Room, Humanities and Social Sciences Division, Thomas Jefferson Building, Room LJ 20, 10 First Street SE, Washington DC 20540-5554
Tel: (202) 707-5537
• Museum of the Confederacy Library, 1201 East Clay Street, Richmond, VA 23219
• National Society, Daughters of the American Revolution Library, 1776 D Street NW, Washington DC 20006-5392
Tel: (202) 879-3229
• Newberry Library, 60 West Walton Street, Chicago, IL 60610-3394
Tel: (312) 943-9090
• New York Genealogical and Biography Society Library, 122 East 58th Street, New York 10022-1939
Tel: (212) 755-8532
• Saint Louis Public Library, History

and Genealogy Department, 1301 Olive Street, Saint Louis, MO 63103
Tel: (314) 539-0386
• Tree Trackers Library, PO Box 1210, Eagle Rock, MO 65641
Tel: (417) 271-3532
• United Daughters of the Confederacy Library, 328 Boulevard, Richmond, VA 232220
• Washington State Library, Temple of Justice, Olympia, WA 98504

SOCIETIES AND SPECIAL INTEREST GROUPS

• African American Family History Association, PO Box 115268, Atlanta, GA 30310
Tel: (404) 349-7405
• American College of Heraldry, PO Box 19347, New Orleans, LA 70179
• The American College of Heraldry, PO Box 1899, Little Rock, AR 72203-1899
• Association of One-name Studies, Richard W. Price and Associates, PO Box 11980, Salt Lake City, UT 84147
Tel: (801) 531-0920
• British Isles FHS of Los Angeles, 2531 Sawtelle Boulevard #134, Los Angeles, CA 90064-3163
• Dutch Family Heritage Society, 2463 Ledgewood Drive, West Jordan, UT 84084
Tel: (801) 967-8400
• Federation of Genealogical Societies, PO Box 3385, Salt Lake City, UT 84110-3385
Tel: (801) 254-2785
• Genealogical Insititute, Family History World, PO Box 22045, Salt Lake City, UT 84122
Tel: (801) 257-6174
• German Genealogical Society of America, PO Box 291818, Los Angeles, CA 90029
Tel: (909) 593-0509
• Jewish Genealogical Society, Inc., PO Box 6398, New York, NY 10128
Tel: (212) 330-8257
• Institute of Early American History and Culture, College of William and Mary, Earl Gregg Swem Library Building, PO Box 8781, Williamsburg, VA 23187
Tel: (804) 221-1110
• International Society of British Genealogy and Family History, PO Box 3115, Salt Lake City, UT 84110-3115
• The Irish Genealogical Foundation, PO Box 7575, Kansas City, MO 64116
Tel: (816) 454-2410
• Irish Genealogical Society International, PO Box 16585, St Paul, MN, 55116-0585
• National Genealogy and History News, Rt. 3, Box 65, Chandler, OK 74834-8504
• National Genealogical Society, 4527 17th St North, Arlington, VA 22207-2363
Tel: (703) 525-0050
Website: http://www.genealogy.org/NGS
• National Society, Daughters of the American Revolution, 1776 D Street NW, Washington DC 20006-5392
Tel: (202) 879-3229
• National Society, Descendants of Early Quakers, 3917 Heritage Hills Drive #104, Bloomington, MN 55437-2633
• New England Historic Genealogical

Society, 99-101 Newbury Street, Boston MA 02116-3087
Tel: (617) 536-5740
Website: http://www.nehgs.org
• Rhode Island Genealogical Society, PO Box 7618, Warwick, RI 012887
• Silicon Valley PAF Users Group, PO Box 23670, San Jose, CA 95153-3670

SPECIALIST PUBLISHERS

• Ancestry Publishing Company, Salt Lake City, UT 84110
• Barnett's Family Tree Book Company, c/o Antique Center of Texas, 1001 West Loop, North Houston, TX 77055
Tel: (713) 684-4633
• Broderbund, PO Box 6125, Novato, CA 94948-6125
• *Family Chronicle*, PO Box 1201, Lewiston, NY 14092-9934
• Family Line Publications, Rear 63 East Main Street, Westminster, MD 21157
Tel: (410) 876-6101 Tel: (800) 876-6103
• Genealogical Publishing Co., Inc., 1001 North Calvert Street, Baltimore, MD 21202
• Genealogy Publishing Service, 448 Ruby Mine Road, Franklin, NC 28734
Tel: (704) 524-7063
• *Genealogical Research Directory*, Mrs Jan Jennings, 3324 Crail Way, Glendale, CA 91206-1107
• *The Genealogical Helper*, Everton Publishers Inc., PO Box 368, Logan, UT 84323-0368
• Heart of the Lakes Publishing, 2989 Lodi Road, PO Box 299, Interlaken, NY 14847-0299
Tel: (607) 532-4997
• Summit Publications, 9605 Vandergriff Road, PO Box 39128, Indianapolis, IN 46239-0128
Tel: (317) 862-3330

COMPUTER INTEREST

• Ancestral File Operations, Family History Library, 35 North West Temple, Salt Lake City, UT 84150
Tel (801) 240-2585
• Brother's Keeper, 6907 Childsdale Road, Rockford, MI 49341
Tel: (616) 866-9422
• The Genealogy Forum on Compuserve, PO Box 5273, Billerica, MA 01822-5273
Tel: (800) 848-8199
• Computer Rooters, PO Box 161693, Sacramento, CA 95816
Tel: (916) 363-8403
• KinQuest Inc, PO Box 873, Bowling Green Station, New York, NY 10274-0873
Tel: (718) 998-6303
• New England Roots Users Group, 232 Underwood Street, Holliston, MA 10746-1627
Tel: (508) 429-7010
• Tulsa Genealogical Society, PO Box 585, Tulsa, OK 74101-0585
Tel: (918) 742-3893

Please note that while every effort has been made to ensure this information is as accurate as possible at the time of publication, addresses and telephone numbers (especially for e-mail and websites) are subject to change beyond the publisher's control.

FURTHER READING

BOOKS

- Barber MD, Henry. *British Family Names*. London, 1894
- Bardsley, Charles Wareing. *A Dictionary of English & Welsh Surnames, with American Instances*. Genealogical Publishing Co., Inc.: Baltimore, 1996
- Begley, Donal F. *Handbook on Irish Genealogy*. (6th edition.) Heraldic Artists Ltd, 1984
- Begley, Donal F. *Irish Genealogy: A Record Finder*, 1987
- Bentley, Elizabeth Petty. *County Courthouse Book*. Genealogical Publishing Co., Inc.: Baltimore, 1990
- Bentley, Elizabeth Petty. *The Genealogist's Address Book*. (3rd edition.) Genealogical Publishing Co., Inc.: Baltimore, 1995
- Blatchford, Robert & Heslop, Geoffrey. *The Genealogical Services Directory*. G.R. Specialist Information Services, 1998
- Bryant Rosier, M.E. *Index to Parishes in Phillimore's Marriages*. Family Tree Magazine, 1998
- Buck, W.S.B. *Examples of Handwriting 1550–1650*. Society of Genealogists, 1982
- Catton, Bruce. *The Penguin Book of the American Civil War*. Penguin Books: London, 1966
- Cheney, Malcolm. *Chronicles of the Damned*. 1992
- Coldham, Peter Wilson. *Child Apprentices in America from Chris's Hospital, London 1617-1778*. Genealogical Publishing Co., Inc.: Baltimore, 1990
- Cole, Jean & Church, Rosemary. *In and Around Record Repositories in Great Britain and Ireland*. Armstrong Boon Marriott Publishing, 1998
- Cole, Jean A. & Titford, John. *Tracing your Family Tree*. 1997
- Colletta, John Philip. *Finding Italian Roots. The Complete Guide for Americans*. Genealogical Publishing Co., Inc.: Baltimore, 1993
- Cottle, Basil. *The Penguin Dictionary of Surnames*. Penguin Books: London, 1978
- Cox, Jane. *New to Kew*. Public Record Office Readers' Guide No 16. PRO Publications, 1997
- Cox, Jane & Colwell, Stella. *Never Been Here Before? A genealogists' guide to the Family Records Centre*. Public Record Office Readers' Guide No 17. PRO Publications, 1997
- Croom, Emily. *The Genealogist's Companion & Sourcebook*. Betterway Books, 1994
- Currer-Briggs, Noel & Gambier, Royston. *Debrett's Family Historian: A Guide to Tracing your Ancestors*. Webb & Bower Ltd, 1981
- Daniels, Jackie & Morris, Christine. *From Schools to W.I.: 150 Years of Education at Walden Road*. Huntingdon & Peterborough Federation of Women's Institutes, 1993
- Dunkling, Leslie. *The Guinness Book of Names*. (6th edition.) 1993

- Federation of Family History Societies (FFSH). *Current Publications on Microfiche by Member Societies*. FFHS, 1994
- FitzHugh, Terrick V. H. *The Dictionary of Genealogy*. Alphabooks, 1985
- Fowler, Simon., Spencer, William. & Tamblin, Stuart. *Army Service Records of the First World War*. Public Record Office Readers' Guide No 19. PRO Publications, 1997
- Gandy, Michael. *Catholic Missions and Registers 1700–1880*. Catholic Family History Society.
- Gibson, Jeremy. *Census Returns 1841–1881 on Microfilm*. (5th edition.) FFHS, 1988
- Gibson, J.S.W. *Probate Jurisdictions: Where to look for Wills*. Gulliver Publishing Co. and the FFHS, 1983
- Gibson, J.S.W. *Quarter Sessions Records for Family Historians*. (2nd edition.) FFHS, 1983
- Gibson, Jeremy & Hampson, Elizabeth. *Marriage, Census and other Indexes for Family Historians*. (4th edition.) FFHS, 1992
- Gibson, Jeremy. & Rogers, Colin. *Coroners' Records in England and Wales*. FFHS, 1988
- Gibson, Jeremy., Webb, Cliff. & Rogers, Colin. *Poor Law Union Records*. FFHS, 1993
- Greenwood, Val D. *The Researcher's Guide to American Genealogy*. (2nd edition.) Genealogical Publishing Co., Inc.: Baltimore, 1990
- Hartley, William G. *The Everything Family Tree Book*. Adams Media Corporation, 1998
- Hawgood, David. *Computers for Family History. An Introduction*. (2nd edition.) Hawgood Computing Ltd, 1987
- Hawgood, David. *Internet for Genealogy*. David Hawgood, 1996
- Heber, Mark D. *Ancestral Trails*. Sutton Publishing: Stroud, 1997
- Hey, David. *The Oxford Companion to Local and Family History*. Oxford University Press: Oxford, 1996
- Hey, David. *The Oxford Guide to Family History*. Oxford University Press: Oxford, 1993
- Humphrey-Smith, C. *Atlas & Index of Parish Registers*. (2nd edition.) Phillimore & Co. Ltd: Chichester, 1995.
- Johnson, Keith. A. & Sainty, Malcolm R. *Genealogical Research Directory, National & International*.
- Jones, George F. *German-American Names*. 1990
- Kemp, Thomas Jay. *International Vital Records Handbook*. (3rd edition.) Genealogical Publishing Co., Inc., 1994
- Lynskey, Marie. *Family Trees. A Manual for their Design, Layout & Display*. Phillimore & Co Ltd, 1996
- MacSorley, M.E. *Genealogical Sources in the United States of America*. M E MacSorley, 1995

- Markwell, F.C. & Saul, Pauline. *Tracing your Ancestors The A-Z Guide*. (3rd edition.) FFHS, 1988
- Martin, C.T. *The Record Interpreter*. Kohler & Coombes, 1979
- McLaughlin, Eve. *Family History from Newspapers*. FFHS, 1987
- Meyer, Mary Keysor. *Meyer's Directory of Genealogical Societies in the USA and Canada*.
- Milligan, E.H. & Thomas, M.J. *My Ancestors Were Quakers*. Society of Genealogists, 1983.
- Munby, Lionel. *Reading Tudor and Stuart Handwriting*. Phillimore & Co. Ltd: Chichester, 1988
- Murphy, Michael. *Newspapers and Local History*. Phillimore & Co. Ltd: Chichester, 1991
- *Oxford Dictionary of English Surnames*. Oxford University Press: Oxford,
- Pontet, Patrick. *Ancestral Research in France*. Patrick Pontet, 1998
- Reaney, P.H. *The Origin of English Surnames*. (3rd edition.) Routledge: London, 1991
- Rogers, Colin D. *The Family Tree Detective*. Manchester University Press: Manchester, 1985
- Room, Adrian. *Brewer's Dictionary of Names, People & Places & Things*. 1992
- Rose, Christine & Ingalls, Kay Germain. *The Complete Idiot's Guide to Genealogy*. Alpha Books, 1997
- Schaefer, C.K. *Genealogical Encyclopedia of the Colonial Americas*. Genealogical Publishing Co., Inc.: Baltimore.
- *Sittingbourne, Milton and District Directory for 1908–9*. W.J. Parrett Ltd, 1908
- Tate, W.E. *The Parish Chest*. Phillimore & Co. Ltd: Chichester, 1983
- Todd, Andrew. *Basic Sources for Family History. 1: Back to the Early 1800s*. Allen & Todd, 1994
- Wheeler, Meg. *Tracing your Roots*. Tiger International Plc, 1996

PERIODICALS

- *Computers in Genealogy*
- *Family Chronicle, The Magazine for Families Researching their Roots*
- *Family History Monthly*.
- *Family History News and Digest*
- *Family Tree Magazine*
- *Genealogical Computing*
- *Genealogical Research Directory*
- *The Genealogical Helper*
- *International Society for British Genealogy and Family History. Newsletter*
- *Irish Family History*
- *The Irish Genealogist*
- *Irish Roots*
- *NEXUS, The Newsmagazine of the New England Historic Genealogical Society*
- *NGS/CIG Digest*
- *Practical Family History*

INDEX

Picture credits:

Abbreviations: t = top; b = below; l = left; r = right; c = center

Touchstone: 5, 7, 10, 12(b), 13(br), 21(b), 22(b), 23(bl), 24(b), 25(b), 26(r), 27(br), 33(b), 61(b), 70, 81(t), 86(cr), 88, 96(b), 104, 109(br), 111, 116(b), 118(tr), 120(br), 121(tr), 121(b), 130, 132(t), 132(b), 133(tl), 133(tr).

The Public Record Office: 6, 17(r), 17(b), 27(t), 27(bl), 35(c), 38, 42 (Crown copyright), 43(l), 49(c) (Crown copyright), 53(tr) (Crown copyright), 58, 59(tl) (Crown copyright), 60 (Crown copyright), 62(b) (Crown copyright), 73(b), (Crown copyright), 74(b), 77(cl) (Crown copyright), 82(t), 85(t), 85(b) (Crown copyright), 90(b) (Crown copyright), 106(b) (Crown copyright), 107(t), 107(b), 114(c), 115(t), 118(bl) (Crown copyright), 119(t) (Crown copyright), 120(t) (Crown copyright), 122(t) (Crown copyright), 122(b) (Crown copyright), 123 (Crown copyright), 124(t).

Solution Pictures: 11(tl), 24(r), 28(t), 31(t), 39(tl), 39(tr), 49(t), 52(br), 57(bl), 57(br), 76(t), 82(b), 84(t), 93(b), 105(t).

Quadrillion Publishing Ltd: 11(tr), 23(br), 40, 47, 54(bl), 56(bl), 56(r), 66(bl), 66(br), 71(t), 71(b), 74 (t), 79(t), 80(t), 82(cr), 86(t), 86(b), 89(b), 96(t), 97(c), 97(b), 105(br), 108(tr), 108(b), 109(bl), 110(bl), 117(b), 118(br), 124 (b), 126(br), 127(bl), 127(br).

Frank Spooner Pictures/Gamma: 11(b), 37(tr),99(tl), 103(br).

Christine Morris: 13(bl), 20, 22(t), 26(t0, 26(b), 30(bl), 33(t), 34, 44(b), 45(t), 46, 48, 63(t), 78(b), 103(t), 116(tr), 116(c), 133(b).

Mary Evans Picture Library: 15(tl), 21(tr), 30(tr), 50(tr), 51(tr), 53(b), 57(cr), 61(tr), 62(t), 64(t), 64(b), 65(t), 72, 76(b), 79(bl), 87(b), 91(b), 94, 95, 98, 99(tr), 100, 102–103, 109(t), 114(b), 126(t), 126(c), 128(b).

Corbis UK Ltd: 21(tl), 52(t), 54(t), 69(bl), 69(br), 92, 106(t), 110(br).

Corbis-Bettman: 55, 68, 75, 93(t), 101(c), 101(br), 128(t), 129(t), 129(c).

Hulton Getty: 41, 45(b), 50(b), 51(tl), 59(b), 67, 73(t), 77(b), 80(b), 81(b), 112(cr), 113(c), 125(tl).

Paul Nightingale: 89 (t), 105(cr), 112(t), 114(t), 117(t), 125(cr), 131 (b).

The publisher would like to thank the following manufacturers for supplying genealogical software for photography:
Generations deluxe edition—Sierra On-Line Inc.
S & N Shareware & demos—S & N Genealogy Supplies.
Family Tree Maker Deluxe 10-CD Set—Broderbund Software Ltd.
Family Tree—Pinenut Publishing.
SoftKey's Family Tree—SoftKey.
Family Origins deluxe—Parsons Technology/Broderbund.
Internet Service Provider CD—AOL.
Internet Service Provider CD—LineOne.

The publishers have made every effort to ensure that all copyright holders have been correctly acknowledged and would like to thank all contributors who have supplied pictures, information, and website pages.